Feminist research in theory and practice

Feminist research in theory and practice

Gayle Letherby

Open University Press
Buckingham · Philadelphia

Open University Press
Celtic Court
22 Ballmoor
Buckingham
MK18 1XW

email: enquiries@openup.co.uk
world wide web: www.openup.co.uk

and
325 Chestnut Street
Philadelphia, PA 19106, USA

First Published 2003

A catalogue record of this book is available from the British Library

ISBN 0 335 20028 1 (pbk)   0 335 20029 X (hbk)

Library of Congress Cataloging-in-Publication Data
  Letherby, Gayle.
    Feminist research in theory and practice / Gayle Letherby.
      p. cm.
    Includes bibliographical references and index.
    ISBN 0-335-20029-X – ISBN 0-335-20028-1 (pbk.)
    1. Women's studies–Methodology. 2. Feminism–Research–Methodology.
  I. Title.
  HQ1180 .L47 2003
  305.4'07–dc21

                                                              2002030369

Typeset by Graphicraft Limited, Hong Kong
Printed in Great Britain by Biddles Ltd, Guildford and King's Lynn

For my mother, Dorothy Thornton, and my father, Ron Thornton (1923–79). With love and gratitude for everything.

Contents

Acknowledgements

Many people have helped me with this book. First and foremost I must thank Jennifer Marchbank and John Shiels, without whose careful critique and positive affirmation I would never have done it. Their support and that of my mum, Dorothy Thornton, got me through the doubts and the sleeplessness.

I am also very grateful to the students and colleagues who have helped to shape my thinking on the issues I consider in this book and to the colleagues and friends who have given me the time and space to work. To the following I owe particular thanks: Paul Bywaters, Pam Cotterill, Maureen Hirsch, Stevi Jackson, Karen Ramsay, Gillian Reynolds, Keith Sharp, Liz Stanley, Ruth Waterhouse, Corinne Wilson.

Thanks also to Jacinta Evans, Cathy Thompson, Clara Waissbein and Jon Ingoldby for being helpful, kind and patient.

Introduction

Contents   Initial thoughts
Definitions and meanings
Feminism and feminist research
Methods, methodology and epistemology
The self and other in feminist research
Issues of 'I' and other
The 'self' as researcher
Myself and feminist research
Introducing myself
Developing academic interests
This book
Relationship to past work
Outline of the book
Notes
Suggested further reading

In this book I consider the variety of methods, methodologies and epistemologies contained within feminist discourses. While, obviously, I shall try to be as fair as possible in presenting and discussing the work of others, I should make it clear from the outset that my own preferred stance is 'auto/ biographical'. Developed through the work of Weber (1949), Mills (1959) and the British Sociological Association Study Group 'Auto/Biography', this approach essentially starts from the aim of making sociological sense of the self – one's own history, development and biography – and in locating oneself in social structures, to understand those structures and extrapolate from this to try to understand and respect others' experiences, feelings and social locations. As I shall detail later, some critics have characterized this approach as introspective, self-indulgent and easy. If pursued properly and thoroughly it is none of these things, as I hope to show. Having said this, I emphasize that a preference for one methodological and epistemological schema should not blinker one to the uses and values of others. Different research topics are best served by different methods and approaches. Variety is an essential ingredient and strength of feminist research – an issue I shall consider and discuss throughout.

In this introductory chapter I outline some of the things that have influenced me in relation to *Feminist Research in Theory and Practice*. I consider the place of this book in relation to particular writing traditions and my own academic and personal biography. I also define key terms and provide a brief outline of the rest of the book.

Initial thoughts

There are currently lots of books concerned with issues of method, methodology and epistemology: books concerned with theory and practice in research. If you go to any academic library or read any academic book catalogue you are likely to discover large numbers of books on 'doing research' and large numbers of books on the philosophy of research practice. So, as well as books (and articles) on the practical aspects of undertaking research there are others on the knowing/doing relationship in research. As Stanley (1990: 13), in the introduction to an edited book concerned with issues of method, methodology and epistemology, writes:

> Methods manuals abound in the social sciences. Soon feminist alternatives will proliferate also. This collection should not be seen as offering 'research advice' of the manual variety. Rather, it should be used as a kind of cookbook: read the recipes; try out those you like but modifying, as good cooks always do, the ingredients and their portions; jettison those you don't like; pass on those you do . . . do not treat these discussions of feminist research processes prescriptively and/or postcriptively, but rather as accounts for readers to relate to variously and discriminatingly.

More than a decade on from Stanley's comments there is certainly a lot of work by feminists concerned with approaches to research. There are edited texts, single and joint authored books and journal articles specifically concerned with 'doing', others with 'knowing'. From my reading, though, I would argue that most of these pieces tend not to be written as 'manuals' but offer alternative positions for consideration in relation to *doing feminist research* and the relationship between this activity and the subsequent *production of knowledge*. They demonstrate (at least in part) the continued academic feminist commitment to 'politically motivated research and politically engaged theory' (Kemp and Squires 1997: 6).

In this book I present my own interpretation of the historical and contemporary debate on *knowing and doing*. Thus, I am concerned with feminist research in theory and practice and I draw on philosophical and theoretical debates and practical research accounts in relation to these issues. Obviously, this account is by no means definitive. As Fonow and Cook (1991: 20) argue, feminist debate about research is dynamic and ongoing, and therefore this book represents only a moment in time (just as research accounts do). Indeed, my representation is not only temporal but partial, in that although I draw on the work of others I could not possibly hope to detail everything that has ever been written about feminist research – and obviously, like anyone, I have my own favourites. Even for those I do consider, it is likely that my interpretation of the work will not always tally with other readers, or the writers themselves.

Some writers suggest that over recent years too much attention has been given to the consideration of knowledge production at the expense of detailing the 'doing' of feminist research: 'Despite the high profile now given to discussing feminist research . . . much of the material published, with a few exceptions, tends to focus on the principles involved in a rather abstract way. This can sometimes be at the expense of exploring the dynamics of actually doing research in the field' (Maynard and Purvis 1994: 1). For me though (and, as this book will demonstrate, for many other writers and researchers) *knowing* and *doing* are intimately related and it is impossible to write about one without consideration of the other. So this book explores the dynamics of research while at the same time considering the issues of doing research within the broader context of the *knowing and doing relationship*. My central concern is the relationship between the *process* and the *product*. I engage with the current debates surrounding these issues and draw on my own work and a wide range of other research writings. Many of my ideas have been formed through discussion with others working in the area as researchers (at all levels from undergraduate onwards) and with teachers and students. This book is concerned with ideas that I and others grapple with when aiming to put theory into practice. Issues of method, methodology and epistemology are not peripheral – they matter. The questions we ask, and the way we choose to ask them, often determine the answers we get, and, as Stanley (1997: 198) argues, are 'the key to understanding and unpacking the overlap between knowledge/ power'. For this reason I believe that these issues are both vital and exciting, not tedious detail. Methods, methodology and epistemology are not things that need to be got out of the way in research reports, articles and books before we get down to the 'important' stuff: the 'findings'. Nor are they things that need to be carefully disguised as if they in some way threaten the 'objective' status of the knowledge presented. As Kelly et al. (1994: 46) note:

> Feminists have been stern critics of 'hygenic research'; the censoring out of the mess, confusion and complexity of doing research, so that the accounts bear little or no relation to the real events. But many of our accounts are full of silences too. These are not simply the outcome of personal choice, but of publishers' insistence that 'methodology' is boring and should be relegated to a short appendix.

This may appear contradictory, given my previous point on the plethora of books concerned with research practice, but it is not when we consider how and where accounts of research practice are published. The view seems to be that research practice is worthy of considerable attention and is a substantive topic in itself, and this is a reflection of the fact that research has itself become a researchable topic (Stanley 1990). Yet when the focus of the book is non-methodological – concerned with family life, work, leisure, issues of representation or whatever – the research practice engaged in is (to continue the cookbook and food analogy) a mere aperitif which needs to be cleared out of the way before the main servings, or alternatively the cheese dish which you may get around to when you have had your fill of the rest. Surely our choice of recipe (method) and the way we prepare and cook the ingredients (methodology) affect the kind of dish (knowledge) we get. Further, different cooks using the same ingredients, because of their different views on cooking and food (epistemology), may produce quite different dishes. It is important that the 'recipe' and the 'cooking process' do not get lost. Thus, issues of method, methodology and epistemology matter to each and every substantive issue that we consider.

Definitions and meanings

Feminism and feminist research

Before going any further it is worth spending a little time outlining some of the main terms at issue. Essentially in this book I am concerned with issues of method, methodology and epistemology and the importance of these issues for feminism and feminists. Feminism, we know, is not a unified project. While all feminists are concerned with understanding why inequality between women and men exists and, relatedly, reasons for the overall subordination of women, feminists do not all agree on where to find the causes of male domination nor how to combat this and achieve liberation for women. Indeed, as Abbott and Wallace (1997: xiii) note: 'There are even disagreements about what the feminist project is about and indeed what women are!'. However, whatever theoretical and epistemological position feminists hold, it is fair to say that all feminists take a critical position on the 'woman question' and argue that: 'The single most distinguished feature of feminist scholarly work has been its overtly political nature and feminism's commitment to material and social change has played a significant role in undermining traditional academic boundaries between the personal and the political' (Kemp and Squires 1997: 4).

Feminism is both 'theory' and 'practice' (i.e. praxis). Feminist researchers start with the political commitment to produce useful knowledge that will make a difference to women's lives through social and individual change. They are concerned to challenge the silences in mainstream research both in relation to the issues studied and the ways in which study is undertaken. Feminist work highlights the fact that the researchers' choice of methods, of research topic and of study group population are always political acts. With this in mind, although there is no such thing as a feminist method, and there is debate over the usefulness and even the existence of a feminist methodology and a feminist epistemology (see below), there is a recognition that 'feminist research practice' (Kelly 1988) is distinguishable from other forms of research. Feminist research practice can be distinguished by the questions feminists ask, the location of the researcher within the process of research and within theorizing, and the intended purpose of the work produced. There is however a tension between theory, practice, politics and research, and much discussion and debate about the knowing/doing relationship within research.

Methods, methodology and epistemology

The meanings of 'method', 'methodology' and 'epistemology' are very different and are often misunderstood and confused. A *method* is a technique, a tool for doing research, for gathering evidence, for collecting data. Examples include surveys, interviews, focus groups and conversation analysis. Thus, there is nothing distinctive about feminist methods and, contrary to popular non-feminist academic opinion, there is in fact no such thing as a 'feminist method' as any method can be used in a pro-feminist or non-feminist way. *Methodology* entails a perspective or framework. Thinking methodologically involves describing and analysing the methods used, evaluating their value, detailing the dilemmas their usage causes and exploring the relationship between the methods that we use and how we use them, and the production and presentation of our data – our 'findings'. Thinking methodologically is theorizing about how we find things out; it is about the relationship between the process and the product of research. There is a feminist approach to thinking about methodology. Within feminism, the term 'feminist methodology' is also sometimes used to describe an ideal approach to doing research – one which is respectful of respondents and acknowledges the subjective involvement of the researcher. This leads us to a question which Cook and Fonow (1990: 71) ask: 'is feminist methodology that which feminist researchers *do* or that which we *aim for*'? An *epistemology* can be defined as a theory of knowledge. (Thinking epistemologically involves a consideration of the relationship between the knower and the known, and issues of epistemology relate to issues of ontology ('being'/the nature of things/that which is knowable). So epistemology is concerned with what counts as legitimate knowledge and what can be known. 'Epistemology' is defined not only as 'theories of knowledge' but also as 'theories of knowledge production'. So in this second meaning methodological reflection (as identified above) is itself an epistemological act.

As Skeggs (1994) argues, the ways in which method, methodology and epistemology are identified in the research process demonstrate the different theoretical positions held by researchers. Differentiating feminist from non-feminist research Skeggs (p. 77) claims that 'feminist research begins from the premise that the nature of reality in western society is unequal and hierarchical'. Thus, feminist research is grounded in political as well as academic concerns. Historically, research has been presented as orderly, coherent and clean: as hygienic (see Kelly et al. 1994). Yet all research is ideological because no one can separate themselves from the world – from their values and opinions, from books they read, from the people they have spoken to and so on. Thus, the product cannot be separated from the means of its production (Olsen 1980) and feminists not only acknowledge this but celebrate it. Being reflexive and open about what we do and how we do it, and the relationship between this and what is known, is crucial for academic feminists as it allows others who read our work to understand the background to the claims that we are making.

With all of this in mind, feminist researchers are concerned to do research which reveals what is going on in women's lives (and men's too, because to fully understand women's lives we need to also understand what men are thinking and experiencing), and to undertake research in a way that is non-exploitative. This is important because historically women and women's concerns have not been given much attention by researchers and when women were included they were presented as 'not male' and therefore as 'other', as not the 'norm', as deviant. Also, research has generally served the purposes of the researcher rather than the researched and been carried out in a way which objectifies respondents. Thus, the concern for feminists is not just with what we do but how and why we do it and the relevance of the techniques and approaches we choose. Feminist research accounts acknowledge the 'messiness' of the research process and consider the detail of doing research and the relationship between this and the knowledge produced.

With all this mess in mind it is also interesting to consider another word that is often used in relation to research – namely, fieldwork. As Clifford (1990: 65) notes, the view that data collection and practical work actively take place in the 'field' has been 'shared by naturalists, geologists, archeologists, ethnographers, missionaries and military officers' and has been further generalized by many researchers to denote the 'place' where all research happens. Further to this, as Spark argues, the 'field' (like nature) has generally been perceived to be feminine and something that is waiting to be conquered by men. The field therefore is 'a female place for ploughing, penetration, exploration and improvement' (Sparke 1996: 214). Despite the obvious sexism in this I think that the field reference is useful in relation to understanding feminist research practice and subsequent research accounts. When we enter a field we make footprints on the land and are likely to disturb the environment. When we leave we may have mud on our shoes, pollen on our clothes. If we leave the gate open this may have serious implications for farmers and their animals. All of this is also relevant to what we find out about the field and its inhabitants. Thus, when doing research (fieldwork) we need to be sensitive to respondents and to the relevance of our own presence in their lives and in the research process.

The self and other in feminist research

Issues of 'I' and other

Already it must be clear that this book is written in the first person. This is not just my preferred style but, I believe, an academic and political necessity in a book about feminist research in theory and practice. As Morley (1996) argues, when we use 'I' we question traditional styles of academic writing where 'we', 'the author' and 'he' are meant to represent distance and object-ivity. 'I' is therefore a way of challenging traditional academic 'authority'. As Fleischman (1998) notes, writing in which the author refers to her/himself as the 'author' or 'we' excludes any reference to the writer's self and implies that they have no involvement with and no responsibility for what they write. Writing as 'I' we take responsibility for what we write. There are dangers here though in that 'I', when linked to the writing of subordin-ate groups, can be intellectually discredited by those with more power and status in the academic community (Morley 1996). Furthermore, in research that sometimes raises emotional as well as intellectual issues, as feminist research often does, the use of 'I' may lead to accusations of 'un-academic' indulgence.

It is also interesting to consider further the language we use in relation to research. In reading research accounts it is possible to find reference to those who are being researched as respondents, subjects, participants or inform-ants. With a focus on the historical objectification of the researched, the words 'subjects' (which can imply full involvement but is also reminiscent of people having things done to them, as in 'the subjects of medical research', and of people who belong to others, as in subjects of a monarch) and 'informants' (people from whom others get information) are often avoided in current research writings. Some researchers (feminists included), with the aim of equalizing the researcher/respondent relationship, have begun to refer to the researched as 'participants'. However, this is problematic too, as it implies an equality in the participation and hence that the researched have more control over the research process than they have in practice. The interactive nature of the interview within my first experience of research as an undergraduate (see p. 10) led me to talk and write about interviews/ conversations and 'respondents'. When I started to write about my doctoral research I also considered using the word 'participant' to describe the respond-ents in the study. However, I subsequently decided against this. Replacing research language with words that are more reminiscent of reciprocal relation-ships negates the balance of power that researchers have, even if researchers do not always experience the research process as a power relationship in their favour. Indeed, renaming would only highlight the objective difference – our possession of the power to define and redefine.

The 'self' as researcher

Having established that, as researchers, we need to acknowledge our respons-ibility for what we write, it is interesting to consider further the role of the 'self' in research and research writing. Box (1986) considers the lack of per-sonal inclusion in academic writing, arguing that readers often turn to the preface of a book for a glimpse of the author as a person. Further, Potts and Price (1995: 102–3) agree that traditionally the self is left out of academic writing and add that:

Academic discourse in general isn't very good at acknowledging the materiality of its own production, the resources and labour that enable its existence . . . Only the acknowledgments page – split off from the main body of the text, whether unnumbered or given Roman numerals, as euphemized recognition of hierarchized 'debts'; intellectual over personal or domestic – gives any due as to the texts' material origins. Our own 'debts' . . . cannot be accounted for in such a way, they cannot be passed off in a ritualized paragraph, summed up and dispensed with before we turn to the proper business of theorizing.[1]

Within sociology (my own academic discipline) Weber (1949) was among the first to write about personal involvement in research. He was concerned about the overt expression of political ideas (and) or prejudices, used for the promotion or advancement by teachers in universities. At the same time he recognized that the personal and political values of the researcher affected the selection and conduct of research, but tried to find ways to minimize the possible biases that could creep in as a result. This tension between subjectivity and objectivity was not really resolved in his work and is still an important issue for feminist research theory and practice (i.e. methodology and method). Weber argued that social scientists need to be as clear as possible about their own values and ideals and how these will affect their work, so as to avoid total subjectivity. Following on from this, Mills (1959: 204) argues: 'The social scientist is not some autonomous being standing outside society. No-one is outside society, the question is where he [sic] stands within it . . .' With reference to the research process it has now become commonplace for the researcher to locate her/himself within the research process and produce 'first' person accounts. This involves a recognition that as researchers we need to realize that our research activities tell us things about ourselves as well as about those we are researching (Steier 1991). Further, there is recognition among social scientists that we need to consider how the researcher as author is positioned in relation to the research process: how the process affects the product in relation to the choice and design of the research, fieldwork and analysis, editorship and presentation (Plummer 1983; Iles 1992; Sparkes 1998).

There are resonances with these views in feminist work but feminists go further in terms of a much more explicit recognition of the researcher's self. Stanley and Wise (1993) argue that to ignore this personal involvement is to downgrade the personal. As Okely (1992: 9) notes:

In the 1970s, the Women's Liberation Movement argued that the 'personal is political'; I contend that in an academic context 'the personal is also theoretical'. This stands against an entrenched tradition which relegates the personal to the periphery and to the 'merely anecdotal': pejoratively contrasted in positivistic social science with generalisable truth.

Thus, as Roberts (1981) argues, personal research accounts give the reader an insight into research by exploring some of the theoretical, practical, ethical and methodological issues raised. Roberts adds that this is an insight denied in traditional texts. Stanley (1991: 209) goes further and argues that all feminist work should be fundamentally concerned with how people come to understand what they do. Thus, in producing feminist work it is important that we recognize the importance of our 'intellectual biography' by providing 'accountable knowledge' in which the reader has access to details of the contextually located reasoning process which gives rise to the 'findings', the 'outcomes'. Further to this, as I have written elsewhere, our personal biographies are also relevant to the research that we do in terms of choice of topic and method, relationship with respondents and analysis and presentation of the 'findings', and this to needs to be acknowledged (Cotterill and Letherby 1993; Letherby 2000b). Overall, we need to acknowledge the location of ourselves in research and writing in order to make it clear that the production of knowledge is a dialectic loaded in favour of the researcher (see e.g. Stanley 1993).

Myself and feminist research

Introducing myself
Just as feminist research accounts should be grounded in the personal and be accountable to readers, so should books concerned with feminist research. Writing auto/biographically – that is, treating oneself as 'subject' and placing one's own experience within the social context – is also an antidote to feeling superior in research relationships and writings. While I attempt in this book to present an overview of writing in the area it will become obvious what my own views are, which writers I favour and which arguments I support. With this in mind it is important for me to introduce myself and acknowledge further some of my influences.

To situate myself, I am a forty-something white woman who came to higher education as a mature student at 28. I was born in Liverpool to parents with little formal education but much spirit of adventure. My father resigned his factory job and we left Liverpool when I was 7 and travelled around Britain and abroad for the next four years. When I was 11 we settled in Cornwall, largely to enable me to have a settled secondary education. I left school at 18 with two A levels and trained and worked as a nursery nurse for the next ten years. My first degree was in sociology and my doctoral research was a feminist sociological study of the experience (predominately women's) of 'infertility' and 'involuntary childlessness'.[2] Having taught part-time alongside my early doctoral work I am now in my ninth year of a full-time permanent post. I teach in sociology, women's studies and criminology. My current research and writing interests include motherhood and non-motherhood, identity, kinship, working and learning in higher education, sex, sexuality, power and oppression and, of course, feminist research – all of which relate to another of my interests: that of auto/biography in research and research writings (see Chapter 6). Throughout my undergraduate degree I was concerned to explore issues of gender and my interest in feminism and women's studies grew during my time as a postgraduate researcher and part-time teacher. My interest in research began in the first year of my undergraduate degree (1987/8). I wrote an essay entitled 'Should sociology take sides?' and was fascinated by what writers such as Weber (1949), Mills (1959) Becker (1971, 1976) and Gouldner (1971) had to say on the subject. Through these interests I began to see how sociology and feminism made sense of my own experience. However, from the reading I did, it appeared that the debate closed in the mid-1970s and had not been considered since. In the middle of my second year, while browsing through the library shelves for a book on another subject, I came across several books written by feminist writers concerned with these issues and soon discovered that the practical, academic and political debates about methodology were far from over.

One of the modules that I now teach is entitled 'Feminist research: approaches and epistemologies'. In this module students and tutors (I teach this module with colleagues) consider the status of different types of knowledge and knowledge production and demonstrate the need for feminist informed research because of silences (both academic and experiential) in traditional knowledge production. We also explore the motivations for, and practicalities of, doing feminist research and consider how practical issues of 'doing' affect our construction and presentation of what we know. Just the kind of things I am concerned with here.

Developing academic interests

My first experience of research took place in 1989/90 and was related to a personal experience earlier in the 1980s. Early in 1984, after several years of discussion on the subject, my (then) husband and I decided to start 'trying for a family'. It took me over a year to become pregnant and I remember the feelings of desperation and helplessness I experienced. I did become pregnant in March 1985 but miscarried at 25 weeks' gestation. My husband rang the doctor several times during the long, painful process, to be told that I should try to get some sleep and he would come and see me in the morning (possibly he thought he was reacting to an 'over reactive/hysterical' woman). Over ten days later when I went back for a check-up he had forgotten who I was. About nine months after that, having not been able to achieve pregnancy again, the doctor's partner told me that getting upset wouldn't do any good, I just had to relax. Several months after this my original doctor talked to me about 'infertility' treatment. He explained that treatment ranged from sperm tests to in-vitro fertilization (IVF) treatment but advised me against 'going that far'. In the 15 months following my miscarriage I grieved for the baby I had lost and began to grieve for those I thought I would never have. It was only with hindsight, informed by feminist sociological work, that I could begin to 'place' the grief that I felt. Some aspects, of course, are not susceptible to feminist, psychological or sociological understanding(s). To my knowledge I have never been pregnant since.

In September 1985 I began an A-level course in sociology at my local college of further education. It was 'sociology by default', as the psychology course I had wanted to take did not run, owing to lack of numbers. Having found sociology both stimulating and challenging, I did not want to give up the subject and consequently, in September 1987, I became a first-year student on a single honours sociology degree in a Midlands polytechnic. The decision to start a college course had to be balanced against my desire to get pregnant.

From the beginning of the course, I knew that an individual dissertation was a course requirement in the third year. Students were able to choose whether to base this piece on their own empirical research or to conduct a library-based piece of scholarship. From the first day of the course I knew that I wanted mine to be based on an empirical study of the experience of miscarriage. I wanted to do this as I felt that the experience was misunderstood and under-researched, yet I was apprehensive about the project. One of the first worries in research concerns the practical matters such as: Would I find enough people to speak to? Would we both feel comfortable during the interview situation? Would I ask the 'right' questions? Would I do justice to their experiences in the writing-up stage? I was also concerned with how I would thank people for what they were giving me and was worried that I might cause the people to whom I spoke distress by reminding them of things they would rather forget. However, I looked forward to the fieldwork and envisaged that my relationship with respondents (especially the women) would be based on the understanding that we shared experience of an event that we felt many other people did not fully understand and that we did not fully understand ourselves (the pain, grief and other complex feelings). To this end I anticipated that each interview would contain some reference to my own experience. So, before the fieldwork began, I tried to write down how I felt about my miscarriage and its effect on my life. Although my miscarriage was an experience of great loss and trauma it also had many positive elements: after a very bad few months I began to feel that my own identity did not depend on a successful pregnancy and I was concerned about how to express this within an interview, if asked. I was worried that my own feelings might appear unrealistic or be of little interest to others. Eventually I decided that the best thing to do was to try and outline exactly how I felt if asked.

Acutely sensitive to all my 'fears' and after doing some preliminary reading around the subject area I embarked on the fieldwork. I interviewed ten women and corresponded with two women and one man. Initially, I rang some miscarriage support groups and attended one support group meeting and also contacted a couple of acquaintances I knew had had miscarriages. Through this I found six women who were willing to talk to/correspond with me. Some of these suggested others or mentioned my research to others who in turn contacted me. The women I spoke to or corresponded with were aged between 31 and 70 years. They were all in a stable relationship with the father of their baby when their miscarriage(s) occurred. They all had between one and three miscarriages. For some the miscarriage was during their first pregnancy, for others the miscarriage(s) occurred in subsequent pregnancies. All the women had living children and one had several grandchildren. All the women I approached were happy to talk to me (the two I corresponded with, rather than talked to, lived a long way away and both sent me a taped account of their experiences). Also, as previously mentioned, some even contacted me and asked if I would like to interview them. Prior to, or at the beginning of, each of the interviews I told each respondent that I had also had a miscarriage. From then on, each interview was peppered with my experiences, questions on what I knew of support groups, statistics etc. and sometimes sentences ended with 'Isn't it?', 'Don't you think?' etc. This kind of response demonstrates both the reflectivity of respondents and the importance of responsiveness and reflexivity in researching feminist issues, among others. Also, it is possible to argue that the way these points are phrased (as questions rather than assertions) shows that the respondents see the research process, at least to some extent, as a relationship.

Committed to representing the experience of all, I had planned to talk to five men about their experience; but they were more difficult to contact. I asked several of my female respondents if their partners would be willing to talk to me. All refused except one, who wrote down a brief description of how he felt. Eventually, I stopped asking women if their partners would speak to me and, although I also knew a man who I considered asking, after so many rejections I was too nervous to do so. This, in terms of feminist research practice, speaks volumes for the practical difficulties involved – not merely that the men may be embarrassed, but that women feel obliged to 'protect' either the men (from embarrassment) or themselves. Also relevant here is the issue of gender and topic. As writers on the subject of miscarriage have argued (e.g. Oakley et al. 1984; Hey 1989), women and men react differently to the experience. Consequently, it appears that most women feel that the experience can only be fully understood by another woman who has had the same experience. Just as most women (including myself) would feel uncomfortable about a male researcher undertaking research on women's experience of miscarriage, perhaps men feel that a woman would not appreciate their feelings. While recognizing that we need to develop a critique of masculinity and the gender order, I also wondered how far it was necessary to 'include' men in a piece of research essentially about women's experience.

Due to other undergraduate work commitments, the fieldwork took place over a period of six months. Nine out of the ten face-to-face interviews took place in the women's homes and one took place in my home. Conscious of the fact that I was taking up their time, I was always concerned to arrive on time. As a non-driver this often caused me last minute panic as a train or bus was late or cancelled, and once I had to take a taxi. However, although I sometimes had to combine walking, bus and train rides on the journey there, the women or their husbands/partners often insisted on taking me some of the way home, making the return journey easier. I was always treated hospitably and offered drinks and biscuits and, on the occasions when the interview was around a mealtime, I was offered 'something more substantial'. Sometimes children were present or came in at some point to talk to us or ask their mothers for something. When partners/husbands were at home they occasionally interrupted or came into the room to 'look for something' or to talk to us. It is likely that some husbands/partners felt alienated by the interview or, alternatively, felt that they should protect their wives/partners from any 'unnecessary' distress. This early experience of research also made me aware of the importance of practical issues as well as methodological ones. Despite interruptions, each interview lasted between half an hour and two hours. I recorded each one successfully except once when, after the first five minutes my batteries ran out and once when the tape ran out and the woman I was interviewing continued to talk.

Although we only met the once, all the women to whom I spoke or with whom I corresponded told me very personal and intimate details about their lives. There was often reference to very negative emotions: grief, anger, pain, jealousy. It is possible to argue that the women to whom I spoke may have found it easy to talk to me because I was someone who had also experienced an event that they had found distressing. I was someone who was likely to understand how they felt and I also legitimated talk about a topic that is generally considered to be taboo. Having said this, some accounts appeared to be more 'personal' and 'private' than others – with more reference to emotions than physical aspects. In this, I was forced to the realization of how the emotional, the sense of self, and the physical were tied intimately into the social definitions of 'womanhood' and 'responsibility'. There were also differing references to my experience – in some interviews I spoke about it briefly while other interviews were much more extensive. Some of the women said that either the experience of talking was useful for them, or they felt relief when an emotion they felt ambivalent, worried or guilty about was shared by me. Again, if miscarriage is a 'normal' and 'natural' event, why these emotions? They can only be induced by the discourses, the ideological points of reference, which define femininity and womanhood in particular ways. Understanding these discourses is central to feminism. The women I had contacted through support groups had had the chance to talk to others who had an understanding of their experiences. However, these women did not necessarily appear to find 'talking' less useful than those who had less opportunity to talk. Of the two tapes that arrived in the post, one was the shortest I transcribed and the other was one of the longest. This second account was one of the most 'private' and was also very emotional. This respondent also wrote in an accompanying letter that she felt the experience had helped her a lot.

Before undertaking this research project, I had never spoken in detail to another woman who had experienced a miscarriage, and I found that in many of the interviews I was able to voice and/or compare some feelings for the first time. Although my primary motive was not initially to find 'people to share my experiences with' but to make reference to an experience which I felt was under-reported, this opportunity to 'talk' was helpful to me personally. The result for me was a period of self-reflection on my miscarriage in particular and my life in general. However, shared gender does not necessarily ensure shared experiences, and I did not always share experiences or opinions with respondents. After each interview, I wrote in my research

diary exactly how I felt. After all but two, the word 'comfortable' was present
in each entry. In one of the two other entries I recorded that I did not feel
totally relaxed. The other interview and journal entry was somewhat different. This particular interview was with a woman who had been a supporter
in a local self-help group for several years. It was also one of the first interviews I undertook and I was rather nervous beforehand. I came away feeling
much worse. The woman was hospitable and pleasant and answered all my
questions at length. However, I also answered a lot of questions about my
own experiences and, throughout, felt uncomfortably as if I was being counselled against my will. I felt as if my openness had backfired on me in this
instance because what I said was misunderstood. For example, my assertion
that I was learning to live with childlessness was misunderstood as a rejection of children altogether and I was 'instructed' to 'find another doctor' and
'keep trying' because 'children are worth it'. I was very distressed and needed
to talk to my mother and tutors about this experience. Although I was initially upset, and questioned again my feelings regarding miscarriage and motherhood, this experience helped me to sort out some of my own ambivalent
feelings, as well as teaching me a lot about the complexities of the research
process and about some of the difficulties and ambivalences of in-depth
interviewing. Finding a 'balance' within the research process is important
within feminist research and a consideration of 'who holds the power' is not
always simple. It is, of course, impossible to know how I would have felt and
acted during the research process had I no prior experience of miscarriage.

Having completed the fieldwork and on leaving the field I embarked on
the data analysis and writing up. After I had finished, more than anything I
felt that I wanted to do more research.[3]

During the first couple of months of my doctoral study I read my dissertation again and was disappointed. Although, at the time of writing, I felt
that it expressed a 'revolutionary' methodology, involving total involvement
of the researcher, on reflection I felt that there was very little of me in
the finished piece. I then decided to look back at the transcripts of each
interview – and found a gap there also. I had faithfully recorded on paper
the respondents' accounts of their physical and emotional experience of
miscarriage, but there was little record of my own experience, even though
I remembered talking about it at length in some instances. Even where
respondents asked me a specific question about my experience or my opinions
or knowledge of the issue, I wrote the question down, but not the answer.
The following is typical of the way I recorded what I said.

CHAT . . . about my experiences

GAYLE . . . talking about support groups and statistics etc.

Rereading the dissertation I saw huge gaps. For example, I had noted one
respondent's experience of the 'disposal' of her baby:

They put my baby down the loo or something and that's awful . . . it's
awful isn't it?

I remember that during the interview my response was immediate and affirmative but I did not include this either in the interview transcription or the dissertation thesis.

This book

Relationship to past work

All of the issues raised in the research account above are relevant to this book. I was concerned in this first piece of research with many of the same issues that I am concerned with in this book. For example, questions like: What is feminist research?; Why do feminist research?; How do you do feminist research?; What value and status does the knowledge we produce from feminist research have? I consider here (as I did in my undergraduate project) practical, ethical, emotional, theoretical and philosophical issues. Thus, I consider the use and appropriateness of different methods: access and recruitment, entering and leaving the field, researching women and researching men, roles and relationships within research, private and public accounts in research, power, ethics and emotion in the research process, issues of auto/biography, insider/outsider status, data analysis and representation and so on. I also consider questions such as: Who is research for?; How can we try to make sure that when our work challenges accepted knowledge that it is taken seriously?; and What is the relationship between theory and research?

Overall, my aim is to consider why, historically, many issues that are relevant to understanding women's lives have remained under-researched, or when researched have been devalued, and I consider how feminists have challenged this through their theoretical and practical approach to doing research. Feminism offers a challenge and a critique to mainstream views on theoretical and practical issues within research and considers why, when challenged, some people go on the attack. As Hill Collins (1989) notes, discussion and debate about the 'philosophy of science' is taken seriously but alternative knowledge claims are challenged for being challenging:

> Alternative knowledge claims, in and of themselves, are rarely threatening to conventional knowledge. Such claims are routinely ignored, discredited, or simply absorbed and marginalized in existing paradigms. Much more threatening is the challenge that alternative epistemologies offer to the basic process used by the powerful to legitimize knowledge claims. If the epistemology used to validate knowledge comes into question, then all prior knowledge claims validated under the dominant model become suspect. An alternative epistemology challenges all certified knowledge and opens up the questions of whether what has been taken to be true can stand the test of alternative ways of validating truth.

This is not to say that all feminists agree and that the challenge is always unified and united. Within feminism itself and specifically in relation to discussion and debate about *feminist research in theory and practice* there are different and diverse views. This is part of the strength of feminist research – it is not static but dynamic – but this in itself can lead to further criticism based on the misguided view that we cannot get our act together. Innovative writing is commonly attacked in this way and the history of male writing is littered with examples. Women's writing of course is more easily dismissed because of the realities of dominance and subordination. This book is written and presented as part of the challenge to these and other attacks on the practice and presentation of feminist research.

Outline of the book

The main body of the book is divided into seven chapters. Chapter 1 is the first of two charting the main debates in feminist epistemology. In it I review feminist critiques of the historical production of 'masculinized' knowledge – that is, knowledge grounded in men's experience. I also consider the relationship between knowledge and language and consider how women have been excluded from the production of both.

In Chapter 2, I again focus on feminist epistemological debates. Here I consider in detail the feminist challenge to masculine-defined epistemologies and consider approaches which focus on commonalities between women based on shared gender. I go on to chart alternative debates which assert that difference and diversity between women is as politically important as male and female differences. Implications for theory and method are considered throughout.

In Chapter 3, I am concerned to explore the relationship between theory and action in the feminist research endeavour. I examine the dialectical relationship between theory and research and, importantly, the impact of feminist research within and beyond the feminist academy.

In Chapter 4, I look specifically at feminist research practice and provide a historical account of the arguments for and against the use of qualitative and quantitative techniques by feminist researchers. Thus I consider available methods and their methodological and epistemological consequences. Some writers have argued that an orthodoxy developed in the early 1980s which equated feminist research with qualitative interviewing. However, I argue that there has always been, and still is, debate around the use of methods.

In Chapter 5, I start from the premise that the basis of all research is a relationship. I consider issues of power, empowerment, ethics and responsibility at all stages of the research process. This includes feminist debates concerning the value of research for the lives of women (and men) specifically involved in the research and women (and men) in general. Yet I do not argue that the power balance is inevitably in favour of the researcher and explore the implications of shifting power for everyone involved in the research process at all stages.

In Chapter 6, I explore the auto/biographical aspects of feminist empirical work. As such I examine the way that the experiences of researchers help them understand those of their respondents. I consider the ways in which the lives of respondents are filtered through the researcher and how the lives of researchers are also present in research relationships and research accounts whether acknowledged or not. I explore the positive and negative aspects of this realization.

In Chapter 7, I am concerned with the ways in which feminist research is received within the wider academic community and by the media and lay audiences. I consider the possible responses of different audiences to feminist research. These include academic audiences and lay audiences, both when our work is presented by us and/or popularized by the media.

Finally, in 'Reflections' I briefly review the main debates in the book and re-emphasize what I see as the pleasure and perils of 'doing feminist research' and the political strengths and possibilities of this approach. Overall, I challenge the view that feminist research is just 'good' research and argue that, although it cannot provide 'the answers', it provides a different and distinct way of looking at the world.

Notes

1 I appreciate that readers are likely to have turned straight to my Acknowledgements section on reading this.
2 I write 'infertility' and 'involuntary childlessness' to highlight the problems of definition.
3 I have written an article on the substantive issues of this work (see Letherby 1993).

Suggested further reading

As noted at the beginning of this introduction there are many books concerned with issues of method, methodology and epistemology. Although obviously not a definitive list, the following are some of my personal favourites:

Berger Gluck, S. and Patai, D. (1991) *Women's Words, Women's Words, Women's Words: The Feminist Practice of Oral History*. London: Routledge.
Fonow, M.M. and Cook, J.A. (eds) (1991) *Beyond Methodology: Feminist Scholarship as Lived Experience*. Bloomington, IN: Indiana University Press.
Maynard, M. and Purvis, J. (1994) *Researching Women's Lives from a Feminist Perspective*. London: Taylor & Francis.
McCarl Neilsen, J. (ed.) (1990) *Feminist Research Methods: Exemplary Readings in the Social Sciences*. Boulder, CO: Westview.
Reinharz, S. (1992) *Feminist Methods in Social Research*. Oxford: Oxford University Press.
Ribbens, J. and Edwards, R. (eds) (1998) *Feminist Dilemmas in Qualitative Research: Public Knowledge and Private Lives*. London: Sage.
Roberts, H. (ed.) (1981) *Doing Feminist Research*. London: Routledge & Kegan Paul.
Stanley, L. (ed.) (1990) *Feminist Praxis: Research, Theory and Epistemology in Feminist Sociology*. London: Routledge.
Stanley, L. and Wise, S. (1993) *Breaking Out Again: Feminist Ontology and Epistemology*. London: Routledge.
Warren, C. (1988) *Gender Issues in Field Research*. Newbury Park, CA: Sage.

Wilkinson, S. and Kitzinger, C. (eds) (1996) *Representing the Other: A Feminism and Psychology Reader*. London: Sage.

The following journals also have lots of relevant articles in them:

Feminism and Psychology
Gender and Society
Journal of Gender Studies
Signs: Journal of Women in Culture and Society
Women's Studies International Forum

Chapter **one**

Educating Rita revisited: knowledge and language in the 'male' academy

Introduction

This chapter is the first of two concerned with issues of epistemology (theories of knowledge and theories of knowledge production). Different epistemologies have characterized different historical times and places. Examples of different epistemological approaches include Greek rationalism, seventeenth- and eighteenth-century empiricisms, eighteenth-century Enlightenment and twentieth-century postmodernism (see McCarl Nielsen 1990 for a further discussion). Stanley and Wise (1993: 188) suggest that:

> An 'epistemology' is a framework or theory for specifying the constitution and generation of knowledge about the social world; that is, it concerns how to

understand the nature of 'reality'. A given epistemological framework specifies not only what 'knowledge' is and how to recognize it, but who are the 'knowers' and by what means someone becomes one, and also the means by which competing knowledge-claims are adjudicated and some rejected in favour of another/others.

It follows therefore that feminist epistemology means feminist ways of knowing and in Chapter 2 I consider this further. Here I am concerned with the status and privilege accorded to different knowledge claims. Many feminist writers have argued that knowledge, reason and science have been 'man-made'. The general idea here is that western societies have been dominated by patriarchy and men have used their positions of power to define issues, structure language and develop theory. Thus, men have been able to promote their own interests and, as a result, all the dominant forms of discourse in western culture – art, media, literature, science, social science and so on – exhibit predominantly male characteristics. This general argument is a central claim of feminist theory but within this it is possible to distinguish a number of different and incompatible positions. In this chapter I outline how particular types of understanding, particular types of theory of the world, have become dominant and consider both who has produced this knowledge and who has access to it. I consider the tension between *authorized knowledge* (the knowledge of the academy) and *experiential knowledge* (knowledge generated from experience) through a consideration of academic disciplines such as sociology and history and through a brief outline of the medicalization of childbirth. I argue that historically the knowledge of the academy, and the male academy at that, has been dominant. Through a brief consideration of language in terms of definition and usage I also consider to what extent women are marginalized by words and the way they are used. I also begin to consider feminist resistance to these male-defined epistemologies both outside and within the academy. Thus, I look at the ways in which some groups of individuals within society are deemed to be 'knowers' and others the 'known' and I am particularly concerned with how views of who is a knower and who is known have historically been rooted in gendered structures and ideas about the masculine rational subject and the feminized object (Millen 1997).

The things men know?

The construction of woman as 'other'
Sociology, my own academic discipline, clearly demonstrates male bias. As Stacey (1981) argues, sociology began at a time when there was a separation of industry from home and sociological attention was on the factory, the marketplace, the state, the public domain, 'the sphere where history is made' (Smith 1974: 6). Thus, as Oakley (1974) argues, the theories and methods of sociology have been built upon, and from, a man's relation to his social world. This, she argues, is because of the sexist interests and personalities of the 'founding fathers', the dominance of men in academic life and the

unquestioning adoption of western societies' stereotypical views regarding gender roles. This theoretical and empirical concentration on the public domain has led to a 'conceptual straightjacket of understanding within which attempts to understand the total society are severely constrained' (Stacey 1981: 189). Even when the 'private' sphere was the subject of theoretical interest it was its 'function' in relation to the public world that was important – for example, functionalist sociologists considered the nuclear family to be ideally suited to modern industrial society and drew on social Darwinism to justify strict gender roles, arguing that women were naturally expressive (caring and nurturing) and men naturally instrumental (Parsons and Bales 1955). There was no consideration of different family types or individuals who did not meet this 'norm' (Bentilsson 1991). Thus, from this perspective, the home – the private sphere – is of little political and theoretical importance as it is merely a place of retreat from the public world.

So what were the 'mothers' doing in the eighteenth, nineteenth and early twentieth centuries and why were they not writing their own accounts of society and social order? The answer is simple. If people are to develop their ideas, write about and publish theory, they need to be serviced. That is, they need to have their bodily and domestic needs met. Many of the wives and daughters of sociology's (and other disciplines') 'great men' were engaged in these tasks: the tasks of domesticity in the private sphere. However, during this time women as a group were not completely silent. They were observing society and recording their thoughts in other ways. Novelists such as Jane Austen, George Eliot (who used a male pseudonym in order to get published), Emily, Charlotte and Anne Brontë, Elizabeth Gaskell and Virginia Woolf, among many others (including of course those not writing in English), commented on the social conditions of the day and on relationships between people. The links between personal and private politics were implicit within the novels of many female writers in the nineteenth and early twentieth century, just as the importance of these links continue to occupy feminist novelists today. Some even wrote about the issue I am concerned with here: the production of and access to 'knowledge'. For example, Anne Elliot in Jane Austen's *Persuasion*: 'Men have had every advantage of us in telling their own story. Education has been theirs in so much higher a degree; the pen has been in their hands. I will not allow books to prove anything' (cited by Evans 1995: 73).

Others were writing in a more overt political way. For example, Mary Wollstonecraft wrote *A Vindication of the Rights of Women* ([1792] 1972) and argued that women should not be excluded from political rights and that it was illogical to regard them as incapable of reasoning. Wollstonecraft portrayed women as intellectually stifled both in their lives as women and by the dominant conceptions of true womanhood, and argued that women should have power over themselves which would include a right to education, civil liberty and emancipation.

Women who spoke out in this way were ridiculed in their respective times since they were seen as trespassing in a domain reserved for men. They were described as 'bluestockings' (a derogatory description of an educated woman) or in the case of Wollstonecraft as a 'hyena in petticoats', and were suspected of 'unnatural longings' to escape from their God-given place: the home (Mills 1991: 31). As Nietzsche wrote: 'When a woman inclines to learning, there is something wrong with her sex apparatus' (Mills 1991: 31).

Perhaps not surprisingly, Wollstonecraft's daughter, Mary Shelley, adopted a fictional form in her critique of masculinized science and technology. The novel, of course, was *Frankenstein* ([1818] 1994). Easlea (1983) argues that *Frankenstein* can be regarded as a major critique of western philosophical thought: a critique especially aimed at natural science and technology, arising out of a gendered body of disciplines (i.e. male dominated disciplines), notably physics, biology and medicine. At the heart of Shelley's novel is a deep concern and unease with what passed for scientific knowledge in the early nineteenth century and *Frankenstein* can be read as a lesson on what can go wrong if science and technology are used to conquer nature rather than working in harmony with it.

So critiques of the male production of knowledge, of 'masculinized knowledge', are not new. But what do we mean by 'masculinized knowledge'? Perhaps it is useful to start by thinking about what we mean by 'knowledge'. Gunew (1990: 14) begins with the process of knowing and argues that knowing can be defined as 'a kind of meaning production, as the way in which we make sense of the world by learning various sets of conventions'. These sets of conventions are systems which help us to share our awareness of the natural and social world. They are interpretive grids through which we experience sensory data – language, music, mathematics, manners and so on. What then is knowledge? Gunew argues that knowledge can be described in territorial terms in that it becomes legitimated within certain institutions – for example, the education system of a particular society. Knowledge here becomes *authorized* and only some can claim 'rights' to it. Further to this, as women were excluded from organized religion, law and politics and from entering educational institutions for many centuries, *authorized knowledge* has historically meant masculinized knowledge.

Conflict between the knowledge of the academy (authorized knowledge) and knowledge drawn from everyday experience (*experiential knowledge*) is an issue of great interest to feminist philosophers and social scientists. Women, alongside many other subordinated groups, have long had their experiential knowledge discounted in favour of the authorized knowledge of the academy. Feminists argue that in the West during the scientific revolution of the sixteenth and seventeenth centuries the scientific knowledge (and knowledge in general) which emerged was fundamentally based on reason and objectivity: an approach to understanding the world generally referred to as Enlightenment. As Gunew (1990) and Wajcman (1991) note, the history of reason is the history of the gendered metaphor, with women being synonymous with non-reason: 'Culture vs. nature, mind vs. body, reason vs. emotion, objectivity vs. subjectivity, the public realm vs. the private realm – in each dichotomy the former must dominate the latter and the latter in each case seems to be systematically associated with the feminine' (Wajcman 1991: 5).

Thus, it was not only the case that women were excluded from education but that knowledge was constructed from a man's perspective and women's exclusion was justified. Male knowledge fostered 'scientific' theories which legitimized this exclusion. Women were argued to have smaller brains than men which, if 'overtaxed', could lead to diminished reproductive and lactating ability, and were also argued to have an inferior form of cell metabolism which caused them to be sluggish, passive and less able to study (e.g. Spencer 1893). That's not all. For example:

> Women's brains are in a certain sense . . . in their wombs.
> Havelock Ellis, 1859–1939 (Mills 1991: 269)

> A woman is but an animal, and an animal not of the highest order.
> Edmund Burke, 1729–97 (Mills 1991: 27)

> Man should be trained for war, and woman for the recreation of the warrior.
> Nietzsche, 1844–1900 (Mills 1991: 248)

Clearly, the views of many earlier thinkers and writers had some influence on this 'scientific', authorized version of womanhood. For example, as Martin Luther (1483–1546) wrote: 'If women get tired of bearing, there is no harm in that; let them die as long as they bear; they were made for that'. (Mills 1991: 168). Much earlier, Aristotle (384–322 BC), who had a lot to say, argued that: 'As between male and female, the former is by nature superior and ruler, the latter inferior and subject' (Grimshaw 1986: 37). Further to this, Aristotle argued that what distinguished human beings from other species was their power of reasoning, which is related to the faculty of speech. However, as Grimshaw adds, according to Aristotle there were certain classes of human beings who were excluded from the full capacities of human reason: namely, slaves and women. He argued that the life of a woman was functional: like slaves they were expected to play a part in providing the necessities of life and they were expected to produce heirs. So for Aristotle woman is 'like the earth that had to be seeded . . . a good belly' (Badinter 1980: 9).

As Oakley (1981: 38) notes, women have historically been characterized as 'sensitive, intuitive, incapable of objectivity and emotional detachment and . . . immersed in the business of making and maintaining personal relationships'. Women are considered naturally weak and easy to exploit and, as the subordinate sex, women's psychological characteristics imply subordination – i.e. they are submissive, passive, docile, dependent, lack initiative, are not able to act, to decide, to think and so on. From this perspective women are more like children than adults in that they are immature, weak and helpless (Oakley 1981; Evans 1997). If women adopt these characteristics they are considered well-adjusted (Miller 1976; Oakley 1981). However, although women have been constructed as weak and hysterical, they have always performed large amounts of physical labour in both the home and outside of it, and on top of this have been, and still are, held responsible for the dominant share of domestic and emotional work (Coppock et al. 1995; Evans 1997; Frith and Kitzinger 1998). In Britain half the workforce is female and women are much more likely to have lower paid, insecure, part-time jobs. To change this would mean that not only would employment laws have to change but comprehensive childcare on a massive scale would have to be provided (Evans 1997). Despite this, the image of women as inferior – both physically and emotionally – is still significant in defining women's lives (e.g. Coppock et al. 1995; Doyal 1995; Evans 1997).

Clearly, sexist thinking has dominated male-defined epistemologies. Historically, men have dominated academic settings and created a male 'scientific' culture characterized by male concerns and grounded in an academic machismo. Women have not only been largely ignored in traditional approaches to knowledge but where they have been considered at all it is only in masculine terms. Women's experiences and concerns were not seen as authentic but as subjective, whereas men's were seen as the basis for the production of true knowledge (Smith 1989). Human equals man and woman is considered in relation to man and as a deviation of his essential humanity: 'she is partial man, or a negative image of man, or a convenient object of man's needs' (Westkott 1990: 59). Woman has been defined exclusively in terms of her relationship to men, which becomes the source from which female stereotypes emerge and are sustained (Westkott 1990: 59). Sociological knowledge portrayed women as men saw them, not as they saw themselves, and therefore played a key role in maintaining women's subordinated and exploited position (Smith 1989). Thus, traditionally, sociology was at best sex-blinkered and at worst sexist (e.g. Smith 1989; Morgan 1981; Abbott and Wallace 1997).

Clearly, as de Beauvoir (1949: 18) puts it, woman has been defined as 'other' to the male norm:

> Humanity is male and man defines woman not in herself but as relative to him; she is not regarded as an autonomous being . . . she is simply what man decrees . . . She is defined and differentiated with reference to man and not he with reference to her; she is incidental, the inessential as opposed to the essential. He is the Subject, he is the Absolute – she the other.

Tensions between authorized and experiential knowledge

Historically, legitimate theory has been bound up with legitimate beliefs and secular and sacred knowledge have often been difficult to disentangle. There has been constant tension between theory based on experience and/or observation and abstract or universal theory. The earliest universities were staffed by theologians and were places where knowledge about a male God was 'disseminated'[1]. Theory represented and claimed an attempt to move beyond the chaos and abstractions of individual experience to objective and universal truth and abstract knowledge. In some respects theory represented the attempt to understand God, and not surprisingly the earliest forms of theory were entwined with theology. Christian philosophies believed that women were inferior and were evil by nature (Daly 1979; Ussher 1991). The myth of Adam and Eve in the Bible emphasized women's role in man's fall from God's grace and this provides a justification for women's oppression as punishment for her sins. Further, to this the 'menstruation taboo', epitomizing as it does men's fear of women, can be traced back through many religions and cultures. Menstruating women have been (and are often still) seen as contaminated and contaminating, and menstruation was/is seen as a curse. As Noddings (1989: 37) argues: 'the menstruating woman was thought to be infected with an evil spirit or to be paying the price for an essential evil spirit that is part of her nature'. Ussher (1991) adds that blood marks women as 'other'. To confirm their lesser status and to ensure that women do not stray, practices such as the use of the chastity belt during the Christian crusades, the witch trials, Chinese foot-binding, female genital mutilation and Indian *suttee* (the Hindu custom of a widow's suicide on her husband's funeral pyre) have all been sanctioned as appropriate ways to treat women (Dworkin 1974; Daly 1979; Ussher 1991). To this we can add the historical and contemporary oppression of women by men through sexual violence and pornography, which although not formally or positively sanctioned is often in reality treated far less seriously than the abuse of men by women (Smith 1989; Ussher 1991).

With particular reference to the suppression of women's experiential knowledge within a misogynistic culture it is useful to consider the suppression of women's role in healing. There is evidence that women have always practised medicine and been involved in healing the sick (e.g. Verslusyen 1981; Webb 1986). Informally women continued to care for the sick and for women in childbirth, and even though they were barred from formal learning they continued to learn from each other. The 'housewife' role in pre-industrial society encompassed a much wider remit than it does today and was synonymous with healing. Women knew about painkillers, digestive aids and anti-inflammatory agents. The care of infants and women in childbirth was also part of their role. Women healers possessed knowledge not available to men and were highly respected within their communities (Webb 1986). Some writers have made links between the campaigns against witches and the suppression of female healing and argue that in the fourteenth through to the seventeenth centuries those who appeared to threaten religious gendered ideology were branded as heretics and accused of witchcraft. Mills (1991: 263) notes that 'witch' originally denoted a man who practised witchcraft (in the year 890) but by the year 1000 it began to be used in relation to women. In 1382 the term 'wisewoman' entered the English language to refer to a woman skilled in the art of white magic: one who dealt in charms against disease and misfortune or malignant 'black' witchcraft, who dealt in healing in general and midwifery in particular. In England more than 90 per cent of those accused were women and the few men who were formally accused tended to be married to an accused 'witch' or to appear jointly with a woman (MacFarlane 1970).

It is interesting to explore further why women were singled out in this way. Between 1300 and 1700, 'medicine' emerged as a male profession and female healers were suppressed. From this perspective we can see the suppression/ridicule of women's knowledge in relation to the development of contemporary medicine and healing: 'If a woman dare to cure without having studied she is a witch and must die' (Ehrenreich and English 1979: 35). The negative term 'witch' was applied by the Christian Church and female healers became associated with witchcraft at a time when society was rapidly changing. The witch-healer-midwife challenged three hierarchies: the supremacy of the Christian Church, of men and of the landed classes. She represented a peasant subculture and the actual or potential power of a minority group. In short, she threatened the established order. Her success in curing illness was defined as an alliance with the devil, a temptation to which the female temperament was held suspect. It is likely that the midwife was particularly threatening, especially the unsuccessful ones who were accused of sacrificing infants to the devil or, worse, killing them while still in the womb (Mills 1991; Ussher 1991). This latter fear was reflected in the likelihood that women asked midwives to assist them when they wanted to abort (Chamberlain 1981).

With all of this in mind, Ehrenreich and English (1979) saw the male concern to take over healing as a central explanation for the witch-hunts. However, as Abbott and Wallace (1997) point out, there is no clear evidence that all or even most women healers were regarded as witches and there is much evidence to suggest that unqualified women continued to practise long after the witch-hunts ceased. The poor had little access to formal medical care until the nineteenth century and the growth of voluntary hospitals, and available evidence suggests that women relied on informal help and advice (about contraception and birth) well into the twentieth century (Abbott and Wallace 1997). Larner (1983) suggests that the main challenge to midwives took place in the eighteenth century when the witch-hunts had finished and in the towns where the professions were stronger and the witch-hunts and trials were not so significant. She accepts that witch-hunting was the hunting of women who did not fulfil the male view of how women ought to conduct themselves, but saw witch-hunting as part of a broader process of social control and an attempt to establish a new Christian social order (see also Hester 1992).

Others argue that changes associated with the Industrial Revolution were the major factors enabling men to achieve control and dominance in medical practice. From this perspective the development of medicine as a science and a profession is also an example of how the making of knowledge, culture and ideology was an integral part of the development of capitalism (e.g. Chamberlain 1981; Smith 1988). As Chamberlain notes, a hierarchy of knowledge was established which paralleled the social hierarchies within society and particular forms of knowledge were identified with class and gender. Medical science became 'masculine', bourgeois science. The view here is that midwifery as a profession has been shaped by both patriarchy and capitalism, and women were displaced through the twin processes of professionalization and masculinization (Witz 1992). The establishment of qualified medical guilds was instrumental in the displacement of women healers as was the development of hospitals. The new, wealthy middle classes in eighteenth-century England provided a market for the medical remedies and treatment offered by the male-dominated guilds (Verslusyen 1981; Hockey 1993).

When women did become involved in (authorized) medicine it was as nurses under the regulation of doctors (Gamarnikow 1978; Hearn 1982; Hockey 1993). The medical management of childbirth, childcare, dying and death changed 'from a structure of control located in a community of untrained women, to one based on a profession of formally trained men' (Oakley 1979: 18). In Britain, the 1858 Medical Act defined a person who could practice as a doctor as 'a qualified medical practitioner'. Women were not excluded as such but they were still not allowed to go to university or become members of medical corporations. The Midwives Act of 1902 confirmed the subordinate status of female midwives and defined their professional skill 'in relation to the expertise and omniscience of the male professional' (Oakley 1979: 21). From April 1905 a midwife was required to pass an examination in order to register her intention to practise as a midwife following criticisms that the Official Register of Certified Midwives contained 'many thousands of absolutely untrained women' who should not be allowed to practise because they had no formal training and did not possess either the scientific knowledge required or the formal education (many could not read and write) to enable them to act in accordance with the dominant scientific rationality of the public sphere (Adams 1993: 152). Midwifery, which was previously an exclusive branch of medicine controlled by women, was taken over by male doctors who served the emerging middle classes. Female midwifes attended poor women who could not afford to pay a doctor (Chamberlain 1981).

Today in the UK the majority of gynaecologists and obstetricians are men and the majority of midwives are women, and although midwives preside over 'normal' births they must contact a doctor if there is a problem. As Kent (2000) notes, what is distinctive about midwifery work is the emotional work involved, although on a positive note the recent movement of midwifery education into higher education is expected by some to result in increased status for midwives. Childbirth is defined as a problem, as indeed is much of female illness, as not only has the organization of modern medicine been constructed around the exclusion of women doctors but it is also based on the view that the male body is norm (Chamberlain 1981; Evans 1997) and that women are inferior both physically and mentally. As Abbott and Wallace (1997) point out, the nineteenth-century portrayal of women as sickly served several purposes in that it created more work for medical men, it underpinned doctors' campaigns against the midwife (as pregnancy was defined as a disease needing qualified medical attention) and it justified exclusion of women from education, the professions and the public sphere in general. Thus, science and medicine contributed to an even more pronounced view of woman as other, and confirmed and continued the view of women as sickly and sickening (Webb 1986; Doyal 1995).

Clearly, different types of knowledge have different values and status and there is a relationship between the body, power and knowledge. Women have been constructed as unable to fully transcend their ties to their bodies and therefore to nature and thus they are incapable of achieving pure rationality. Hence, women were defined as both contaminating and contaminated 'other'. They have not only been excluded from the academy but from any claim to full subjecthood: they are not only excluded from rationality but rationality itself has been defined as against the feminine and traditional female roles (Potts and Price 1995).

Further tales of exclusion

Just as the academy has traditionally made entry for women difficult, if not impossible, the knowledge produced arose out of the gendered perspectives and experiences of those who produced it. In other words, the perspective and experiences of men. However, as Smith (1988) and Evans (1997) note, most people do not participate in the making of culture and only a very small group of men have been involved in knowledge production:

> As a result the perspectives, concerns, and interests of only one sex and one class are represented as general. Only one sex, and class are directly and actively involved in producing, debating and developing its ideas, creating its art, in forming its medical and psychological conceptions, in framing its laws, its political principles, its educational values and objectives.
>
> (Smith 1988: 19–20)

Clearly, the dominant group in society has the greatest influence in determining a culture's overall outlook and as part of this the dominant group is able to legitimize its own superior position and to subordinate and exclude the perspectives of others – that is, women in general, non-white men, homosexual men and disabled men among others (de Beauvoir 1949; Smith 1988; Hill Collins 1994). Thus, the dominant group is the model for 'normal human relationships' and a one-sided standpoint has come to be seen as natural, obvious and general, while a one-sided set of interests preoccupy intellectual and creative work (Smith 1988: 20). Culture is created and manufactured by men in positions of dominance whose perspective is built on the silence of women and other 'others'. It then becomes 'normal' to treat others as subordinates: to denigrate them and oppose actions towards equality. Yet dominant groups will tend to suppress conflict. They will see any questioning of the 'normal' situations threatening and activities by subordinates in this direction will be perceived with alarm. Thus, it is possible to argue that patriarchal assumptions in male thinking have at the least led to a systematic misrepresentation of women's (and other excluded people's) experience of the world or, worse, led male theorists either to ignore women's views and interests and/or to denigrate the role of women. Having considered this in relation to sociology it is interesting to take a brief look at several other disciplines and discourses.

As women were believed to be guided by natural instinct and to be ultimately unchangeable, they were considered uninteresting and not worth studying. In anthropology, for example, female-specific activities such as gathering were devalued and seen as having little importance. Hunting – a male job – was seen as important both to survival and to evolution, in that men were thought to develop cooperative and technical skills through hunting as well as 'bringing home the bacon', and women and their dependent infants were presented as being totally reliant upon men. However, Slocum (1982) notes that the study of modern hunter-gatherers suggests that women can usually gather enough to support themselves and their families, and that in these groups gathering provides the major portion of the diet.

Likewise, in history the focus has been on male activity and achievement. As in sociology, history has been concerned with the public sphere, with national and international politics and the growth of industry and commerce (Hannam 1993; Alcoff 1996). However, recent research has shown that women were active in many of the events that 'made history' but they have been systematically left out of the official record. Private and public documents have revealed information not only on women's personal lives and family relationships but also concerning their involvement in economics and politics. A few 'great' and 'exceptional' women have been singled out for attention – for example, in the UK, Florence Nightingale, Elizabeth Fry, Josephine Butler and Elizabeth Garrett Anderson – but even here the focus has been on emphasizing how these women displayed feminine qualities such as caring and 'saintliness' (Hannam 1993). Conversely, women have also been noticed when engaged in activities traditionally seen as masculine – for example at times of war, when women took up the jobs at home while the men went to fight (Hannam 1993). On the whole though, history appears to have been 'made' by men:

> Of our fathers we always know some fact or some distinction. They were soldiers or they were sailors. They failed that office or they made that law, but of our mothers, our grandmothers what remains is nothing but a tradition. One was beautiful, one was red-haired, one was kissed by a queen. We know nothing of them except their names and the dates of their marriages and the numbers of children they bore.
>
> (Woolf [1929] 1977: 45)

Similarly, in psychology, women have been measured against a male standard and have been seen as wanting; women were identified as 'overtly' dependent and emotional compared to standard psychological profiles. The 'founding fathers' of psychology all drew on the science of evolution, and argued that women were less highly evolved and possessed only primitive mental abilities and that men were more mathematically and spatially competent (Wilkinson 1986). This is relevant today in that discrimination against women in the professions is still justified in some contemporary writing with reference to psychological 'findings' which suggest that men are more competitive and, surprise surprise, more mathematically and spatially competent (for more detail see Wilkinson 1991a, 1991b, 1996).

In the latter half of the twentieth century (particularly since the 1970s) things began to change. Since this time larger numbers of women have entered the academy and begun to do different kinds of research, research that has focused on the lives of women and validated their experience. However, this was difficult as the academic conventions and theoretical frameworks in existence were not appropriate for the study of women. As a result, attempts to uncover the hidden history of women, an anthropology of women, a less biased psychology of women and so on were not easy. For example 'politics' was defined as what occurs in government, as influenced by business and labour unions, and within this definition women were not included as significant political agents. It was therefore necessary for feminist political scientists to redefine politics to include anything concerning relations of power and privilege (e.g. personal and intimate relations in the private and the public sphere) and to examine power in terms of who has it and who uses it and how (see for example Lovenduski and Randall 1993). This shift of interest which includes attention to the private sphere was not only important in substantive terms but, as I shall highlight later (see Chapters 2 and 3), had important methodological implications in terms of the development of a reflexive research process.

Language and male authority

Man-made language?
It is useful to consider the production and prevalence of masculinized/authorized knowledge further through a consideration of language. Many feminists have been critical of the way language is constructed and have argued that language is 'man-made' in that, through language men have been able to dominate knowledge production in the arts and in culture in general. This means that our understanding of the world, what we know as reality, is based on the male view, on (certain) men's experience. The argument is circular in that, as Smith (1988) notes, the dominant ideas in any society are mediated through language, both in written texts and through verbal communication. Hence, because women have been excluded from the making of knowledge and culture, women's experiences, interests and their ways of knowing the world are not represented. This has meant that women have not been able to make sense of the world through their own experience, but only through the experience of men. In other words, ways of knowing have been made *for* women, not *by* women. In *Man-Made Language* Spender (1980) points out that both sexes can generate meanings – ways of knowing, of understanding – but women have not been at the centre of power. Therefore they have not been in a position to have their meanings taken seriously enough to represent a genuine challenge to dominant (masculinist) representations. Therein, meanings, which are different from those generated by men have been cut off from the mainstream and frequently lost. Spender argues that language is not neutral and not simply a means of ordering and classifying the world; rather it is a powerful method of manipulating and

creating reality. So, as Spender notes, even when men claim that language is not sexist their usage gives them away. She quotes Alma Graham:

> In practice, the sexist assumption that man is a species of males becomes the fact. Erich Fromm certainly seemed to think so when he wrote that man's 'vital interests' were 'life, food, access to females etc.'. Loren Eisley implied it when he wrote of man that 'his back aches, he ruptures easily, his women have difficulties in childbirth . . .' If these writers had been using *man* in the sense of the human species rather than males, they would have written that man's vital interests are life, food and access to the opposite sex, and that man suffers backaches, ruptures easily and has difficulties in giving birth.
>
> (Spender 1980: 155–6)

A similar example is given by Evans (1995: 73) who cites a male social scientist who argued that 'people in all societies have wives'. From this perspective, in patriarchal societies language is used to create masculinzed social reality where women are portrayed as subordinate to men.

The English language is biased in favour of the male in both syntax and semantics. There are more words that denote men, with some notable exceptions. For example, there are no words to describe female sexual power, but over 200 describing women's promiscuity (Spender 1980). The majority of words denoting men are positive, while those referring to women are mostly negative. For example, the *Oxford English Dictionary* defines a spinster as 'A woman still unmarried; especially one beyond the usual age for marriage' whereas a bachelor is defined as 'an unmarried man of marriageable age'. So, as Mills (1991: 226) notes, 'A bachelor of course is never too old to marry but an unmarried women once past childbearing age becomes an old maid' and an old maid is 'a prim nervous person of either sex who frets about inconsequential details'. Clearly this is just one example of how women are defined as lesser. Here are some more:

> Woman can be no more than a dumb ANIMAL (see BIRD, BITCH, FILLY, MOUSE, etc) . . . She can be CONTAINER and/or contents (see DISH) . . . Her CLOTHING can signify the whole woman (as in MUFF, SKIRT, PETTICOAT, etc) and/or woman as PART OBJECT, as in an expression like 'a bit of skirt'. A woman feels her VAGINA to be just one part of her body but words like CUNT, TWAT, BEAVER etc are used to denote all of her.
>
> (Mills 1991: xvii)

Interestingly, too, some of the worst insults directed at men have reference to women. Men are criticized for behaving like women, as in 'sissy', 'old woman', 'big girl's blouse', or by being associated with them, as in 'mummy's boy', 'son of a bitch'. Also, some of the most offensive (directed at women and at men) refer to women's genitalia, as in 'stupid cunt' and 'stupid twat'. Spender (1980) argues that men's monopoly of language creates the belief that there is one single reality. Within the confines of this reality is one single truth which can be viewed objectively. Furthermore, women have internalized this belief and by internalizing men's view of the world, women have helped to sustain it. Spender draws on Oakley's (1979) study of childbirth to illustrate this and argues that there is a 'conspiracy of silence' which surrounds the event and many women experiencing child-birth for the first time have been critical of their mothers and women friends for not telling them about the alternative female reality – in other words 'having a baby hurts'. Childbirth is not always an experience of rapturous joy, it is not something that every woman forgets quickly and some women feel awful for weeks, months, years afterwards. Thus, from this perspective 'the joy of childbirth' is a male reality – one seen from the perspective of a spectator. Men obviously do know something about childbirth: many babies are delivered by men and men are often present; but what is important here is the fact that men as doctors have been able to construct the knowledge – 'the truth' – about women's experience. If women speak out and challenge the authorized version they are dismissed as unfortunate exceptions or as disturbed and hysterical (interestingly, the word 'hysteric' is defined as 'of the womb', hysteria being thought to occur more often in women than in men!) (Oakley 1979; Spender 1980; Ussher 1991).

Thus, men's monopoly of authorized knowledge has meant the silencing of women. It has also meant their exclusion from public life – from science, art and literature, politics, law and economics – historically, any occupation where they might challenge the authority of men (Ussher 1991). The legacy of this is still evident not just in the numbers of female politicians, scient-ists or artists that we can name but also in the fact that we use the prefix of 'women' to describe women politicians, women artists, women doctors and feminize gender-neutral job descriptions (e.g. waiter(waitress), author(ess), sculptor(sculptress) and so on).

It would seem that language is exclusive, powerful and 'man-made'. In reaction to this, Daly (1979) argues that women should reclaim the lan-guage, indeed create their own. Further to this, Spender (1982) argues that there are distinct male and female realities and that reality is not objective but socially constructed. Therefore, women's experience and, importantly, the naming of that experience, is valid. Daly (1979) argues that part of this 'naming' involves 'recycling' or 'depolluting' words. As an example here we could return to the word 'spinster' which was originally based on the Old English root 'spinnan' which means to spin, and the suffix 'estre' which means 'one who spins'. In the fourteenth century, 'spinster' became appended to the names of women spinners to denote their occupation, and as Mills (1991) argues, during the Middle Ages it seems likely that spinsters enjoyed a higher status than women working in the clothing industry in subsequent genera-tions, and it was not until the seventeenth century that 'spinster' became the English legal designation for an unmarried woman. Another example is the word 'gossip' – which actually means 'a woman's female friend invited to be present at a birth to be a sponsor'. In the word's original sense, 'God-sibb' meant 'godparent', then sponsor and advocate, then it became a relative, then a woman friend, then 'a person, mostly a woman, of light and trifling character, especially one who delights in idle talk, a newsmonger, a tatler' (Mills 1991: 108). With these kinds of example in mind Daly (1979) argues that male language equals mind rape. So, she argues, there is a need to leave male language behind and empower women through language.

It's only words

However, there are many critics of this approach. Other writers and theorists accept that language does exclude, trivialize and demean women not least because of the sexist norm for humanity being man and mankind. But accepting that language is systematically sexist and plays an active role in the symbolic positioning of women as inferior to men is not the same as accepting that language structures reality. Many feminists reject Spender's and Daly's arguments as linguistic determinism, arguing that this approach reduces reality to language alone. Here, language appears to have a life of its own and it alone creates reality. There is no recognition of the fact that inequality is a product of social structures and social relations (Segal 1987; Mills 1991; Cameron 1985; Black and Coward 1998). Further, the view that language structures reality leaves little or no escape for transforming relations between men and women and leads to a separatist and a defensive and reactionary politics which places women outside mainstream politics and makes it impossible for women and men to communicate, as they have different languages. Overall, this view supports the idea of a distinct male and female reality which writes women out of history just as patriarchal history does, and dooms all women to silence – that is to say, men have power because men generate meanings and men generate meanings because they have power (see e.g. Segal 1987; Black and Coward 1998).

Also, as Cameron (1985) notes, there is always scope for creativity in language, and meanings do shift and change. Definitions are not static and closed. For example, with feminist influence the *work* aspect of housework is taken seriously by many. Also, words can be reclaimed and can be used ironically by women when still used derogatorily by some. Examples are the names given to some feminist publications such as *Spare Rib, Trouble and Strife*, *Shrew* and *Red Rag*. In current society, ancestor (rather than forefather), chair or chairperson (rather than chairman), police officer (rather than policeman) and the critique of 'he' as the generic term to refer to all people is commonplace. Many publishing houses, professional organizations and educational institutions have anti-sexist (and other anti-discriminatory) policies and practices. So social change clearly does affect the meaning and usage of words. However, as Cameron (1985) adds, in the minds of misogynists, language can always be sexist as, even though we may wish to import a positive sense to a word traditionally used to insult and demean women, if this meaning is not understood by others we are not any further forward.

An example of the tension here can be found in current concerns over political correctness. As Frye (1992) notes, political correctness was once viewed positively, whereas now political incorrectness is in many circles a term of positive evaluation generally used to express a sort of pride in resistance to what is claimed to be the banal moralizing of the politically correct. Thus, political correctness is described as righteous bullying or leftist fascism (Frye 1992; Kessler-Harris 1992). The result is a devaluing of political correctness, and when questioning sexist (racist, homophobic, disablist and so on) sentiments or behaviour it is possible to be asked whether bald people should be described as cranially advantaged or short people as vertically challenged.

Clearly, the relationship between language and power is complex and language can be a tool of oppression. However, it can also be a weapon in the struggle against patriarchy (Cameron 1985; Mills 1991). Language does not determine reality in a fixed way but it does provide dominant frames of reference and dominant meanings which we attach to experiences at any one time. We need to recognize that language reflects the centrality of power and authority and that we need to study how particular groups are able to control specific institutions which are able to construct dominant frameworks of meaning (e.g. academia, media, government), and consider how and why meanings are constructed into theory, into truth. Feminism is an interesting case in point here. It is useful to consider why many girls and women concerned about gender identity and gender roles in a way that could be defined as feminist reject any feminist identification (Griffin 1989; Letherby 1997). A couple of years ago I bought myself a UK monthly magazine, *New Woman* to read on a train journey. At that time the magazine was devoting the last page of each edition to a dictionary of important words for women. In the edition I bought, the letter of the month was F. Examples included:

F is for   **Female friends**: what would we do without them?
           Fat: a feminist issue.
           Frigid: a term used for women when we don't fancy sex.

So there were several terms which could be regarded as feminist in the list, which makes the final word and its accompanying definition ever more disturbing:

Feminism: we still need it but we want a new name for it.

Similarly, Toynbee (2000: 8) was disappointed when the three female comedians of the UK show *Smack the Pony* described their programme as 'Not a feminist show' and adds that, like all women who say 'I'm not a feminist but . . .' they have many complaints about women's position in society. Clearly, many women today are still afraid of being stereotyped as bra-burning, man-hating lesbians and are not aware of, or feel unable to acknowledge the impact of, feminism on their lives.

Like critics of Daly and Spender I support the view that language alone does not determine reality and in order to avoid what Segal (1987: 37) calls a 'politics of despair and retreat' we need to develop a sophisticated critique of language and language use. However, the early work of Spender, Daly and others should not be dismissed lightly as it initiated an important area of debate for feminists and highlights issues still relevant today to the study of language (see Gibbon 1999).

Storming the doors of academia

It was only very slowly and grudgingly that the various doors of education and academia were, at least in principle, opened to women and girls. In the UK, middle-class Victorian boys were educated at boarding school and encouraged to increase their physical and intellectual abilities. However, girls were kept at home and prepared for a life of domesticity and childbirth. Schooling for the working classes was not made compulsory until the late 1800s, and when it was the emphasis was on obedience, punctuality, clean-liness and deference to authority. Although literacy skills were taught, there was more concern with morality and discipline. As Abbott and Wallace (1997: 90) note, the aim was to produce 'a skilled and docile male work force and more domesticated wives, mothers and domestic servants'. Successive educational commentators and education acts continued these sexist assump-tions even though there were attempts to address class inequality.

Historically, arguments concerning biological differences between males and females have been used to strengthen the view that differential curricula for boys and girls was appropriate. Following the 1944 Education Act for girls who won a place to grammar school (which they achieved only by gaining 5 per cent higher marks than boys) the emphasis was on the aca-demic. For the majority of girls though, the emphasis was still on education for domesticity. Evidence suggests that in secondary coeducational schools girls' and boys' 'choices' and achievements are even more sex-stereotyped. Coeducational schools are really boys' schools and girls have to fit in (Skelton 1993). Although there now appears to be more equality in terms of co-education and equal access and achievement, girls are still disadvantaged and channelled into particular subject areas, and their participation is not taken seriously. Not surprisingly, now that girls are doing better than boys at all levels of secondary education the underachievement of boys is a problem in a way that the underachievement of girls never was (e.g. see Francis and Skelton 2001). There are presently proactive moves to encourage boys academically.

It is possible to argue that the expansion of higher education in the 1980s and 1990s benefited women more than men, in that in 1995 there were two and a half times more women in the system than in 1970/1 (Abbott and Wallace 1997). However, in practice men remain in privileged positions (Evans 1997). It is still difficult for women who work in higher education to get their research funded and published (Ward and Grant 1991) and both in the 'new' and the 'old' universities women academics remain in a very small minority, representing only 25 per cent of full-time staff. Historically and to date women have been concentrated in lower grades and in less secure posts. They are often on short-term contracts and are paid, on average, less than their male colleagues. Recent reports also suggest that women academics are severely underpaid and represent only a minority of professors and top managers (see, e.g. Bagilhole 1994; AUT 1999, 2000). Women predominate in the humanities and social sciences and the scientific population is, even now, one that is overwhelmingly male, which in itself is a consequence of the attribution of masculinity to scientific thought (Fox Keller 1990; Millen 1997). The following quote not only highlights this point but is relevant to many of the issues considered in this chapter:

> It used to be commonplace to hear scientists, teachers, and parents assert quite baldly that women cannot, should not be scientists, that they lack the strength, and clarity of mind for an occupation that properly belongs to men. Now that the women's movement has made offensive such naked assertions, open acknow- ledgement of the continuing belief in the intrinsic masculinity of scientific thought has become less fashionable. It continues, however, to find daily expression in the language of metaphors we use to describe science. When we dub the objective sciences 'hard' as opposed to the softer, i.e. more subjective, branches of know- ledge, we implicitly invoke a sexual metaphor, in which 'hard' is of course mascu- line and 'soft' feminine. Quite generally, facts are 'hard', feeling 'soft', 'feminization' has become synonymous with sentimentalization. A woman thinking scientific- ally or objectively is thinking 'like a man'; conversely, a man pursuing nonrational, nonscientific arguing is arguing 'like a woman'.
>
> (Fox Keller 1990: 43)

Due to the sexist ideologies that prevail within education, feminists have historically been torn between a desire to gain entry to the forbidden and difficult territories of academia and a desire to create their own education space. Wollstonecraft and de Beauvoir wanted women to have equal access to education and to be able to practise alongside men in the professions. Others like Woolf (1938) argued for the value of a separate women's college. In the 1970s, Rich joined the debate and argued for an educational environ- ment which replaced hierarchies and power structures with collective work and promoted research on issues of central concern to women and the community: 'women-centred knowledge' (see Rich 1986). As Potts and Price (1995) note, women entering the academy as feminists during the 1970s and the 1980s worked to develop a distinct and explicit feminist approach, dis- tinguished not least by its critical attitude to male-defined knowledge. Femi- nist academics were concerned to explore the links between the body, power and knowledge, with these intellectual interests mirroring the political de- mand for women to have control over their own bodies. Robinson (1993: 14) notes that, when women's studies developed, feminists wondered whether women should engage with theory at all and it was felt by some that it was best to focus on the practical and the political and to denounce the theoreti- cal theory has been used as a weapon by men against women. However this position ignores the fact that women have always theorized, despite the sexist assumptions that have assigned men with logic and reason and women with intuition and emotion. So theory itself is not inherently male, even if it has been used to justify women's position of inequality (Spender 1983). Thus, what was needed was a redefinition of theory and theorizing and as Evans (1983: 228) notes: 'Women's Studies has a most important part to play in ensuring that knowledge, itself a form of social power, is not produced solely in the interests of the powerful and influential'.

The presence of more women in women's studies and elsewhere in the academy has led to an increased critique not just of the knowledge produced but of the systems and institutions in which this production takes place. Thus, there is a considerable amount of research and autobiographical writing by women working in higher education which suggests that women academics are more likely to carry a multiple burden of managing home and work (e.g. Leonard and Malina 1994; Munn-Giddings 1998; Letherby 2000a) and suffer from the burden of emotional labour at work in the way that they are expected to care more than men for the emotional needs of students (and sometimes colleagues), as well as academic needs (e.g. Culley and Portuges 1985; Cotterill and Waterhouse 1998; Letherby and Shiels 2001). There is also much evidence that women experience sexism at work from male colleagues (e.g. Butler and Landells 1995; Humm 1996), that marginalization is accentuated by other differences such as age, sexuality, ethnicity and disability (e.g. Corrin 1994; Gibson 1996; Maguire 1996; French 1998) and that some women who have 'made it' do so by distancing themselves from other women and from feminism (Bagilhole 1994). It is possible to see the sense in this as those of us who teach women's studies and/or promote feminist ideas are likely to be accused of bias (even trivia) despite the bias of the history of knowledge (Flax 1987). Male academics do not have to justify themselves and their interests in the same way.

There is also evidence that issues of competition are difficult for women who define themselves as feminist and/or women-centred. As Keller and Moglen (1987: 505) note, the Women's Movement's 'emphasis on mutuality, concern and support' can be 'tremendously difficult to implement in the real world situation of the current academic market'. Although feminists have stressed collaboration rather than competition, sometimes, this is difficult to achieve, for, as Bagilhole (1994) and Kerman (1995) both suggest, women working in male-dominated environments have few others to collaborate with. Also, as Pritchard and Deem (1999) argue (specifically in relation to further education although the point is generalizable), women in management positions who want to work with an ethos of facilitation, support and empowerment often find themselves forced, by the processes and structures of the institution, to become a different kind of manager than they would want. In terms of career the historical (male) higher education linear model that starts with early undergraduate experience, followed by a smooth upward progression through the ranks associated with increased income and prestige is now outmoded (e.g. Weiner 1996; Blaxter et al. 1998). Ironically, this has resulted in a widening of career opportunities but an increased number of insecure positions, and a reduction in career satisfaction and progression possibilities, particularly for women who often enter late and are more likely to have a 'broken' career owing to family responsibilities (Weiner 1996).

Research and writing on the student experience also demonstrates that life is often difficult for women students. The experience of Rita in Willie Russell's play – the title of which I have included in the title of this chapter – provides a fictional account of female students' position in higher education. Rita's father, speaking to her husband, says: 'If that was a wife of mine I'd drown her' (cited by Coppock et al. 1995: 128). These kinds of attitude are reflected in the difficulties that women who combine family life and education have, which are in turn compounded by the fact that both the family and higher education are 'greedy institutions' (e.g. Edwards 1993; Acker 1994). Further, as Thomas (1990) argues, higher education can be contradictory and confusing for women as it prepares them for high-status jobs while not always challenging expected 'feminine' roles and behaviour. Further, within the current academic climate where large numbers of students are intended to be processed through general purpose courses as cheaply as possible (Epstein 1995), academics may be viewed as providing a service or even selling a product (e.g. Epstein 1995; Morley and Walsh 1995; Skeggs 1995). This is accentuated not only by the introduction of fees and student loans but by the increased stress on support and evaluation systems that actively encourage students to see themselves as consumers (see Marchbank and Letherby 2002 for further discussion). This in turn, of course, increases the burden on academics.

However, there are more women students, researchers, teachers and managers in further and higher education than ever before and as Evans (1995) argues, education is no longer just about DWMs (dead white males). In many subjects and on many levels there has been a concentrated challenge to the orthodoxies of the past. The curriculum has broadened and is less rigid in its subject demarcation and the critique of knowledge production is part of (some) academic study. Feminists and others working outside of western assumptions have been influential in these changes. As Evans (1997: 122) notes: 'feminists can claim to have developed one of the now great critical traditions within the Western academy, that of suggesting that the universalisitc assumptions of knowledge in our society are false, and partial, because they are drawn from the experience of only one sex'.

To return to my own discipline, as Abbott and Wallace (1997) note, sociologists can no longer afford to ignore women and gender divisions and there is much discussion about the changes needed for the biases of the past to be overthrown. Yet, they add, the struggle is ongoing and feminist sociology is still ghettoized and marginalized by many – or (and perhaps this is worse), the approaches and methods of feminist academics are adopted by mainstream writers with no acknowledgement of the debt to feminism. With these tensions and problems perhaps, as Gray (1994: 75) argues, it is necessary to remain ambivalent about our position in academia as this enables 'reflexivity, negotiations, movements and communication'. This is better than either complete acceptance of the 'current system' or a rejection of academia.

End points

As reported here, it is fair to argue that the history of knowledge production is masculine in that, until recently, it was largely men (but only a small group of men) who produced and had access to it and male identity was confirmed and accorded a high status by it. Morgan (1981) notes that academic discourse is, in reality, a male discourse hiding behind the labels of science, rationality and scholarship. Resistance to this masculine monopoly has not been easy:

> those who control the schools, the media and other cultural institutions are generally skilled in establishing their view of reality as superior to alternative interpretations. While an oppressed group's experiences may put them in a position to see things differently, their lack of control over the apparatuses of society that sustain ideological hegemony makes the articulation of their self-defined standpoint difficult. Groups unequal in power are correspondingly unequal in their access to the resources necessary to implement their perspectives outside their particular group.
>
> One key reason that standpoints of oppressed groups are discredited and suppressed by the more powerful is that self-defined standpoints can stimulate oppressed groups to resist their domination.
>
> (Hill Collins 1994: 83–4)

Some of Hill Collins' points have been considered in this chapter. Others such as whether the 'oppressed' can see the 'truth' more clearly than the 'oppressors' I will consider in Chapter 2. For now I would like to make two brief points that need to be considered in relation to all I have written so far.

First, despite the ways in which women have been misunderstood, ignored, excluded, denigrated and abused, it is important not to characterize them as inevitable passive victims and men as inevitable or deliberate oppressors, constantly wielding power. As Annandale and Clark (1996: 33) note, we must remain: '. . . cognizant of the possibility that "patriarchal discourse need not be seen as homogeneous and uniformly oppressive" . . . for women or uniformly liberating and unproblematic for men, and that women do not need to be portrayed as inevitable victims and men as victors'. Thus, men can be victims, women can be powerful, men and women often share experiences of powerlessness and, as I shall consider in Chapter 2, an understanding of the differences between women in terms of power and privilege is a vital part of the feminist project. We also know that women challenge, negotiate and resist. Indeed, in the latter part of this chapter I have highlighted some of the ways in which women have successfully challenged mainstream notions of 'who should know what'. With reference to another issue considered here, namely that of childbirth, we know too that both mothers and their midwives have fought for women's right to determine their own labour experience and make their own choices (e.g. Cornwell 1994; Doyal 1995; Kirkham 1997).

A review of the feminist literature from the 1970s to the 1990s suggests that the underlying theoretical model of woman-as-victim has largely disappeared and women are recognized as agents as well as victims operating in diverse and diffuse power structures and discourses of power in society (Evans 1997). However, as all feminist work to some extent 'problematizes' the position of women it is possible to argue that this supports traditional views of men as 'unproblematic'. Further to this, Evans adds that it is important not to forget that men are also governed by the rules of gender, while acknowledging that the rules work more often to their advantage.

The second point that I want to make returns me to a consideration of histories of knowledge. This time, though, I am concerned with the history of women's knowledge. Like Wilkinson (1996) I believe that we need to build on the valuable insights and the mistakes of previous generations of feminists (from both the first and second wave of feminism). Otherwise we have to continually begin at the beginning, to reinvent the wheel, to reach the same dead ends rather than benefiting from the efforts of our predecessors (Spender 1982; Wilkinson 1996). With this in mind my aim in this book is to add to debates while at the same time acknowledging their place in the process.

Note

1 The word 'dissemination' is used widely by researchers to describe the presentation of research material just as the word 'seminal' is used to describe a ground-breaking piece of research or writing. It is worth knowing that both 'dissemination' and 'seminal' have their roots in the word 'semen' ('the impregnating fluid of male animals') with the definition of dissemination being 'to scatter abroad as in sowing seed' and the definition of seminal being 'having the properties of seed; containing the possibility of future development'.

Suggested further reading

For a general overview of feminist thinking and critique see Evans, M. (1997) *Introducing Contemporary Feminist Thought* (Cambridge: Polity). For detail on knowledge and language see Segal, J. (1987) *Is the Future Female? Troubled Thoughts on Contemporary Feminism* (London: Virago); Smith, D. (1988) *The Everyday World as Problematic: A Feminist Sociology* (Milton Keynes: Open University Press); Gunew, S. (ed.) (1990) *Feminist Knowledge: Critique and Construct* (London: Routledge); and (1991) *A Reader in Feminist Knowledge* (London: Routledge); Mills, J. (1991) *Womanwords* (London: Virago); and Gibbon, M. (1999) *Feminist Perspectives on Language* (London: Longman).

For good edited texts with lots of articles about the experience of women in higher education, see Davies, S. Lubelska, C. and Quinn, J. (eds) (1994) *Changing the Subject: Women in Higher Education* (London: Taylor & Francis); Morley, L. and Walsh, V. (eds) (1995) *Feminist Academics: Creative Agents for Change* (London: Taylor & Francis) and (1996) *Breaking Boundaries: Women in Higher Education* (London: Taylor & Francis); Malina, D. and Maslin-Prothero, S. (eds) (1998) *Surviving the Academy: Feminist Perspectives* (London: Taylor & Francis); and Anderson, P. and Williams, J. (2001) *Identity and Difference in Higher Education: 'Outsiders Within'* (Aldershot: Ashgate).

For further reading on gender and education in general see, for example, Acker, S. (1994) *Gendered Education* (Buckingham: Open University Press); Arnot, M., David, M. and Weiner, G. (1999) *Closing the Gender Gap* (Cambridge: Polity); and Francis, B. and Skelton, C. (eds) (2001) *Investigating Gender: Contemporary Perspectives in Education* (Buckingham: Open University Press).

two

United we stand? The feminist reconstruction of knowledge

Introduction

In Chapter 1 my concern was with how the production of knowledge has been dominated by men throughout history and the implications of this both for the ways in which women have been defined and for their access to 'knowledge'. I also outlined some academic (and practical) resistance to 'male' authorized knowledge, and in this chapter I further consider academic feminism's resistance to male-defined ways of knowing. Not surprisingly, the authorized view of women's experience and the associated expected behaviour of women has often made women feel anxious, guilty, fearful and frightened, as it sets up an ideal that women are often unable to meet.

Historically, women have felt discrepancies between how they felt and experienced the world and the 'official definition' of their identity. However, as many writers suggest, the history of women's resistance is long (e.g. Rowbotham 1992; Lovenduski and Randall 1993; Doyal 1995; Evans 1997). This resistance is practical and political as well as academic and intellectual and, indeed, the two are often related. Here I am concerned largely with intellectual resistance. It is necessary to consider this as it is not only important for feminists to analyse gender relations and how they are constructed and experienced, but also to locate theory within wider 'philosophic contexts' (Flax 1987: 171).

As I argued in Chapter 1, male-defined epistemologies deny the importance of the experiential, the private and the personal so it is not surprising that, within feminism, the focus is often on the experiential and the private rather than the abstract and the public. Drawing on Smith (1988), Maynard (1994: 14) notes that:

> A focus on experience has been seen as a way of challenging women's previous silence about their own condition and in doing so confronting the 'experts' and dominant males with the limitations of their knowledge and comprehension. Feminism must begin with experience, it has been argued, since it is only from such a vantage point that it is possible to see the extent to which women's worlds are organized in ways which differ from those of men.

Further to this, early second-wave feminism was concerned to discover the cause of women's oppression and to locate this oppression in the social structure. As Williams (1996) notes, women's oppression was 'variously thought to be caused by capitalism, patriarchy, capitalist patriarchy, patriarchal capitalism, a dual system of exploitation and oppression or patriarchy as male control over women's sexuality, fertility and/or labour' (p. 66). Whatever the cause, the common emphasis here was towards 'the solidarity to be drawn from the commonalities of oppression that women shared as women' (p. 66).

Grass-roots campaigns by women in the 1970s and 1980s, which focused on developing separatist solutions to women's problems through the development of women's refuges and well-women health groups as well as campaigns such as Greenham Common, led to a perspective that stressed women's 'otherness' as a positive identity. As Williams (1996: 66) adds, this approach did successfully begin to challenge the traditional masculine-based view of the world. Yet, it was itself challenged for its own conception of 'woman' which was homogeneous and based on the false premise that differences between women were less important than what united them. Men, in other words, were the 'common enemy' (Smeeth 1990). Thus, as Adams (1994) notes, early second-wave feminist theory did not accommodate groups of women who could not identify with the white, middle-class, heterosexual women at the forefront of the Women's Movement. This led to debate about differences between and among women and the splintering of the Women's Movement, which as Kemp and Squires (1997: 4) note, despite 'oft-presumed unity', occurred almost simultaneously with the growth of second-wave feminism.

Alongside this, within academic feminism, was the development of multiple theoretical perspectives and in this chapter I am concerned with how feminist epistemological approaches challenge mainstream positions and the tensions and differences within feminist debate. I consider various positions and highlight problems of definition and differences of interpretation and meaning in relation to different feminist epistemological approaches. I also consider approaches which insist on a focus on women and approaches which aim to deconstruct the category 'woman'. I am aware of the dangers here. As Stanley (1999) argues, if we focus on distinct approaches and emphasize their differences we risk dividing feminist explanations into disparate positions, which is inappropriate as it implies mutual exclusivity, whereas many feminists have sympathies with aspects of each approach. This model also implies a historical, linear development of ideas which is also inaccurate (see e.g. Stanley and Wise 1993; Waugh 1998). Another danger suggested by some is that searching for a feminist knowledge, feminist science, feminist sociology, psychology, economics, history and so on is actually a contradiction because, if achieved, feminism will reproduce the power relations it questions (see e.g. Morley 1996; Harding 1997). However, it is useful to look at the differences between the modernist (feminist empiricism and feminist standpoint) approaches and the postmodernist approaches in order to consider whether, as several writers have suggested, there has been a 'paradigm shift' (from the material and the structural to the cultural and the postmodern) within feminism or, alternatively, whether supporters of these approaches are engaged in a productive dialogue with each other (see e.g. Maynard 1994; Zalewski 2000).

Thus, my aim is not to reconstruct the divisions but to explore the problems of 'finding a position', which I demonstrate further by identifying differences within as well as between approaches. I consider throughout the links between epistemology and research and with all of the above problems in mind I tentatively outline my own favoured approach and position.

Stand by your woman

Feminist empiricism
Harding (1990) suggests that in terms of the male academy, feminist empiricism can be seen as the least threatening of feminist epistemologies as it leaves intact much of science and philosophy's traditional understanding of the principles of adequate inquiry – that is, it seeks to use 'traditional' methods and approaches more 'appropriately', challenging the way methods are used rather than challenging the methods themselves and/or the ultimate scientific goal. Feminist empiricism is a foundationalist approach which does not critique the norms of science itself but the way in which the scientific method has been practised. From this perspective sexist and racist 'findings' are the result of sexist and racist practices: 'Everybody knows that permitting only men to interview only men about both men's and women's beliefs and

behaviours is just plain bad science' (Harding 1994: 105). What has passed for science is in fact the world represented by men from their perspective, and what looks like objectivity is really sexism as the kinds of questions social science has traditionally asked have systematically excluded women and their interests (Smart 1990). Women and pro-feminist men who are more likely to notice androcentric biases cannot only make the male scientific community aware of where others have gone wrong but they, with their awareness of the biases in traditional gender-blinkered work, can do 'good' science. Thus, feminist knowledge is better or truer because it is derived from the perspective of the outsider, the 'other', and includes women's experience in research as central rather than as marginal and deviant.

So, feminist empiricism is based on the foundationalist principles found within the modernist, Enlightenment tradition in that its supporters advocate the view of a single and universal social world where truth exists independently of the knower. Feminist empiricists are concerned to investigate and present 'real' science rather than the faulty science that results from masculine assumptions and ways of working. Feminist empiricism represents a threat to our traditional notion of what science is and suggests the need for a 'successor science': a science that will investigate and theorize the social world from the perspective of women. Eichler (1988), for example, argues that we can avoid sexism (and presumably other discriminatory practices) in research by paying attention to the research design, the execution of methods, evaluation and analysis. There is also a need to make it clear who the research is about and who is being researched. So, feminist empiricism suggests that feminists are more likely than others to achieve 'good science' and this challenges the view that the social identity (including the gender) of the researcher is irrelevant to the value of the result, and also challenges the belief that science must be protected from all politics. However, it does not challenge the view that 'the truth is out there' waiting to be discovered. Thus, the 'value freedom' of traditional research is challenged but not the empiricist goals (see Stanley and Wise 1983; Abbott and Wallace 1997; Millen 1997 for further discussion).

Feminist standpoint epistemology

Feminist standpoint epistemology – or as it is sometimes alternatively referred to, 'women's experience epistemology', 'cultural feminism' or even 'eco feminism' (depending on which text one reads) – also begins from the view that 'masculine' science is bad science and suggests the importance of developing a 'successor science' to existing dominant social science paradigms: an approach that would lead to a 'holistic, integrated, connected knowledge' as opposed to an 'analytically orientated and masculine form of knowledge' (Millen 1997: 7.2). Those who support this approach also argue that experience should be the starting point for any knowledge production and insist on the need to investigate and theorize the social world from the perspective of women. Thus, feminist standpoint epistemology starts from the position that the 'personal is political' while the traditional masculinist approach denies and downgrades the personal. Like feminist empiricism this is a foundationalist approach based on an insistence that 'truth' exists independently of the knower. Millen (1997) suggests that feminist standpoint epistemology draws on Marxist ideas about the role of the proletariat and suggests that women are an oppressed class and as such have the ability not only to understand their own experiences of oppression but to see their oppressors, and therefore the world in general, more clearly. Thus, female experience is not an invalid basis for knowledge but in fact a more valid basis for knowledge because 'it gives access to a wider conception of truth via the insight into the oppressor' (Millen 1997: 7.2). It is not just that the oppressed see more – their own experience and that of the privileged – but also that their knowledge emerges through their struggle against oppression: in this instance the struggle against men. So:

> To achieve a feminist standpoint one must engage in the intellectual and political struggle necessary to see natural and social life from the point of view of that disdained activity which produces women's social experiences instead of from the partial and perverse perspective available for the 'ruling gender' experience of men.
>
> (Harding 1987: 185)

Supporters of this approach argue that masculinized knowledge has (inaccurately) defined women's experience and they reject male 'objectivity' as a basis for a feminist epistemology, arguing that reality, defined as it is by men, has little meaning for women. Like feminist empiricism, feminist standpoint epistemology involves a critique of the research process. Its supporters recognize that the production of knowledge is a political act in that the researcher's own personhood is always part of research. A feminist standpoint is therefore grounded in the experience of women who are reflexively engaged in a struggle, and knowledge arises from this intellectual and political engagement (Smart 1990). Objectivity is possible but involves the critical scrutiny of all aspects of the research process and, as Harding (1991, 1993) argues, traditional notions of objectivity are 'weak' because the researchers' own values, assumptions and so on are hidden:

> Knowledge claims are always socially situated, and the failure by dominant groups critically and systematically to interrogate their advantaged social situation and the effect of such advantages on their beliefs leaves their social situation a scientifically and epistemologically disadvantaged one for generating knowledge. Moreover, these accounts end up legitimating exploitative 'practical politics' even when those who produce them have good intentions.
>
> (1993: 54)

For the supporters of feminist standpoint epistemology, reflexivity within research is not a problem but a scientific resource, and the use of reflexivity leads to 'strong' objectivity. Thus, 'All knowledge is based on experience, and standpoint theorists claim their research is scientifically preferable because it originates in and is tested against a more complete and less distorted kind of experience than malestream' (Stanley and Wise 1993: 293). Furthermore,

Harding (1993) suggests that the activities of the dominant group set limits on how everyone understands themselves and the world but the activities of marginalized groups provide more useful starting points as they generate the most critical questions about the status quo. So, feminist standpoint epistemology:

> sets out a rigorous 'logic of discovery' intended to maximize the objectivity of the results of research and thereby to produce knowledge that can be *for* marginalized people (and those who would know what the marginalized can know) rather than *for* the use only of dominated groups in their project of administering and managing the lives of the marginalized.
>
> (Harding 1993: 56, original emphasis)

Thus, as McCarl Nielsen (1990: 25) notes, the implication here is that developing a specifically feminist epistemology based on women's experience and perspective will lead to more accurate, more complex knowledge and a better world.

There are some problems here. First, the standpoint concept can imply that one group's perspective is more real, more accurate and better than others. There is an objective reality waiting to be discovered and we have access to a greater truth through an understanding of womanhood. So this approach can and has been used to replace male supremacy with female supremacy and support binary positions (i.e. all men are like this and all women are like that), accepting the essentially masculinist myth of feminine intuition and subjectivity and making this the basis for an epistemology. Given patriarchal structures of power and privilege (the fact that men still hold privileged positions in the education system, the media, politics and so on), means that women are colluding in their own oppression (Grosz 1990; see also Annandale 1998).

Second, the recognition of male dominance in both the public and the private spheres is an essential starting point for feminism but it is not enough that feminism concern itself solely with men's dominance over women. We have to consider women's differences and the power that some women have over others, and the interests that women sometimes share with men. In other words, shared gender does not automatically break down other barriers by unique forms of communication and understanding. Female oppression varies in both nature and degree and it is simplistic to assume that all women identify with each other on the basis of gender alone. Women's lives are contradictory, with conflicting interests in different systems of power. Gender is only one source of power and for many women gender oppression has not been their primary concern (e.g. black women may find that they have more in common with black men in the struggle against racism). Western women benefit from the exploitation of women in the developing world as producers of cheap food, clothing and contraceptives and, as bell hooks (1984) notes, black women often work under white women, so why should they join with women who exploit them? Thus, multiple systems of oppression frame everyone's lives and everyone's life is subject to varying amounts of penalty and privilege (Collins 1990). So we should avoid a position which implies that there is 'only one experience' which (as Flax 1987 argues) can only be built upon the suppression of voices of persons with experiences unlike those who are in a position to define. Further, the view that the more oppressed or more disadvantaged group has the greatest potential for knowledge implies that the greater the oppression the broader or more inclusive one's potential knowledge, and this could lead to an unproductive discussion about hierarchies of oppression (i.e. who is more oppressed, and how do we prove this anyway, and therefore potentially more knowledgeable – Hekman 1997). Even if we can find the most oppressed group of all, how do we know that their way of seeing is the most true (Harding 1986), as it is not the only alternative reality to the traditional male authorized view? There is also an implication that a person, or group of people, who stop being subordinated lose their double vision (Cain 1990). All women are different from each other and each woman has multiple (or fractured) identities, any one of which might arguably provide a standpoint for knowledge. With this in mind, Hill Collins (1989) argues that black women have access to an Afrocentric culture that white women do not and therefore they have a wider angle of vision than white women. However, she challenges the view that the more oppressed a person is the more 'accurate' is their view of the world and argues that black women's views of the world are not necessarily better, but are different from, white women's.

Some supporters of this approach focus on biology, which is problematic. Griffin (1983: 1), for example, suggests that 'those of us who are born female are often less severely alienated from nature than are most men'. There is also a tendency in much standpoint writing to liken womanhood to motherhood (e.g. Griffin 1983; Ruddick 1990) and/or womanly qualities of care and superior moral values (Gilligan 1982). This of course could be seen as contrary to the feminist insistence that the association of nurturance with womanhood is socially constructed, not biologically determined. Further, there is a danger that a focus on motherhood and motherly qualities places women who are unable to have children or who choose not to as 'other' to woman/womanhood (see Letherby 1994, 1999 for further discussion). Some supporters of feminist standpoint epistemology leave traditional definitions of women unchallenged and resist instead the traditional value given to women and womanhood. Thus, they revisit the ways in which women have been identified with particular characteristics and roles and, rather than pointing to the negative consequences of women's identification with the natural realm, celebrate the identification of women with nature (Alcoff 1988; Wajcman 1991). From this perspective there is a recognition of the value of the so-called feminine qualities: commitments to care, to emotion, to the natural. Thus:

> Women's biological capacity for motherhood was seen as connected to an innate selflessness born of their responsibility for ensuring the continuity of life. Nurturing and caring instincts are essential to the fulfilment of their responsibility. Conversely, men's inability to give has made them disrespectful of human and natural life, resulting in wars and ecological disasters. From this perspective, a new

feminist science would embrace feminine intuition and subjectivity and end the ruthless exploitation of natural resources. Rejecting patriarchal science, this vision celebrates human values and virtues and endorses the close relationship between women's bodies, women's culture and the natural order.

(Wajcman 1991: 7)

As Wajcman (1991) notes, many of the values being ascribed to women here originated in the historical subordination of women. Their association with nature, procreation, nurturance and so on lies at the very heart of traditional sexist conceptions of women (see Chapter 1). Clearly, the view of an innate 'womanhood' can and has been used in a patriarchal culture to keep women 'in their place'. A further, and related, problem is that feminist standpoint epistemology has tended not to give much attention to men and masculinity. Smart (1990) notes that as standpoint feminism has arisen from a grass-roots concern to protect women and to reveal the victimization of women, it has not been sympathetic to the study of masculinity(ies). The suggestion here is that standpoint feminism has been an entirely defensive stance with no recognition that women and men's lives sometimes intersect. This can backfire and perpetuate the view that women are 'the problem' (see e.g. Annandale and Clarke 1996 who, writing specifically about issues of reproduction, argue that concentrating on women compounds the view that reproduction is women's responsibility and it is women's fault when things go wrong).

Having said all of this it is important to appreciate the value of this approach in its insistence in viewing traditionally defined female characteristics in a different and much more positive way (Alcoff 1988; Kemp and Squires 1997). Feminist standpoint epistemology provides a way of naming the oppression of women which is grounded in the truth of women's lives and provides a challenge to the masculine definition of truth and method. Research and autobiographical writing by women suggests that many women experience life and knowledge in different ways from men and these ways have been positioned as subjective, irrational – as 'other' – by masculinist ideals of valid ways of knowing (e.g. Hill Collins 1989; Millen 1997): 'The fact that women belong to a group which has the capacity for procreation and mothering and the fact that men belong to a group that has the capacity to carry out, and does, acts of rape and violence against women must intrude into the consciousness of being male and female' (Bell & Klein 1996: 297–8). As Stanley and Wise (1993) note, women do experience reality differently just by having 'different' bodies and 'different' physical experiences (the use of quotation marks here is borrowed from Stanley and Wise who note that we should be wary of the use of the word 'different' as this sets male bodies, or particular male bodies, and experience as the norm). This 'difference' identifies women as 'other' so they are bound to be experienced as threatening and treated with scorn, puzzlement, dismissal and even violence. Millen (1997) argues that we need to incorporate these feminine ways of knowing and therefore classify women as well as men as knowers. Thus, as J. Evans (1995) suggests we need a sophisticated reading of feminist standpoint epistemology that challenges the limitations and celebrates the value of this approach. Cain (1990: 135) suggests that standpoint is a relational position constituted by politics, theory, theoretical reflexivity and not biology: 'What is important is to reflect upon a uniquely fractured site, reclaim it as a standpoint for knowledge production and political work and use this theoretical reflection to understand the relationship with other sites and standpoints'. Harding (1993) argues that the claim that women's lives provide a better starting point for thought is not about arguing for *one* position. Drawing on the work of Smith (1991) and Hill Collins (1990) she suggests that starting from the thoughts of different people with different experiences from our own helps to increase our ability to understand the perspectives of the powerful and the less powerful.

Furthermore, and interestingly, when searching for an epistemology based on the experience of African American women, the values and ideas that African writers identify as being characteristically 'black' are often very similar to those claimed by white feminist scholars as being characteristically female, which implies that material conditions of oppression can vary dramatically and yet generate some uniformity in the epistemologies of subordinate groups (Hill Collins 1989). However, in terms of knowledge construction and production, taking a standpoint remains problematic for, as Stanley and Wise (1990, 1993) argue, once we acknowledge the existence of several standpoints it becomes impossible to talk about 'strong objectivity' as a means of establishing superior or 'better knowledge' because there will always be alternative knowledge claims arising from contextually grounded knowledge of different standpoints.

I am what I am, or am I?

The importance of 'difference'

As Maynard (1994b) notes, the concept of 'difference' has a long history in relation to western feminism. Difference was not used as a word by first-wave feminists but these women were concerned with how women were the same as or 'different' from men, as well as how women's experience was affected by factors such as class and so on. Second-wave feminists have implicitly or explicitly employed the term 'difference' to point to the inequalities and disadvantages that women experience when compared to men, and more recently 'difference' has been used with another connotation referring to the 'differences' between women themselves. Maynard (1994b) adds that there are two formulations of 'difference': one which focuses on diversity of experience and another concerned with difference as informed by postmodernist thinking.

With reference to 'difference' as diversity of experience, assumptions that gender unites women more powerfully than other 'differences' has been challenged. Ethnicity, class, sexual identity and so on all affect our life chances and life experience. Thus as Lorde (1984) notes: 'There is a pretence to a homogeneity of experience covered by the word *sisterhood* that does not in fact exist'. Arguably, the second-wave feminist movement was largely a white, middle-class, heterosexual one, and with the importance of diversity of experience in mind there was a growing insistence on the need for a politics of identity which did not focus on women as a homogeneous group but recognized diversity between women (e.g. Kemp and Squires 1997). This was empowering for those women who saw themselves as outside the 'mainstream' of feminism because it validated and affirmed the experiences of groups of women who share both a positive identification and a specific oppression (Adams 1994). This was not just important in practical terms but also in theoretical terms. For example, a focus on white middle-class heterosexual women's experience results in the diversity of the experience of black women, working-class women, lesbians (and so on), effectively placing them as 'other' (e.g. Davis 1981; bell hooks 1982; Stanley and Wise 1993).

Taking ethnicity as an example, we know that 'race' adversely affects black women's experiences in relation to areas such as education, work and health (e.g. Mizra 1992; Afshar and Maynard 1994; Douglas 1998) and that whereas white feminist researchers have focused on the family as a place of subordination and oppression, black feminists have shown that for some women the family can be an arena for resistance and solidarity against racism (Carby 1982; bell hooks 1982; see also Jackson 1993 for further discussion). Also, 'race' is not a coherent category and the lives of those usually classified together under the label 'black' can be very different. Thus, culture, class, religion, nationality, sexuality, age and so on, in addition to gender, can all have an impact on women's lives and it is necessary to challenge the homogeneity of experience previously ascribed to women by virtue of being 'black'. For example, as Douglas (1998) notes, the health status of black and minority ethnic women in the UK reflects the interaction between their experiences of race, gender, class and culture. So, health and well-being are determined in these groups of women by a complex mixture of social and psychological influences and biological and genetic factors. Black women are not a homogeneous group with uniform needs for:

> They may be South Asian, Asian, Chinese, Vietnamese, African or African-Caribbean. They may have been born in the UK, may have migrated recently and may be refugees. They may have disabilities, be older, be lesbian. In attempting to examine the need for appropriate health services for black and minority ethnic women the similarities and differences in needs of black women must always be paramount . . .
>
> (Douglas 1998: 70)

Further, as Maynard (1994b) points out, individuals do not have to be black to experience racism, as attention to the historical and contemporary experience of Jewish and Irish people demonstrates.

Thus, attention to diversity of experience among women is essential. However, it is important to be aware of potential problems here. As bell hooks (1986) argues 'organising around your oppression' may provide an excuse for many privileged women to ignore their own status and their oppression of others. Also, there is a danger of an inherent competitiveness – a sort of hierarchy of oppression which implies that black women are more oppressed than white, black lesbians more oppressed than black heterosexual women and so on. As Hill Collins (1989) argues, oppression cannot be quantified and compared, and adding layers of oppression does not produce a potentially clearer standpoint. This implies the existence of a supposed norm and can result in women retreating into ghettoized positions (Maynard 1994b). If this happens it is then impossible to generalize about women's oppression in a useful way and/or to take a feminist position. A focus on diversity can therefore lead to problems in collaboration and ultimate depoliticization.

Postmodernism or poststructuralism?

As Waugh (1998: 177) notes, the term 'postmodernism' means much more than an approach to theory and has 'come to designate a bewilderingly diverse array of cultural practices, writers, artists, thinkers and theoretical accounts of late modernity'. With reference to feminist postmodernism, Smart (1990) notes that we are mistaken if we depict it as the third stage following feminist empiricism and feminist standpoint epistemology, or if we view it as a synthesis of these two approaches. Feminist postmodernism does not try to resolve the problems of other positions; rather it starts from a different place and proceeds in other directions (p. 81). Much postmodern analysis is rooted in philosophy and aesthetics and the term 'postmodernism' was first used in the 1950s. Smart suggests that in the case of feminism it started in political practice and began with the separate demise of sisterhood, Marxism and other 'grand' theories. As Waugh (1998) notes, postmodernism represents a more radical change in thinking than that of feminist empiricism or feminist standpoint epistemology, in that it completely rejects the possibility of the objective collection of facts and insists that knowledge is rooted in the values and interests of particular groups. From this perspective there are no universal theories and any attempt to establish a theory, a truth, is oppressive, whether from the perspective of men within a traditional authorized approach or from the perspective of women. Thus, feminist postmodernism (like other forms of postmodernism) rejects any claim to knowledge which makes an explicit appeal to a (grand) theory. A core element of postmodernism is the rejection of one reality which arises from 'the falsely universalizing perspective of the master' (Harding 1987: 188). However, unlike standpoint feminism, it does not seek to impose a different unitary reality. Rather, it refers to subjugated knowledges, which tell different stories and have different specificities.

Thus, feminist postmodernism takes issue with the whole notion of a standpoint (Millen 1997: 7.6). There are no overarching truths, no answers, only partial knowledges which are constructed in the specifics of time and place (Williams 1996). Postmodernism opposes all forms of essentialism and is a theory which disregards the notion of unitary categories and the possibility of access to a single, objective form of reality. From this perspective there is no such thing as the category 'woman', no such thing as a stable, coherent self, no such thing as patriarchy. None of us can speak for 'woman' because no such person exists except within a specific set of relations. The view here, as Alcoff (1988) points out, is that if we attempt to define women, characterize, or speak for women we are duplicating misogynist strategies. Thus, as Millen (1997: 7.7) notes:

> Instead of privileging female or feminine standpoint, FPM [feminist postmodernism] suggests that there is a variety of contradictory and conflicting standpoints, of social discourses, none of which should be privileged: there is no point trying to construct a standpoint theory which will give us a better, fuller, more power-neutral knowledge because such knowledge does not exist (Hekman 1990; Nicholson 1990). The search for a unitary notion of 'truth' about the world is impossible, a relic of the sterile Enlightenment: knowledge is 'partial, profane and fragmented' (McLennan 1995). Rather than seeking out a unifying epistemology, albeit one which incorporates gender, we should be constructing multiple discourses.

So the aim of feminism ceases to be the establishment of the feminist truth and becomes the deconstruction of truth. There is a shift away from treating knowledge as ultimately objective (and hence able to reveal the concealed truth) towards recognizing that knowledge is part of power and that power is ubiquitous. Feminist knowledge therefore becomes part of a multiplicity of resistances (Smart 1990). For postmodernists there is not one truth but many truths, none of which is privileged, and these different truths exist within different discourses (Flax 1987; Abbott and Wallace 1997). Thus, a postmodernist is concerned with explaining the discursive procedures whereby human beings gain an understanding of their common world, a discourse being a set of ideas, a framework within which possible ideas can be set and the conceptual sieve which passes some ideas as well-formed and rejects others as incoherent. Arguments happen within discourses and discourses determine what may be thought and what may not be thought in a given context, and thus what it makes sense to do and what makes no sense. Truth is what the discourse allows to be true and knowledge is constructed through discourse. There is nothing outside discourse, no objective reality or self and the self is deconstructed into multiple modes and forms of identities, existing only at the intersection of discourses (Maynard 1994b).[1] From this perspective all feminists can do is present alternative accounts – to question and to challenge. There is no truth awaiting our discovery, only 'truth' to be invented through the creative uses of language. Thus, as J. Evans (1995: 125) notes, postmodernism admits to no narrative that automatically subsumes women and relegates them to second place, nor does it admit to one that puts women first. Thus, unlike varieties of feminism which allow for differences between women in terms of social structure – social class, ethnicity, age and so on – postmodernists argue a thoroughly relativistic position which denies the possibility of *any* form of 'authorized' knowledge.

Some feminists (e.g. Flax 1987; Butler 1990; Hekman 1990) insist that feminism is inherently postmodern, as feminist notions of self, knowledge and truth are contradictory to those of the Enlightenment and feminism and postmodernism are the only theories that represent a critique of the Enlightenment legacy of modernism. As Jackson (1992) argues, this is correct in that feminism does aim to deconstruct the taken for granted, especially concerning gender relations, and does challenge the sexism in language and the view of objective masculine science. As Waugh (1998: 179–80) suggests:

> Historically, the rise of second-wave feminism coincided with a growing incredulity towards universal truth-claims. Yet feminism has, to some extent, always been 'post-modern'. Feminists have shown how Enlightenment discourses universalise white, Western, middle class male experience and have thus exposed the buried strategies of domination implicit in the ideal of objective knowledge. Feminists as well as postmodernists have long recognised the need for a new ethics responsive to technological changes and shifts in the understanding between the relations of power and knowledge. Feminism has provided its own critique of essentialist and foundationalist assumptions, arguing, for example, that gender is not a consequence of anatomy and that social institutions do not reflect universal truths about human nature.

The connection or not between feminism and postmodernism has stimulated a great deal of debate. As Zalewski (2000: 130) argues, postmodernist feminists insist that modernist feminists 'decide in advance what women are (or should be) and then proceed to base their explanations and prescriptions on this'. She suggests that postmodern feminists have no wish to define or determine women and insists that 'the uncertainty that results from abandonment of the belief in the certainty of the subject' does not mean that politics is impossible because 'to demonstrate how women are represented and constructed in and by language is itself a political act'. So, says Zalewski, postmodernist feminists are concerned with how the category 'woman' is defined, represented and made to appear natural, rather than holding onto any definite idea *about* women. Their critique of modernist feminisms is that they challenge Enlightenment thought by rejecting its epistemology as fundamentally male biased and yet at the same time look to the methods of modernism on which to base a politics of feminism.

However, some writers suggest that postmodernism poses some serious problems for feminism. Alcoff (1988: 420) asks:

> If gender is simply a social construct, the need and even the possibility of a feminist politics becomes immediately problematic. What can we demand in the name of women if 'women' do not exist and demands in their name simply reinforce the myth that they do? How can we speak out against sexism as detrimental to the interests of women if the category is a fiction?

Similarly, Jackson (1992: 28) notes that if we insist that feminist meanings are no more valid than any other, how can we claim that the 'feminist reading of forced sexual intercourse as rape is any more valid than the rapist's interpretation of it as pleasurable seduction?'

Thus, scepticism about truth and knowledge raises questions not only about the possibility of any theory of women's subordination but also about the systematic description of subordination, or even that subordination exists at all. From a postmodernist perspective we cannot make the claim that it is wrong to oppress women because we do not know what we mean by women, nor whose criteria we are using to argue for oppression (Hartsock 1990; Abbott and Wallace 1997). Furthermore, although feminist postmodernism suggests that there is a need to focus on meaning and language, this denies any reality outside of the discursive. As Maynard (1994a) notes, discourses are variably available to more and less privileged people and we are not all able to take advantage of them.

Further, as Ramazanoglu (1993) argues, women's experiences suggest that men can have power that is in a real sense a form of domination backed by force, and that this domination cannot be seen simply as a product of discourse but must also be understood as 'extra-discursive' or relating to wider realities than those of discourse – to other social relations. This includes relations between men and women and between women with different experiences, which are each affected by the social construction of appropriate gender roles which are related to biological and material differences. It is necessary to consider 'extra-discursive' influences not least to acknowledge that women (people) can be active agents and not passive victims. As Weedon (1987: 125) notes: 'Although the subject . . . is socially constructed in discursive practices, she none the less exists as a thinking, feeling and social subject and agent, capable of resistance and innovations produced out of the clash between contradictory subject positions and practices'.

With all of this in mind, Di Stefano (1990) argues that postmodernist theory had more meaning for men than for women. She suggests that white, privileged men were central to the development of Enlightenment theory, and can now afford to subject that legacy to critical scrutiny. Hartsock (1990) says that it is particularly interesting that, just at a time when previously silenced populations have begun to speak for themselves, postmodernism tells us that seeking a liberating 'truth' about women is theoretically suspect. As Scott (1998: 1.3) argues: 'The radical uncertainty that post-modernism introduced into academic feminism arrived at a time when feminism's worldly success in having the problems of gender inequality acknowledged as social problems was peaking, and a "backlash" against feminism had begun'.

As Millen (1997: 7.8) notes, feminist postmodernism exposes the tension at the heart of feminist theory and feminist research in its critique of traditional epistemology and methods, and provides a powerful critique of the relationship between power and knowledge. However, the particular form this critique takes could seriously undermine the political role of feminist research with its focus on gender relations and inequalities. Further, philosophically, postmodernism itself could be argued to be self-defeating as it attacks the notion of 'grand theory' while setting itself up as a theory itself: the 'no truth except within a discourse' theory.

Finding a position

Focusing on the material

'. . . while gender relations could potentially take an infinite number of forms, in actuality there are widely repeated features . . .' (Humphries 1998: 1.12).

We know that the material conditions of women's lives worldwide are worse than those of men. Worldwide, women are poorly represented in ranks of power, policy and decision making (see e.g. Lovenduski and Randall 1993; Humphries 1998; Marchbank 2000). Women work more and their labour is of less value (see e.g. Jackson 1993; Witz 1993; Doyal 1995) and care work and emotion work are also gendered with women more likely to bear multiple burdens both at home and at work (see e.g. Hochschild 1983, 1990; Graham 1984; James 1989; Delphy and Leonard 1992; Finch and Mason 1993; Duncombe and Marsden 1998; Marchbank 2000). Despite supposed sexual liberation, heterosexual relationships and the patriarchal family are supported by all social institutions and lesbians are marginalized and disadvantaged in legislation and family life (Reinhold 1994; Caradine 1996). Divorced and never-married women with children and older women dependent on state pensions and social security benefits are often the poorest in society (Pascall 1997). Further, the double standard of sexual morality means that the sexual reputation of a woman is much more precarious than that of a man (Smith 1989; Lees 1997; Ussher 1997). Violence against women is often supported, even promoted, by the media and not given serious attention by the criminal justice system (Stanko 1985; Morgan 1989; Lees 1996; Gregory and Lees 1999; Gillespie 2000) and, further, to humiliate is to 'feminize' (Dawson 1994; Newburn and Stanko 1994). On the other hand, women who kill or attack men (even after years of abuse) are likely to be punished much more severely than men who attack or kill women (Smith 1989; Lloyd 1995; Lees 1997). Violence against women is often sanctioned by culture and/or religion as in foot-binding and female genital mutilation (see e.g. Showalter 1987; Ussher 1991; Van der Kwaak 1992; Blake 1994) and arguably internalised by women themselves trying to meet an ideal as in anorexia and cosmetic surgery (Freedman 1988; Malson 1996; Greer 1999). With all of this in mind, economic, social and cultural factors prevent many women from meeting their physical and psychological health needs (Wilkinson and Kitzinger 1994; Doyal 1995, 1998). Thus, as Blake (1994: 678) argues: 'Gender differences are not only biologically determined, culturally constructed, or politically imposed, but also ways of living in a body and thus of being in the world'.

Despite all of this, several feminists have suggested that there is a 'turn to culture' (Barrett 1992; Kemp and Squires 1997) within academic feminism: a shift away from structural concerns such as capitalism and patriarchy and an emphasis on culture, sexuality, symbolization and representation. Yet, as Maynard (1994b: 20), drawing on Hall (1992), argues:

> ... it is one thing to argue such a shift has taken place but another to imply that this renders a concern with materiality redundant: 'It is, after all possible to acknowledge the significance of culture and discourse and some of the problems to which they may give rise in speaking about the social world, without denying that events, relations and structures do have conditions of existence and real effects outside the sphere of the discursive.

The value of difference

'... shared material conditions cannot transcend divisions among women created by race, social class, religion, sexual orientation and ethnicity' (Hill Collins 1994: 83).

As Maynard (1994b) notes (and the previous section suggests), although universalizations are untenable it is possible to talk of general properties and to highlight similarities as well as differences in women's experiences. It is clearly the case that women share experiences across cultures. Therefore, although categories/variables such as woman, race and class are not unitary this does not mean that they are meaningless. Such terms stand for 'the social construction of a particular set of people facing – albeit with large internal differences – a common material reality because [it is] one based in a common oppression/exploitation' (Stanley 1990: 152). This material reality of course includes representations and categorizations as well as physical material circumstances, and there is no need to conclude that such a position leads to essentialism (Riley 1988; Maynard 1994b). As Maynard (1994b) adds, discussions of difference have, rightly, drawn attention to serious problems which existed in the narrowly-defined nature and over-generalizations of previous work about women by western feminists. It is necessary to problematize categories such as 'race' (which are often used homogeneously) and challenge deterministic and stereotypical definitions of womanhood. Thus it is important to be aware of the complex nature of difference and diversity – for example:

> On certain dimensions, Black women may more closely resemble Black men, on others, white women, and on still others, Black women may stand apart from both groups ... Deborah K. King describes this phenomenon as a 'both/or' orientation, the act of being simultaneously a member of a group and yet standing apart from it.
>
> (Hill Collins 1994: 86)

With this in mind, bell hooks (1984) suggests that sisterhood, which implies an approach shared by all women, should make way for solidarity. This enables different groups of women to support each other without insisting that their situation is identical.

Feminist standpoints or feminist epistemologies?

I have suggested in this chapter that there are problems and tensions with both 'successor science' (feminist empiricism and feminist standpoint epistemology) and completely relativist (feminist postmodernism) approaches. Yet, there is value in these approaches also. Thus, many writers argue for the development of a position/approach which avoids crude essentialism and crude difference/deconstructivism (Alcoff 1988; Maynard 1994a; Doyal 1995) – a position which retains a commitment to an emancipatory project (Kemp and Squires 1997; Waugh 1998) and yet dispenses with 'absolute' epistemological foundations (Maynard 1994b).

bell hooks (1986) suggests that feminism is possible not because women share the same experiences, but because it is possible to federate around common resistance to all forms of oppression. Therefore, the aim is not to establish a 'feminist standpoint' as a generator of *true* stories about social life, but rather feminist oppositions and criticisms of *fake* stories, to lead to an understanding of women's lives that both illuminates their experiences and is respectful of them. There is, however, a further problem here. How do we know what stories are false if we do not have a feminist standpoint from which to view them? Thus, perhaps, it is better to speak as Stanley and Wise (1990) do, of 'feminist standpoints' (emphasis added) or a wider notion of a 'feminist standpoint' that incorporates a number of feminisms. Differences do exist between women, so the category 'woman' needs to be carefully defined in order to focus on ontological separations as well as similarities. There is a common material reality that all women share which is characterized by inequality, exploitation and oppression, but women are not all oppressed in the same way. It is therefore important to recognize that while oppression is common, the forms it takes are conditioned by race, age, sexuality and other structural, historical and geographical differences between women. 'Woman' can be argued to be a: 'socially and politically constructed category, the ontological basis of which lies in a set of experiences rooted in the material world', and yet 'the experience of "women" is ontologically fractured and complex because we do not all share one single and unseamed reality' (Stanley and Wise 1990: 21–2). Di Stephano (1990: 78) deals with the complexity of this when she argues that it is necessary to be aware that gender functions as 'a difference that makes a difference even if it can no longer claim the legitimating mantle of *the* difference'.

From this position there cannot be a feminist science as there is no reality out there waiting to be discovered, to be known, but there are many subjective experiences. Yet, women, and other groups of people (e.g. black people, disabled people) do have a commonality of experience and oppression (Stanley and Wise 1993). Further to this, black writers have emphasized the importance of recognizing that experience does not necessarily equal 'truth'. Rather it provides the basis from which to address both the similarities and the contradictions in women's lives and to develop theories as to how these might be understood collectively (Collins 1990; Brah 1992). As Brah says, the notion of experience is important 'as a practice of making sense, both symbolically and narratively; as struggle over material conditions and over meaning' (1992: 141), and further is both individual and collective as in individual biography or collective histories which enable us to see how groups are positioned in social structural terms (Brah 1991, 1992).

Yet, Cain (1990) argues that it is possible to develop a 'successor science', though she argues that it would be useful to escape the connotations of the term 'science' and aim to produce 'good quality knowledge' which should suggest that, however it is authenticated, the knowledge produced should not be accepted uncritically. Interestingly, the German word *Wissenschaft*, which is used to describe 'organized' knowledge or argument, is viewed equally when preceded by *Natur-*(natural) and *Geistes-*(social). The prescriptive/restrictive/ positivistic sense seems to be an Anglo/Franco construct (see Chapter 3 for further discussion). Harding (1986) suggests that successor science projects may be the best weapon women have in their engagement with men's knowledge at this stage in the struggle, whereas others suggest that there are unacknowledged similarities between modernist and postmodernist approaches:

> the construction of a gulf between modernist and postmodernist feminisms seems radically at odds with the postmodern claim to want to destabilise dualisms; surely the feminist modernist/postmodernist divide is a prime example of a dualism to be destabilised rather than reinforced? Even more than this, one can argue that the feminist modernist/postmodernist dualism is a prime example of the illusion of such a divide. Modernist feminisms paradigmatically challenge Enlightenment thought by rejecting its epistemology as fundamentally male biased . . . Yet at the same time modernist feminism has looked to the methods of modernism on which to base a politics of feminism. As such, there is a profound ambiguity in feminism: it challenges modernist epistemology but is located in the emancipatory impulses of modernism. So in a sense all feminisms are in an anomalous position *vis-à-vis* the modernist/postmodernist debate. The idea of a gulf seems inadequate to capture this intriguing ambiguity. Instead it encourages a policing and disciplining set of strategies.
>
> (Zalewski 2000: 139–40)

This suggests that rather than accepting the idea that there has been a 'paradigm shift' within feminism we need to acknowledge the fact that many feminists have sympathies with more than one approach and that feminist standpoint epistemology and feminist postmodernism have much to learn from each other's insights and successes (see e.g. Maynard 1994a; Stanley 1999; Zalewski 2000).

Harding (1993) suggests that the varieties of all feminist epistemologies that we have should be regarded as 'transitional epistemologies' and not be constructed as finished products but as part of an ongoing practical struggle. Furthermore, there is much contention over what is a standpoint and who is a postmodernist and many writers and thinkers are labelled in ways that they themselves challenge (see e.g. a recent debate in the journal *Signs*).[2] I appreciate that the approach I have taken here is problematic in that it separates out arguments and theories. I also accept that my reading differs from that of others. This chapter represents my interpretation of feminist debates on the construction and status of knowledge.

End points

As noted in Chapter 1 many feminists have made a significant contribution to the understanding of the connection between power and knowledge. Feminists have pointed out how, historically, knowledge and knowledge claims have been intimately tied to relations of dominance and exclusion. As highlighted here, this attention has led to debate and discussion within feminism about the nature and status of feminist knowledge. Yet, this debate has added to rather than threatened the value of feminist epistemologies and as Scott (1998: 1.5) argues:

> Despite the challenges to the possibility of 'truer' and more complete knowledge, and feminists' increasing awareness of the variety and complexity of women's experience, feminist research has continued. It may be more circumspect in its claims, but a fundamental link remains between listening to what people have to say about their lives and identifying patterns and relationships which expose the operations of power and oppression.

Furthermore, as Scott adds, feminists have been concerned to ground their research in a feminism-friendly epistemology and have concerned themselves with knowledge production and the role of the researcher in the process of knowledge production. Stanley (1999) argues that this 'intellectual craftswomanship' is just as important to the critical project of feminism as the analytical and political engagement with substantive issues that affect individuals' lives. With this in mind, in the remainder of this book I explore further the dynamic relationship between the process and the product of research and consider further the position of the feminist researcher.

To end this chapter, and as a challenge to those who would argue that academic feminism is the poor political sister to grass-roots feminism, it is useful to draw on Humm (1997: 17) who argues that theory alone cannot create social change, nor can it be dismissed: 'The feminist fight is not on the page but in the home, at work and on the streets. But the struggle comes from ideas. Feminist theory is a river fed by different feminisms and different feminists'.

Notes

1 It is interesting to compare this to Spender and Daly's arguments as outlined in Chapter 1.
2 In an article in *Signs: Journal of Women in Culture and Society* Hekman (1997) described several writers as 'standpoint theorists'. In replies to this article several of said writers argued that they were not (e.g. Harding 1997; Hartsock 1997; Hill Collins 1997; Smith 1997).

Suggested further reading

For further, similar and different discussion of the issues considered in this chapter the following are useful: Gelsthorpe, L. and Morris, A. (eds) (1990) *Feminist Perspectives in Criminology* (Buckingham: Open University Press); Nicholson, L.J. (ed.) (1990) *Feminism/Postmodernism* (London: Routledge); Alcoff, L. and Porter, E. (eds) (1993) *Feminist Epistemologies* (London: Routledge); Maynard, M. (1994) Methods, Practice and Epistemology: the debate about feminism and research, in M. Maynard and J. Purvis (eds) *Researching Women's Lives from a Feminist Perspective* (London: Taylor & Francis); and (1994) 'Race', gender and the concept of 'difference' in feminist thought, in H. Afshar and M. Maynard (1994) *The Dynamics of 'Race' and Gender: Some Feminist Interventions* (London: Taylor & Francis); Abbott, P. and Wallace, C. (1997) *An Introduction to Sociology: Feminist Perspectives* (London: Routledge); and Jackson, S. and Jones, G. (1998) *Contemporary Feminist Theories* (Edinburgh: Edinburgh University). Also, readers such as Evans, M. (1994) *The Woman Question* (London: Sage); and Kemp, S. and Squires, J. (1997) *Feminisms* (Oxford: Oxford University Press) provide really useful collections of feminist writings.

three

Doing it for ourselves: feminist research as theory in action

Introduction

In Chapter 2 I considered the complexities of various feminist epistemological positions. I highlighted the problems for feminists in 'taking a position' and argued that it is necessary to recognize both the importance of the material and the importance of difference. I also began to hint at the implications of this for research in terms of the difficulties in being 'objective' and the need to acknowledge the importance of the researcher's self within research. In this chapter I consider further the relationship between theory and research. When thinking about the importance of theory it is worth remembering that everyone is a theorist: we all think, analyse, interpret and reflect in order to make sense of our lives and our theories are always open to change and development (Cain 1990; Stanley 1991; Hall 1992; Abbott and Wallace 1997). Theoretical perspectives provide frameworks to explain and make sense of what is going on, and in attempting to take account of all the 'facts' social theory tries to be more systematic about explanations and ideas while at the same time being open to challenge and refutations (Abbott and Wallace 1997). A theoretical perspective provides us with a framework within which we can explain and account for our observations of social life (e.g. social class, patriarchy, the isolated nuclear family). It also suggests the type of questions we should be asking (and the variety of ways in which they might be asked), draws our attention to certain kinds of events rather than others and provides us with ways of answering questions. (Cain 1990; Abbott and Wallace 1997).

For many feminists, feminist research *is* feminist theory in action. Feminist theory has political aims in that it celebrates and is grounded in the daily experiences of women (and men), and by focusing on experience it is able to challenge mainstream/malestream knowledge. Furthermore, as Scott (1998: 1.6) notes, the relationship between theory and experience is dynamic: 'Experience may be the starting point for feminist research but it is in the analysis of experience that the potential for change lies without denying that behind the text are lives'.

So the aim is to understand the world and change it (e.g. Stanley 1990), and to do this we need to take the experience of our respondents seriously. We also, as Cain argues, need 'to take our own theory seriously' and 'use the theory to make sense of . . . experience' (1986: 265). This is 'an interpretive and synthesizing process which *connects* experience to understanding' (Maynard 1994a: 24). The way we theorize has implications for the knowledge we get and like Stanley and Wise (1993) and Cain (1990) I agree that we need to take our experience of research seriously, because the methodological approach we take also affects the resultant product. In other words, we need to consider the relationship between the process and the product. Thus, we need to theorize on the method and approach and aim to produce 'unalienated knowledge' in feminist terms: '. . . unalienated knowledge is that which concretely and analytically locates the product of the academic feminist labour process within a concrete analysis of the process of production itself' (Stanley 1990: 12).

This woman-centred approach to understanding research should not be mistaken as being completely synonymous with *feminist standpoint epistemology*, as described in Chapter 2, despite the use of the word 'standpoint' by both McCarl Nielsen and Smith:

> Feminist *standpoints* begin with but do not end with women's experiences, and as in the case of other standpoint epistemologies, they are more than perspectives. They involve a level of awareness and consciousness about one's social location and this location's relation to one's lived experiences.
>
> (McCarl Nielsen 1990: 24, emphasis added)

> The *standpoint* of women therefore as I am deploying it here cannot be equated with perspective or worldview. It does not universalize a particular experience, it

is rather a method, that at the outset of inquiry, creates the space for an absent subject, and an absent experience that is to be filled with the presence and spoken experience of actual women speaking and in the actualities of their everyday worlds.

(Smith 1988: 106–7, emphasis added)

Thus, taking a feminist standpoint to research means adopting a position which does not 'add' women in but begins from their perspective: adopting a feminist methodological standpoint.

In this chapter and the next I consider the relationship between theory and research – the link between what we know and how we gather knowledge; the link between knowledge and knowledge production, the process and the product – and demonstrate that there is a dynamic relationship between the construction of theory and the collection of data. Specifically in this chapter I focus on the critique of mainstream theory through a consideration of the support for, and critique of, the 'quest for science', the 'generation of theory from data' and the development of a feminized approach in terms of knowledge production, reflexivity and representation.

In Chapter 2 I argued against both the strong objectivity of *feminist standpoint epistemology* and the complete relativism of *feminist postmodernism* and argued for a position that celebrates the multiplicity of viewpoints and positions among women while still acknowledging the importance of collectivity between women. Here, and in line with this approach, I also argue for a midway position and contend that while feminist research cannot claim to have epistemic privilege and thus is unable to reveal a 'truth', it is possible to argue that, while recognizing that we do not uncover the one and only truth, we should aim to make our work illustrative of women's experience. Within this I also begin to consider debates concerning the inclusion of men in feminist research.

A critique of malestream theory

The quest for 'science'

As noted in Chapter 1 the unquestioned authority of the scientific method as the best way to study both natural and social phenomena has dominated recent history. Within this, as McCarl Nieslen (1990) notes, *objectivism* (the view that there is an objective world that is knowable) versus *relativism* (the view that there is no final truth that we can agree on) has characterized western discourses on knowledge.

Within objectivism there is a clear view that the neutral knower can be separated from what is known, that different researchers exposed to the same data would replicate results and that it is possible to generalize from this type of research to wider social and natural populations. It is believed that this approach guarantees objective inquiry and is valid for the investigation of any sort of phenomenon in the social as well as the natural world (e.g. McCarl Nielsen 1990; Stanley and Wise 1993; Oakley 1999). Indeed, physics was/is considered the model of science: 'the most real of sciences'.

The social sciences were shaped by the advances of natural science and technology in the eighteenth and nineteenth centuries and this led to social scientists adopting the same view of the social world as natural scientists had of the natural world. So the social world was believed to be made up of 'social facts' that could be studied in much the same way as 'natural' facts were – i.e. there is one reality and it can be discovered. From this perspective theory is neutral, objective and value-free and the research process needs to be likewise. In their struggle to distinguish themselves and their disciplines from the natural sciences, social scientists were concerned to find a distinct 'scientific' approach and method (Oakley 1999). This involved a rejection (first in Europe and later in the USA) of the experimental method and the adoption of the survey method. Indeed, quantitative methods were accepted as the dominant approach within the social sciences until the 1960s. Thus, as Oakley (1999: 159–60) suggests: 'The survey method within social science owes its origins to the need men felt . . . for an empirically based social research that would explain social transformation not just at the level of the local community but more broadly and that would provide a basis for concrete social policies'.

Those that aim for 'scientific' social science would argue that research is linear and is characterized in terms of the objectivity of its method and the value-neutrality of the 'scientist'. A single unseamed reality exists 'out there' which the researcher can investigate and explain as it 'really' is, independent of observer effects (Stanley and Wise 1993: 6). The research process is value-free, coherent and orderly – in fact 'hygienic' (Stanley and Wise 1993; Kelly et al. 1994) – and all that a researcher has to do is follow the rules. Early social scientists accepted this approach uncritically, including its implication that the identity of researchers is irrelevant (even though at the same time women were thought to be the best interviewers because of their assumed 'feminine' skills – see Chapter 4). This meant that researchers and theorists were able to leave their gender and accompanying positions of institutional power and privilege unquestioned (Skeggs 1994: 78). The emphasis here is on *deductivism*: hypotheses are formulated and then tested to assess their validity. Resulting findings are fed back into, and absorbed by, the theory. In many texts (feminist and others) this approach is referred to as *positivism*.

However, there is a danger of oversimplification here. As Oakley, drawing on historical studies of the sciences and social sciences, argues, equating positivism with 'science' is problematic:

> However you look at it, positivism is the work of the devil. Anyone who believes that hypotheses need to be warranted, anyone who uses numerical data or statistics, anyone who is concerned about representativeness or generalizability or the credibility of research findings is liable to be deemed a 'positivist'.
>
> (Oakley 1999: 156)

Oakley suggests that one problem with this is that the term 'positivism' ceased long ago to have any useful function as there is considerable confusion over what it means. Furthermore, and relatedly, there is confusion over the meaning of 'science', and much of what social scientists implicitly refer to as 'science' is not recognizable within science itself. Indeed, natural scientists themselves disagree over whether they are describing the world or constructing an image of it (Maynard 1994a: 13). 'Natural' science covers many approaches and the methods and subject matter of physics as previously noted (often seen as the epitome of 'scientific' science) are specific and not relevant even to other natural sciences, let alone the social sciences. Furthermore, science does not consist of a unitary set of methods and procedures, nor does it unproblematically uncover causal laws through a linear, evolutionary process (Oakley 1999).

Positivism and the use of quantitative methods are not necessarily the same thing and there are aspects of quantitative research which are not directly attributable to either positivism or the practices of the natural sciences (see Bryman 1988; Maynard 1994a; Oakley 1999). While there are some quantitative social scientists who regard themselves as neutral observers producing objective and value-free 'facts', others do not and acknowledge that all methods (including those that involve figures and numbers) constitute a construction. So, as Maynard (1994a) notes, positivism is not intrinsic to quantitative research even though historically many textbooks do not make a distinction between the two.

While accepting that quantitative research is not necessarily positivistic research there is much feminist (and other) criticism of the use of numbers to 'prove facts' in social life. Census data is seen as value-neutral and is often used by researchers to 'prove' points about such matters as migration, employment, housing and so on. Yet, as Oakley (1999: 158) notes, the 'categories chosen for which data are collected, are themselves far from neutral'. In Britain there has been considerable criticism of the census and associated data collection. Factual questions such as those about the accommodation in which one lives are value-laden and vary from country to country. For example, it is possible to determine whether or not a person lives in highrise housing from the French census, whereas in Britain this is not possible (Williams and May 1996: 113). Furthermore, until the last (2001) census ethnicity was not even a category in the British census and it is still not possible to determine the amount of time a person spends on voluntary work. Furthermore, the way most official statistics are collected limits the extent to which they can be used for purposes other than those originally intended. As McFarlane (1990) argues, because of the way they are increasingly shaped by the demands of the government, official statistics are anything but neutral, objective and value-free. Indeed, there are many examples that demonstrate that statistics are a social product, including the number of changes in the definition of unemployment in the UK (from the 1980s onwards), all of which served to reduce the total; the removal of tables detailing 'sensitive' data from government and other reports (Roberts 1990); and the traditional recording of men as 'head of household' even though women and men in the same household do not always share a social class or educational level (Chapman 1992). With examples such as this in mind,

Jayaratne and Stewart (1991) point out that feminist critique suggests that quantitative research in particular is not used to overcome social problems and treats individuals as islands out of context of their real lives. With specific reference to women's experience the view is that much quantitative research has at best misunderstood and at worst misrepresented women and therefore compounded the view of woman as 'not a man' and therefore as a deviation from the norm or as simply to be disregarded. Thus, statistical analysis can and has assisted in the construction of woman as 'other'.

This criticism of the quantitative is therefore a criticism of crude data collection and analysis and it is not so much quantification that is the problem but an over-reliance on quantification and/or poor quantification (e.g. see Eichler 1988; Gelsthorpe 1990, 1992).

Generating theory from research

Although phenomenological approaches predate the 1950s, 'positivism' as a philosophical tradition came under increased attack at this time with critics arguing that there was no such thing as an objective, neutral or disinterested perspective, that we are all socially and historically located and that this influences the knowledge we produce. This inevitably involves addressing the issue of relativism. The idea here is that all knowledge is ideological and socially constructed and 'positivism' is particularly guilty of denying the social processes by which 'social facts' arise as data (McCarl Nielsen 1990; Holmwood 1995). So, the '"monologue" of positivism should be replaced by a "dialogue" between inquirers and those who are the subjects [sic] of inquiry' (Holmwood 1995: 413). Drawing on the work of Gouldner (1971), Holmwood (1995) adds that an emphasis on dialogue leads to the suggestion of a need for a reflexive practice which acknowledges the similarities between social scientists and their respondents. The critique was aimed not just at the philosophical foundations of positivism but also at the methods used, the argument being that quantitative questions distorted rather than reflected individuals' meanings (Maynard 1994a).

An approach often known as the 'naturalist' approach developed in reaction to positivism with proponents arguing that it is not possible or desirable for theories to direct research. Instead, research should be ethnographic and describe life 'as it is', from which theories should be developed.

As Morgan (1981) points out, the early critics of the 'scientific' approach were still largely male and their research also tended to focus on male experience. An oft-quoted example of an early critique is the influential study of (male) youth culture by Paul Willis (1977, 1978). In the study, class was a focus and Willis gave a voice to an underprivileged section of society, yet women were absent except as portrayed through the sexist attitudes of the male respondents (Morley 1996; Millen 1997). Willis himself described young women as unforthcoming and unwilling to talk. He wrote that they retreated in giggles when asked questions and Morley (1996: 13) argues that Willis saw this as a symptom of the young women's social inadequacies rather than a result of his presence as a male researcher.

Yet, there were differences in terms of analysis and theory construction in this approach that at first appeared attractive to feminists. One such attraction was the focus on induction (theory emerging from data) rather than deduction (theory-testing). 'Grounded theory' is theory developed from data and aims to be faithful to the reality of situations. Thus, a grounded theory is one that is 'inductively derived from the study of the phenomenon it represents' (Strauss and Corbin 1990: 23). From this perspective the researcher does not begin with a theory and then prove it but allows the relevant theory to emerge from the data (Strauss and Corbin 1990).

So, central to grounded theory is the belief that the researcher elicits theory from data with the aim of theory following data rather than preceding it. Grounded theoreticians are advised to maintain an attitude of scepticism as all theoretical explanations should be regarded as provisional. With this in mind researchers are encouraged to minimize researcher-imposed definitions by, for example, not undertaking an extensive literature review before beginning data collection (Reinharz 1983). Everything should be checked out, played against the data and never accepted as fact.

Due to the concern to locate theory in respondents' worlds and the desire to reject abstract theory, grounded theory was seen as highly compatible with feminism (Morley 1996: 140). But many feminist theorists who initially rejected deductivism now reject grounded theory on the basis that no study (feminist or otherwise) can be completely inductive or solely based on grounded theory, as no work is free of politics and all work is theoretically grounded (Maynard 1994a; Morley 1996). As Stanley and Wise (1990: 22) argue, 'researchers cannot have "empty heads" in the way inductivism proposes' so one must acknowledge intellectual and personal presence. With specific reference to feminism, Kelly et al. (1994: 156) argue that 'As feminists we cannot argue that theory emerges from research, since we start from a theoretical perspective that takes gender as a fundamental organizer of social life'. Moreover, as they and others argue, any piece of research refers to what has gone before by adding in levels of complexity or challenging previous perspectives. What research should provide is modification, reworkings, extensions and/or critiques of existing theory and the creation of new concepts.

Feminist critiques and alternatives

As I have argued feminists (and others) have been critical of traditional researchers – both those who take 'scientific' and 'naturalistic' approaches – whose choice of topics and methods support sexist and élitist attitudes and practices. In sum the argument is that both 'scientific' and 'naturalistic' research is ideological and has therefore tended to ignore gender differences, gender relationships and the problems and possibilities of each: 'Masculine ideologies are the creation of masculine subjectivity; they are neither objective nor value free nor inclusively 'human'. Feminism implies that we recognize fully the inadequacy for us, the distortion, of male-centred ideologies and that we proceed to think and act out of that recognition' (Rich 1986: 207, cited by Stanley and Wise 1993: 59).

There is critique of method, methodology and epistemology and the following have all been cited:

- the selection of sexist and élitist research topics;
- biased research design including the use of male-only respondents;
- exploitative relationships between researcher and researched and within research teams;
- claims to false objectivity (by those who seek the scientific);
- inaccurate interpretation and over-generalization of findings – including the application of theory to women from research on men (see Jayaratne and Stewart 1991 for further discussion).

As Stanley and Wise (1991: 266) note, many research accounts suggest that research is orderly and coherent and admits to no 'idiosyncrasies, quirks and problems'. The implication is that if things do go wrong then it is the researcher who is not doing things correctly. The relevance of the researcher's self within the research process is completely removed from the public account of research and there is no reference to the process, to the research relationship, to issues of power and emotion. Because of this, Reinharz (1984: 95) compared traditional research to rape where researchers 'take, hit and run' and 'intrude into their subjects' [sic] privacy, disrupt their perceptions, utilize false pretences, manipulate the relationship, and give little or nothing in return'. Writing specifically about sociology, Stanley and Wise (1993: 139) reflect on the implications of this not just for the researched but for the 'product of research': the data, findings, results and conclusions:

> 'Truth' is seen to lie within and be produced out of aggregates interpreted by the objective and removed observer – the sociologist – and compared with and assessed against theoretical understandings. The upshot of all this is that sociologists . . . frequently describe people's accounts as invalid and inadequate interpretations of the social reality which they experience and live.

Feminists insist that it is not possible for researchers to be completely detached from their work: emotional involvement cannot be controlled by mere effort of will and this subjective element in research should be acknowledged, even welcomed. Furthermore, researchers are not the only people involved in research and respondents are also likely to have an emotional and political involvement with the research. Thus, respondents have their own view of the researcher and the purpose of the research, and present themselves and their stories accordingly (Cotterill and Letherby 1993; Stanley and Wise 1993; Lee-Treweek and Linkogle 2000; see also Chapter 6). With all of this in mind it is necessary to present a personalized discussion of the research process, admit the relevance of interests, identities and histories of writers, researchers and respondents and expose these for analysis (Scott 1998: 1.6). This involvement with research exists at all levels of our work and all types of research. Like Stanley and Wise (1993) I argue that 'hygienic research' is a myth which presents a simplistic and often misleading view of research. All research, whether relying on the collection of primary data or the study of secondary sources involves a relationship between researcher and researched because researchers have opinions and views, likes and dislikes (Cotterill and Letherby 1993, 1994; Stanley and Wise 1993).

In the 1980s there was much concern and discussion among feminists about the best ways to replace the 'value-free objectivity' of traditional research with 'conscious subjectivity' (Klein 1983 cited by Wilkinson 1986: 16). Klein argued that this was an approach that was not only more honest but helped to break down the power relationship between researcher and researched. By explaining how they feel about the research, making it clear that their experiences affect their approach to, and interpretation of, the research, and admitting that the 'results' are their interpretations of people's lives and experiences, researchers make themselves much more vulnerable personally and academically. Finch (1984), writing specifically about feminist sociology, supported Becker's (1976) view that sociology is inevitably a political endeavour and sociologists should take the position of the underdog. She argued that feminist researchers did not need to 'assume' the position of the underdog when researching women because they shared the same powerless position. Oakley (1981) took this further and went so far as to suggest that non-hierarchical interviews between women could lead to friendship between the researcher and the researched (see Chapter 6 for further discussion).

However, there are also potential problems with this approach that it is important to be aware of. We know (see Chapter 2) that women are divided by other variables – for example, race, class, age and so on – and this is likely to affect the research process. Also, as McRobbie (1982) and Finch (1984) argue, the very fact that women are 'happy to talk' may be an indication of their powerlessness and researchers need to be very careful that information given so freely cannot be used against those who give it. Many others agree with this and add that some objectification of the researched is inevitable, as the researcher has ultimate control over the material when they 'walk away with' the data (e.g. Ramazanoglu 1989; Ribbens 1989; Cotterill 1992) (for further discussion see Chapters 4, 5 and 6).

We also need to be careful not to replace one set of expert views with another. Research from a feminist methodological standpoint involves the researcher taking women's experience seriously and being openly subjective and reflexive of herself and the research process, which includes planning, doing fieldwork and interpreting and presenting research findings. As Oakley later wrote: 'The prominence given within the feminist methodological literature to the importance of understanding what methods "do" both to research participants (sic) and to research "findings" has been very important in reconstituting knowledge-claims and in helping to develop a more democratic social science' (1998: 709).

Furthermore, feminists acknowledge that researchers of the social world are faced with an already 'first order' theorized material social reality in that respondents themselves theorize about their own lives. Thus, 'people observe, categorize, analyse, reach conclusions' (Stanley 1991: 208). So, the label of 'academic feminism' must not become the legitimation for a new form of expertise and theory should be:

- derived from experience, continually subject to revision in the light of that experience;
- . . . reflexive and self-reflexive and accessible to everyone (not just to theoreticians as a 'special' kind of person); and
- certainly not to be treated as sacrosanct and enshrined in 'texts' to be endlessly pored over like chicken entrails.

(Stanley and Wise 1990: 24)

Thus, feminists are working within established critically reflexive modes of thought while adding to, challenging and developing this tradition.

The problem of objectivity and bias

Having established that feminists were and are concerned to provide a radical alternative to mainstream research approaches, it is worth giving a little further attention to the supposed issues of 'objectivity' and 'bias'. Even today structured interviews or questionnaires are often designed and used to minimize 'bias' through standardization of questions and data collection. There is still a pervasive view that, in 'stimulus response fashion', if you standardize the stimulus then any variation seen in responses will be a true measure (Mason 1996: 40). As highlighted above, feminists have often pointed to the shallowness of objectivity (or male subjectivity) and the value of subjectivity. Because of the focus on subjectivity and the self-confessed political element in feminist work it is open to much criticism of bias – what Morley (1996: 128–9) calls the 'hidden discourse of purity and danger' – with feminists perceived as pollutants of the otherwise 'hygienic' research process. Hammersley and Gomm (1997: 1.8) outline the opportunities for bias in both quantitative and qualitative work: 'The most commonly recognized source is commitments that are external to the research process, such as political attitudes, which discourage the discovery of uncomfortable facts and/or encourage the presentation of spurious "findings". But there are also sources of bias that stem from the research process itself'.

They go on to argue that commitment to a particular perspective may lead to partial or even distorted collection, interpretation and production of data. In survey research, for example, the questions asked and the way they are asked may be affected or distorted. In qualitative research there is even more danger of the researcher 'going native' and producing an uncritical and biased interpretation. Hammersley and Gomm (1997) argue that these problems of bias are widely recognized and add that there are different possible motivations for doing research but that the researcher should be particularly motivated by the wish to produce 'truth'. 'Knowledge production', they argue, must be systematically forefronted in the collection, analysis and presentation of evidence.

Feminists themselves have entered the debate, and as Jayaratne and Stewart (1991: 227) suggest, the association of objectivity with masculinity led some feminists to reject objectivity and focus on the negative consequences of the obsessiveness with 'scientific objectivity', which is in turn associated (historically, though not logically) with quantification. As Jayaratne and Stewart note, feminist criticisms have focused on several important points including:

- 'objective' science has often been sexist (therefore not 'objective');
- the glorification of 'objectivity' leads to the imposition of hierarchies in research relationships; and
- the idealization of 'objectivity' has ignored significant personal subjectivity-based knowledge.

This has led some feminists to suggest that we should 'openly abandon the quest for better "neutral" knowledge replacing it with a clear emancipatory commitment to knowledge from the standpoint of women's experience and feminist theory' (McLennon 1995 cited by Millen 1997: 6.5). Many feminists (and others) argue that bias is in fact inevitable and that the only thing we can do is to aim to make bias visible. Furthermore, it is better to understand the complexities within research rather than to pretend that they can be controlled, and biased sources can themselves result in useful data.

However, some feminists argue that there may be a danger in abandoning the pursuit of objectivity completely. As Jayaratne and Stewart (1991) suggest, while it is necessary to revalue the subjective, removing ourselves from the pursuit of objectivity and rationality effectively leaves the terrain of rational thought to men alone – thus perpetuating the system which excluded us in the first place. Furthermore, as Gelsthorpe (1992: 214 drawing on DuBois 1983) argues: 'Crucially . . . a rejection of the notion of "objectivity" and a focus on experience in *method* does not mean a rejection of the need to be critical, rigorous and accurate'.

Rather, as Gelsthorpe (p. 214) adds, it means that we should make our 'interpretive schemes explicit': what Stanley (1999) calls the production of 'accountable knowledge' or 'unalienated knowledge' to produce 'good and useful knowledge' rather than 'less good and useful knowledge' (Cain 1990) (see also Jayaratne and Stewart 1991; Oakley 1998, 2000 and later discussion in this chapter).

In defence of the view that feminism's political focus and its 'active commitment to some other goal than the production of knowledge' (Hammersley and Gomm 1997: 5.1) means that it is guilty of bias and 'culpable systematic error' we can again turn to the point that no research is free from ideological influences. As Holland and Ramazanoglu (1994) argue, 'there is no technique or methodological logic that can neutralize the social nature of interpretation' (cited by Morley 1996: 142). Morley (1996: 142) goes further: 'The difference with feminist research is that it admits it!' Ironically, this acknowledgement of subjectivity by feminists and the associated 'super-sensitivity' to the relevance of the personhood of the researcher could feasibly lead to the conclusion that our work is more objective, in that our work, if not value-free, is value-explicit. Personally, though, I prefer to speak of 'theorized subjectivity', as 'objectivity' has so many connections with the traditional, authorized, masculine knowledge of the past.

However, this does not mean that feminists are not acutely sensitive to and concerned with issues of bias in the research process and they worry about over-identification, even manipulation, of respondents (more of this later in Chapters 4, 5 and 6). We are aware that we do not always get it right. With this in mind it is useful to reflect on the following extract. Although Skeggs is writing specifically about qualitative work, her points are generalizable and indicate that our research writings should not just tell us about the lives of our respondents but should also tell us something about knowledge construction itself:

> Feminist ethnography can contribute to a wider feminist project by giving knowledge a practical relevance and by exposing the constructions of knowledge as a form of control and categorization. Feminist ethnography can account for the practice of different women, at different times, in different places. It can increase the specificity of analysis by providing an economic, institutional, social and discursive context. It can bring into question universalistic or homogenous theories which speak from a position of privilege. Feminist ethnography shows how women make history but not in the conditions of their own choosing. It can show how feminist ethnographers do the same.
>
> (Skeggs 1994: 88)

While acknowledging the importance of theorizing on our own subjectivity I try to avoid the word 'bias' as it seems to me to have become an overused term which is often used abusively or defensively by anyone who feels challenged by a discussion of the political aspects of the research process. This is not to say that issues of objectivity and subjectivity have not dominated a large part of the literature, but the equation of subjectivity with bias is simplistic.

A feminized approach

'Defining' feminist research
Reading different books and articles written by feminists it is possible to find similarities in the definition of what constitutes a feminist research process. The following are just a few examples, most of which I have already referred to. Cook and Fonow (1990: 80) focus on the need for research to *mean* something, to lead to change in women's lives and talk about

> the search for techniques which analyze and record the historical process of change and ultimately the transfer of such methodological tools to the subjects [sic] of research so they might confront their oppression and formulate their own plan of action. Thus, 'the truth of a theory is not dependent on the application of certain methodological principles and rules but on its potential to orient the processes of praxis toward progressive emancipation and humanization' [Mies 1983: 124]. Feminist research is, thus, not research about women but research for women to be used in transforming their sexist society . . .

Scott (1998) on the other hand argues for an approach which is accountable to others, insisting on the production of unalienated knowledge which is cognizant of power difference and emotion.

Attention to the literature suggests further that feminist researchers should:

- give continuous and reflexive attention to the significance of gender as an aspect of all social life and within research, and consider further the significance of other differences between women and (some argue) the relevance of men's lives to a feminist understanding of the world;
- provide a challenge to the norm of 'objectivity' that assumes knowledge can be collected in a pure, uncontaminated way;
- value the personal and the private as worthy of study;
- develop non-exploitative relationships within research;
- value reflexivity and emotion as a source of insight as well as an essential part of research.

To this list Fonow and Cook (1991) add that feminist approaches to research are often characterized by an emphasis on creativity, spontaneity and improvisation in selection of both topic and method, which includes a tendency to use already given situations both as the focus of investigation and as a means of collecting data.

For me (at least) all of these points are important. All relate to the subordinate nature of women's status within traditional/mainstream research and in wider society and, although it is not an exhaustive list, it gives a good indication of most feminists' views on the research process. Put more simply:

> any research may be considered 'feminist' which incorporates two main aims; a sensitivity of the role of gender within society and the differential experiences of males and females and a critical approach to the tools of research on society, the structures of methodology and epistemology within which 'knowledge' is placed within the public domain . . .
>
> (Millen 1997: 6.3)

Ramazanoglu (1989) argues that research from a feminist methodological standpoint should provide understandings of women's experience as they understand it, interpreted in the light of feminist conceptions of gender relations. Yet, as Temple (1997: 1.6) notes: 'There are many varieties of feminism and many ways of being feminist . . . There are points of commonality . . . [and] the presence of different voices and epistemologies are one of its strengths'. The debates, discussions, contradictions, compromises and alliances presented in this book need to be read in the light of a realization of this difference and commonality.

Bringing women in?

Harding (1987: 8) notes that studying women is not new, yet studying them from the perspective of their own experiences so that women can understand themselves and their social world has 'virtually no history at all'. The first step, then, is to make women's lives visible, the result being not only a clearer picture of women's experience but a better understanding of the whole cultural and historical experience of women (and of men). Smith (1988) insists that researchers must begin with real, concrete people and their actual lives if research is to do more than reaffirm the dominant ideologies about women and their place in the world. Here is it possible to see the relevance of a grounded approach even if there are problems with a wholehearted adoption of grounded theory.

Thus, as suggested above, it is important not just to do more research on women but to develop an appropriate approach. For some this means that feminist research should be instrumental in producing a research 'for women'. However, this point needs some further explanation, as it appears to mean different things to different writers. Some argue that it means taking women's experiences in their own right with no reference to a male 'standard'. Others go further and argue that the main beneficiaries of research should be the researched (e.g. Ehrlich 1976; Mies 1983). Supporters of this approach insist that research should be emancipatory (e.g. Cook and Fonow 1990; Stanley 1990; Kelly et al. 1994; Oakley 1998) and should not just describe the world but help to change it. The ultimate goal is the eventual end of social and economic conditions that oppress women. Thus, as Klein (1983) argues, criticism and corrective research is not enough, as visibility does not guarantee change because society is still 'man-made'.

Oakley (2000) gives an example of a research project that could be described as 'sociology/research of women' rather than 'sociology/research for women'. She cites a large research project on the social origins of depression by Brown and Harris (1976) and notes that the study resulted in a convincing explanation of the relationship between depression and the life events and socioeconomic circumstances of women. However, no connection was made between women's depression and their oppression. There was no concern with whether or how women defined themselves as depressed, but only with how the state of women's mental health could be exposed and fit into a system of classification developed by a profession of 'experts' on mental health (psychiatrists). Also, the researchers did not begin with a desire to study the situation of women or set out to give women a chance to understand their experience as determined by the social structure of the society in which they lived. The primary aim of the research was to study depression and women were selected as respondents because they are easier (and therefore cheaper) to interview, being more likely than men to be at home and therefore available during the day.

None the less, there are problems attached to undertaking 'research for women'. Cannon (1989) argues that many researchers feel guilty that they have nothing to give back to the people who have given them so much, yet as McRobbie (1982) argues, many individuals freely give information about their lives without wanting anything back. A 'research for women' stance could cause feminists to reject or neglect findings that undermine women. Kelly (1978: 229) insists that this is more likely to lead to 'eventual backlash' than to solve any problems. Also, as Stanley and Wise (1993) argue, the implication that research should always lead to action condemns the search for knowledge for its own sake. But research for its own sake is an essential precondition for informed action.

Advocating a 'research for women' approach could be interpreted as insisting on research about women only, but many feminists agree with Morgan (1981) who argues that 'taking gender seriously' means bringing men back in. Morgan also stresses that if we accept that man is not the norm nor woman the deviation, we need to consider the social construction of both femininity and masculinity (see p. 39). Further support of this is supplied by Oakley (2000) who cites a project by Belenky et al. (1986) who studied a group of American women and their experiences and problems as lecturers and 'knowers'. They chose a women-only respondent group, arguing that male experience had already been fully and powerfully articulated. Yet, as Oakley says, how can we be sure that the approaches to knowing described by Belenky et al. are ways women know rather than ways people know? Women were interviewed to construct a generalized account of something that happens to both men and women, but ways of knowing are affected by social position and gender is only one aspect of social position. It is important to consider the experience of men to uncover the similarities as well as the differences between us (women and men) and to highlight the differences between men, just as we do the differences between women (Annandale and Clark 1996). Furthermore, in a patriarchal world it is important to discover what men think and feel: about themselves, about women, about the world they live in (see e.g. Scott and Porter 1983; Laws 1990; Foster 1994; Ramsay 1996). However, including men can have its problems. For example, McKee and O'Brien (1983) report that it is often difficult to get men to talk, especially about family matters, and thus men generally have less to say and take less time to say it. Issues of power (and safety) within the research process are also relevant here, and may be exacerbated by the gender order when women researchers include men as respondents in their studies (Reynolds 1993) (see Chapter 6 for further discussion).

Reflexivity and representation
Stanley (1996: 43) argues that there are four major feminist positions with regard to representation:

- Acceptance of the conventional foundationalist view of research, that there is a single reality 'out there' which good research can depict and explain, and accordingly, that there is a one-to-one relationship between reality and representation in (good) feminist research.
- Recognition of (moral, ethical, political) issues concerning power in the research and writing process, in particular the power of the researcher through (often unacknowledged) knowledge-claims that written research both can and should represent the realities of other people's, here women's, lives.
- Recognition of (intellectual, epistemological) issues regarding both the foundationalist supposition of a single and unseamed reality 'out there', and also of making representational claims: that is, rejection of the assumption that it is possible to represent (using any or all possible forms) in a one-to-one way.

- Insistence that the issues involved (of either the second or the third kind) are so great that the only adequate feminist response is to eschew the representation of other lives altogether.

Position one reduces us to a type of feminist positivism which can only lead to the privileging of one reality over others: one feminist standpoint which, as highlighted in Chapter 2, is untenable. Position four leads to a 'dead end' for the feminist project or leads us to the conclusion that we can only research 'others like ourselves', which would involve, as Wilkinson and Kitzinger (1996: 10) call it, 'speaking only for ourselves'. Yet, as Wilkinson and Kitzinger point out (and I shall explore this further in Chapter 6), this is difficult as it becomes increasingly problematic to define just who US or WE are. This leaves us with positions two and three, which broadly speaking encompass most feminist research today.

Wilkinson and Kitzinger (1996: 18) point out that 'our work should not be so much about the other as about the interplay between the researcher and the Other'. But as they themselves add, 'any feminists want both to enable the voices of Others to be heard, and to create social and political change for or on behalf of those Others' (p. 20). This involves us in a struggle between acknowledgement of the impossibility of full representation and the assertion that our work makes a difference.

As highlighted earlier, a reflexive and critical approach to research is not the province of feminists alone but as Williams (1993: 579) argues, feminists have been particularly 'concerned with showing the situatedness of representational claims'. This means the researcher locating herself in the written accounts of the research and acknowledging that all accounts should be seen as representations of reality and should be open to 'critical feminist analytical enquiry' (Stanley and Wise 1993: 200). Stanley (1991: 209) describes the relationship between 'intellectual autobiography' and 'authorized knowledge', and the relationship between feminist research and feminist theory, thus:

> Feminist theory would be directly derived from 'experience' whether this is experience of a survey or interview or an ethnographic research project, or whether it is experience of reading and analysing historical or contemporary documents. Thus its analysis would centre on an explication of the 'intellectual autobiography' of the feminist researcher/theoretician: it would produce *accountable* knowledge, in which the reader would have access to details of the contextually-located reasoning processes which give rise to 'the findings', the outcomes.

Thus, we need to acknowledge that as researchers we are people with our own 'responses, values, beliefs and prejudices' (Morley 1996: 139) and that respondents as well as researchers are reflexive, theorizing individuals: 'people who observe, categorize, analyse and reach conclusions' (Stanley 1991: 208). Thus, research relationships are complex encounters and the 'reports' that arise from them are complex too. Pamela Cotterill and I (writing specifically about qualitative research) have suggested that this means that we need to acknowledge the relevance of our personal as well as our intellectual autobiographies (Cotterill and Letherby 1993).

Stanley and Wise (1993) argue for a methodological and epistemological position which they call *feminist fractured foundationalist epistemology:* a position that does not dispute the existence of truth and a material reality but acknowledges that judgements about them are always relative to the context in which such knowledge is produced. From this perspective researchers have the responsibility of providing accounts of their research process so that readers can have access to the procedures which underlie the way knowledge is presented and constructed by the researcher. Stanley and Wise also insist that the researcher does not claim an intellectual superiority over respondents. Yet, as Maynard (1994a) and Abbott and Wallace (1997) suggest, there is a problem with this position because of the difficulty of defining all accounts as equal with no way of selecting between them. With this in mind, and from my own research experiences, while I agree with Stanley and Wise that as researchers we are not intellectually superior to our respondents, I do think it is important that we acknowledge our own intellectual privileges. As researchers, we often have access to much more information – both academic and experiential (through the collection of data) – than our respondents. Obviously, we refer to these when we 'adjudicate' between respondents' accounts and between respondents' views and our own. We analyse our data with reference to our discipline training as well as our own values and prejudices. We have the final say and the possibility of reflecting on the research experience that respondents do not have. With this in mind I would suggest that we are not only privileged but are also 'superior': we have a right to be regarded as a 'knower' in a way that our respondents do not.

Furthermore, respondents are themselves often aware of, and even supportive of, this 'intellectual privilege'. Wolf (1996: 26) notes that participatory research 'can entail very disparate levels of input from research subjects' [*sic*] and respondents may not want this type of involvement, and instead prefer the researcher to 'speak for them'. When undertaking my own doctoral research on the experience (predominantly women's) of 'infertility' and 'involuntary childlessness', Annie (one of my respondents) described me as her 'little soapbox', telling me that she could have her say through me without identifying herself publicly. Similarly, Scott (1998: 4.4), writing about her research on ritual abuse, notes:

> My informants [*sic*] were well aware that their immediate accounts were often deemed inadequate, and they wanted to be spoken for by someone who could claim a different level of knowledge to that of the everyday. This did not mean my interviewees believed I had a superior ability to understand or analyse ritual abuse than they did, rather they recognised my location within the 'academic mode of production' and its role in producing what counts as knowledge and deciding what does not. Knowing that the media, legal and psychiatric systems largely characterised them as unreliable witnesses to their own experiences, they were hopeful that 'being researched' could transform their experiential knowledge into legitimate academic discourse . . .

Thus, there may be a tension between the desire to give women a voice and the making of knowledge (e.g. Maynard and Purvis 1994; Millen 1997), not least because individuals may not necessarily possess the knowledge or have the desire to explain everything about their lives. We do 'take away their words' and then analyse the data from our own political, personal and intellectual perspective. So, as Fine (1994: 22) argues, research involves 'carving out pieces of narrative evidence that we select, edit and deploy, to border our arguments'. Thus, research may involve some misrepresentation of respondents' words/meanings/experiences but a final decision is necessary if feminist research is to say anything at all, have any effect at all, and not be concerned solely with issues of representation rather than 'reality' itself (Kelly et al. 1994). With reference to the equalizing of research relationships and the point of research, Patai's views are challenging and useful:

> The self-righteous tone that at times characterizes feminist work may be merely a capitulation to feminist discourse, which, like any other discourse draws boundaries that define what we see and fail to see, what we accept and contest . . . Neither purity nor danger resides in calling one's research 'feminist'. But no controversy attends the fact that too much ignorance exists in the world to allow us to await perfect research methods before proceeding. Ultimately we have to make up our minds whether our research is worth doing or not, and then determine how to go about it in ways that let it best serve our stated goals.
>
> (Patai 1991: 150)

Any researcher who explores the experience of others and attempts to theorize on this experience is involved in selection and rejection of aspects of the data: qualitative or quantitative, primary or secondary. The first aspect of selection and rejection takes place in the preparation and fieldwork process. The researcher sets the questions, the context of the respondents' 'stories' and thus frames the rest of the respondents' responses. Selection and rejection also takes place during analysis and the presentation of the data. Not only are certain aspects of data drawn on and included or rejected and left out but also, sometimes, so are certain people. The full, individual identities of respondents cannot be known during the process of research and it is inevitable that they get more diluted in the translation. Yet, as I have already acknowledged, and will explore in more detail later, it is important that as researchers we do not over-pacify our respondents by defining them as inevitable victims of research. I find Skeggs' (1994: 86–7) description of her own research experience helpful here:

> The selection and organization of the transcripts makes the process of representation explicit, although, in reading, this process may remain implicit. After much deliberation and for purposes of coherence, I chose accounts and transcripts which operated as theoretical dramatic indicators to exemplify the structural relations as they were lived at the level of everydayness. The accounts were considered to be a product of the particular moment in which they were made. Social construction theorists – in the field of the sociology of knowledge – would argue that I constructed the world of the participants through my representations. I did not. I partially represented their social productions. For that is all that can be achieved . . . I

do not have the power (nor do any individuals) to socially produce the lives of young women.

End points

As I have highlighted in this chapter, feminist researchers, in exposing the hollowness of the 'scientific' claims of others and in theorizing on their own practice argue that knowledge is a material product: 'something which is specific to time and place and person, and so which is contextual, grounded and material, as well as being rooted in the "point of view" of particular knowledge producers . . .' (Stanley 1997: 204). For feminists, adopting a feminist methodological standpoint is an essential part of our political practice and our social and intellectual being. The critical reflexivity that this entails should be a constant aspect of our research, for we need to be aware that 'calling a piece of work feminist does not necessarily mean that it is' (Morley 1996: 133). I am not suggesting that a 'perfect model of the researcher/ researched relationship' can be achieved, nor that 'feminist research is feminist politics' (Glucksmann 1994: 150). It is important that 'a concern with the internal dynamics of the research situation' does not take 'precedence over what the research is ostensibly about' (Glucksmann 1994: 150), but given the 'dirtiness' of so-called 'hygienic' research and the associated damage to the data collected (and potentially to the lives of those represented) it is important that we consciously make our practices as transparent as possible.

Suggested further reading

For more discussion on critiques of mainstream theory and feminist alternatives see, for example: Stanley, L. and Wise, S. (1993) *Breaking Out Again: Feminist Ontology and Feminist Epistemology* (London: Routledge); Oakley, A. (1999) *People's ways of knowing: gender and methodology*, in S. Hood, B. Mayall and S. Oliver (eds) *Critical Issues in Social Research: Power and Prejudice* (Buckingham: Open University Press), and (2000) *Experiments in Knowing: Gender and Method in the Social Sciences* (Cambridge: Polity). Hammersley and Gomm (1997), Temple (1997) and Humphries (1997) engage in debates about bias in the journal *Sociological Research Online* (www.socresonline.org). For more detail on feminist research practice see the suggested reading at the end of the Introduction.

Chapter four

Quoting and counting: the qualitative/quantitative divide

Introduction

As highlighted in Chapter 3, many feminists have been critical of the traditional use of quantitative methods and argued for the use of the qualitative. Adding to this debate, Oakley (1999, 2000) argues that quantitative and qualitative methods tended to be portrayed as mutually antagonistic ideal types. However, this is an oversimplification for, as Reinharz (1992) notes, feminist researchers have used all of the existing methods available as well as inventing some new ones. To demonstrate this, in her book *Feminist Methods in Social Research*, she states that her emphasis is on the plural: that is, methods not method. Like Reinharz and others (e.g. Jayaratne and Stewart 1991; Stanley and Wise 1993; Kelly et al. 1994), I would argue that there is a danger in the use of the word 'method' as this can suggest that there is one (or two or three) method(s) that feminists *must* use. Rather, it is important to stress that it is not the use of a particular method or methods which characterizes a researcher or a project as feminist, but the way in which the method(s) are *used*.

In this chapter I consider the issue of method further and detail some of the methods that feminists use. I also consider the relationship between the feminist use of methods and the non-feminist use of methods. I begin by focusing on the qualitative/quantitative debate and consider in detail one of the most prevailing myths about feminist research – namely that feminists only do qualitative research, and further that the only qualitative method they use is the semi-structured in-depth interview. I begin with a brief history of the interview and then outline the debate between feminists and others (and among feminists) about the value of qualitative and quantitative methods for the 'production of knowledge' from a feminist perspective.

In this chapter I give examples of some of the methods that feminists have used to try to understand and represent women's (and men's) lives. This includes attention to:

- life histories, interviews, focus groups and conversational analysis;
- diaries, letters, documents and text;
- questionnaires and statistics;
- participant and non-participant observation.

I also consider multi-method research and detail some innovative methods and approaches. Throughout I draw on actual examples of feminist research in relation to the methods considered. Overall, although I do not claim to have considered all the methods and approaches ever used by feminists, I aim to demonstrate that feminist research practices must be recognized as a plurality (Reinharz 1992: 4).

A short history of the interview

'Tools' of research

In order to further the development of a real 'science of society' (see Chapter 3) it was necessary that when the interview was used it was used 'hygienically': as an instrument, a 'tool' which enabled the collection of data. Methodological textbooks as late as the 1950s and 1960s advised that when interviews were necessary the following of 'rules' would ensure the maintenance of detachment and thus objectivity. For example, students were warned of the dangers of 'over-rapport' and advised to ensure the passivity of the interviewee by parrying questions (Oakley 1981). So it appears that the interview was, historically, a masculine method used to obtain authorized knowledge. The rules were clear: '. . . the interview is not simply a conversation. It is, rather, a pseudo-conversation. In order to be successful, it must have all the warmth and personality exchange of a conversation with the clarity and guidelines of scientific searching' (Goode and Hatt 1952, cited by Oakley 1990: 32–3).

This requirement means that the interview must be seen as: '. . . a specialised pattern of verbal interaction – initiated for a specific purpose, and focussed on some specific content areas, with consequent elimination of extraneous material' (Kanh and Cannell 1957 cited by Oakley 1990: 31). Thus, within this tradition, the interviewer is instructed to be 'friendly but not too friendly' and to develop a balance between the 'warmth required to generate "rapport" and the detachment necessary to see the interviewee as an object under surveillance' (Oakley 1981: 33). All of this can be summarized as follows: 'The interviewer's manner should be friendly, courteous, conversational and unbiased. He [sic] should be neither too grim nor too effusive; neither too talkative nor too timid . . . A brief remark about the weather, the family pets, flowers or children will often serve to break the ice (Sellitz et al. 1965 cited by Oakley 1990: 34).

Thus, the interviewer and interviewee have each to be socialized into 'correct' interview behaviour to ensure that the interview remains an appropriate tool for the collection of 'objective', 'scientific' data. The interviewer's role is that of asking questions and promoting rapport and it is important that they do not pass judgment or answer questions. So, when asked questions, the interviewer needs to laugh them off, shake their head, tell the respondent that they have not really thought of this previously or that they will give their view/opinion/story when the interview is over. The interviewee on the other hand is expected to be passive and subordinate: the one who answers the questions and does not direct, in any way, the process of research. So the essential characteristics of this formal type of interviewing are as follows: the interviewer should interact with the respondent on a minimal basis and be completely neutral and in control; the interviewer's job is that of a noter of responses; when asked what a question means they may only repeat the question and neither body language nor verbal cues should 'bias' the answers. The result of all of this, the argument goes, is that the interview can be conducted by any other researcher/interviewer and the same 'results' would be obtained.

The establishment of the interview, based on these masculine principles, is ironic because as Warren (1988) notes women historically have often been seen as 'good' interviewers with a 'special talent for fieldwork' (an interesting point given the use of the word 'he' in the Sellitz quote above, especially as Sellitz is a woman). Women have been thought to have a superior ability to communicate and gain 'confessional rapport'. That is, they are able to put people at ease by drawing on assumed 'feminine' skills and roles as nurturers, communicators, emotional labourers, even as sexually available individuals. Further to this, women interviewers are perceived as less threatening and so, it is thought, it is more likely that both male and female respondents will be willing to talk to them about personal, private and intimate issues. Warren (1988) suggests that this view has not been universal but has been given enough support to ensure that male research directors often seek women research assistants. Perhaps this also has something to do with the sexualization of women at work where research assistants, like secretaries, may be expected to be the 'office wife' to their male boss (see Pringle 1989). Yet despite, or maybe because of, the view of women as 'good' interviewers there were warnings against over-rapport:

> Some interviewers are no doubt better than others at establishing what the psychologists call 'rapport' and some may even be too good at it . . . there is something to be said for the interviewer who, while friendly and interested does not get too emotionally involved with the respondent and his [sic] problems . . . what one asks is that the interviewer's personality should be neither over-aggressive nor over-sociable. Pleasantness and a business-like nature is the ideal combination.
>
> (Moser 1958 cited by Oakley 1990: 34)

Yet, as Oakley (1981) further notes, this is ironic as it rests on a mis-definition of rapport which, as defined in the *Oxford English Dictionary*, actually means 'a sympathetic relationship'.

Developing a participatory model

With all of this in mind Oakley (1981) argues that this style of interviewing, which by defining the interviewee as subordinate, supports the male 'paradigm of inquiry' and supposedly results in the 'perfect interview' is 'morally indefensible'. She adds that the best way to find out about people's lives is through non-hierarchical relationships where the interviewer is prepared to invest their own personal identity in the research relationship, answering questions and sharing knowledge. Drawing on her own research with new mothers she suggests that when asked, 'Which hole does the baby come out?' or 'Does an epidural ever paralyse women?' it is wrong not to answer (1981: 48). She argues that the interview should be a mutual interaction in which the researcher is open and gives something of herself by talking about herself, by answering questions when asked and perhaps feeding back some findings to respondents when writing up. This type of reciprocity, she argues, invites intimacy and, as mentioned earlier (see Chapter 3), in Oakley's experience led to continuing relationships as she was still in touch with a third of her respondents four years after her fieldwork finished and four of these women had become close friends. Clearly, respondents have more control over this type of interview which means, in turn, that they have more control over the whole process of research. Thus, this form of interviewing breaks down the hierarchy between researcher and respondent – the respondent is not 'objectified' nor placed in a passive role, but plays an active part in the research process. The essential characteristics of this type of interview are that the interview process should be interactive; the researcher should be responsive to the language and concepts used by the respondent; and she should give of herself as well as 'obtaining information' from the respondent. In sum, both the researcher and the interview should be flexible. Thus, this 'participatory model' for research aims to produce non-hierarchical and non-manipulative research relationships which break down the separation between researchers and respondents (Reinharz 1983).

The differences between quantitative and qualitative research techniques are often expressed through the two extremes of interviewing styles: the formal (quantitative) and the informal (qualitative). The most formal type of interview is fully structured and the wording of questions and the order in which they are asked is the same from one interview to the next. The interviewer has an interview schedule and often has to place ticks in answer boxes corresponding to the respondent's answers (examples may be found in government questionnaires, social attitudes surveys and market research). The most informal interview is the unstructured in-depth interview. Here the interviewer may simply have a list of topics which they want the respondent to talk about and each interviewer phrases the questions as they wish and asks them in the order that seems appropriate, or may even negotiate with respondents about the content and structure of the interview. This approach also gives the respondent scope to be involved in research design in that, if they raise issues not previously thought of by the researcher and make clear which issues they think are the most important, this is noted by the researcher. Here the focus is on the interaction.

Yet, as Collins (1998: 1.3) notes, it is misleading and ultimately unhelpful to speak of the interview in terms of the 'structured' and the 'unstructured'. He argues that even the most unstructured interview is structured in a number of subtle ways in that it is the interviewer who initiates the interview and, therefore, it is the interviewer who determines the nature of the event. Further, an interview is an event which most people will understand to consist of particular roles and rules, shaped by a particular structure. Also, as noted in Chapter 3, the unstructured interview has had its 'own brand of machismo' with its image of the male researcher 'bringing back news from the fringes of society, the lower depths, the mean streets' (Morgan 1981: 87). So the view that qualitative methods are inherently preferable because of their non-sexism is also simplistic.

The qualitative/quantitative debate in feminism

Establishing the parameters of the debate

As previously noted, Oakley (1981) was one of the first to advocate the participative use of qualitative in-depth interviews to best find out about people's lives. This approach is not only viewed by many as politically correct and 'morally responsible' but is clearly very relevant in terms of the development of an approach which is grounded in the experience of women.

Letting women speak for themselves and (in part at least) set the research agenda is likely to produce work which can be used by women to challenge stereotypes, oppression and exploitation (see e.g. Stanley 1990; Reinharz 1992; Maynard and Purvis 1994; Wilkinson and Kitzinger 1996).

Oakley's (1981) piece, with its emphasis on the development of a 'participatory model', was very influential and many researchers and writers aiming to 'break down research hierarchies' begin with a reference to Oakley's work. Both new and more experienced researchers find her arguments empowering when challenging the male model of detachment and objectivity. Also, as Maynard (1994a) notes, this method seems particularly relevant when 'doing feminist research' as many of the issues that feminists have been concerned to put on the agenda – namely the private, the emotional and the subjective – lend themselves more readily to open-ended strategies. Some writers suggest that this has encouraged the unproblematic adoption of the in-depth interview as 'the feminist method'. Oakley herself, in a more recent piece (1998: 716) has written that 'To be a feminist social scientist one must have a certain allegiance to the qualitative paradigm'.

However, I would suggest that her argument is inaccurate in two ways. First, there is a large body of writing which suggests that the in-depth interview may not always be appropriate to the issue or the respondent group and, even when it is, it can be used clumsily or even exploitatively. Second, there is evidence that there are many other methods that feminists use or have used.

Methods and critiques

With reference to a critique of the in-depth interview, many writers have pointed to the potentially exploitative nature of this method. Various writers have suggested that, when arguing for the 'participatory model' as enabling the collection of better data, Oakley (1981) ignored potentially exploitative elements of this relationship (see e.g. Cotterill 1992; Kelly et al. 1994; Collins 1998). For example, as Kelly et al. (1994) argue, women may not want to share their experiences with another woman and even if they do this may not always be of personal benefit. Finch (1984) argues that friendly researchers are likely to bring forward vulnerable people who reveal very private aspects of their lives and because of this respondents ideally need to know how to protect themselves from interviewers. Also, as we know, women are divided by variables other than gender (see Chapter 2). Cotterill (1992) adds that power is likely to shift between respondent and researcher during research but that once that researcher walks away with the data she or he is in control. Thus, the generation of data through appealing to sisterhood is a simplistic view of feminist research (see e.g. Ramazanoglu 1989; Ribbens 1989; Cotterill 1992; Marshall 1994; Millen 1997). With this in mind there has been a more sophisticated consideration of the dynamics of power in the research relationship (see e.g. Maynard and Purvis 1994; Wilkinson and Kitzinger 1996; Ribbens and Edwards 1998; see also Chapter 5 for further discussion).

Furthermore, small-scale studies do not tell us everything we need to know about women's lives. For example, using the case of work on sexual abuse and domestic violence, Kelly et al. (1994) argue that most research in this area is based on small-scale interviews and on the experience of women who are happy to make their lives public, much of it focusing on the experience of women in refuges. As Kelly et al. note, it is not clear whether the data collected can be extrapolated to women in general and/or applied to those women suffering abuse but who have not voiced their experiences (e.g. women who have not accessed refuges may have very different things to say). In their research on this issue, Kelly et al. preferred to use question-naires which combined yes/no answers with in-depth questions which allowed respondents to participate anonymously. None the less, Kelly et al. describe Oakley's (1981) piece on interviewing as a classic and suggest that what she offers is an account of how the interview in its traditional form can be adapted in relation to feminist practice in terms of researcher/respondent relationships and in terms of the representation of the lived experience of respondents. They suggest that it is necessary to at least try to transform quantitative methods similarly. Furthermore, as Jayaratne (1983: 158–9) argues, it is important to have quantitative evidence which will counter the 'pervasive and influential quantitative sexist research which has and continues to be generated in the social sciences'. She adds that in order to achieve this we may need to change some of the traditional procedures.

The 'gendered paradigm' divide

So we must avoid what Oakley (1998) calls the 'gendered paradigm divide' where qualitative work is associated with feminine values and in-depth approaches and quantitative work are associated with masculine and/or posit-ivistic approaches (see e.g. Stanley and Wise 1990; Randall 1991; Henwood and Pidgeon 1995; Millen 1997). A continued association of the interview as 'women's work' compounds more established sexist views about women as good listeners and ignores the hard emotion work which is now an acknow-ledged aspect of much of the research undertaken by (female and male) researchers. Similarly, equating men with quantitative methods continues and confirms stereotypes about men's superior numerical abilities and their lack of emotional skill (see e.g. Warren 1988; Ramsay 1996; Lee-Treweek and Linkogle 2000; see also Chapter 5).

Oakley (1998: 708) notes that (as highlighted in Chapter 3) the 'critique of quantitative' has overlapped with the 'critique of mainstream/malestream' and the danger is that quantitative and qualitative approaches are represented as 'mutually exclusive ideal types' (p. 709). She cites Reinharz (1990: 294) who suggests that 'The quantitative is the Establishment and the qualitative is the social movement protesting the Establishment. The quantitative is the regular army and the qualitative the resistance. The qualitative approach is the outside trying to get in . . .'. Here, quantitative methods are seen as hard, rational, scientific, objective, reliable and replicable and qualitative methods are seen as feminine, soft, intuitive, subjective, holistic, rich and deep. Oakley suggests that this is another example of science and the quantitative being seen as the same thing and this needs to be challenged:

> The more we speak the language of the 'paradigm argument', the more we use history to hide behind it; instead of looking forward to what an emancipatory (social) science could offer people's wellbeing, we lose ourselves in a socially constructed drama of gender, where the social relations of femininity and masculinity prescribe and proscribe, not only ways of knowing, but what it is that we do know.
>
> (1998: 725)

So the danger here is that feminists can exclude themselves from certain types of knowledge and ways of knowing.

Research-specific methods

Feminist research practice requires a critical stance towards existing methods and methodology and this must include a critique of the methods used by feminists themselves. Quantitative and qualitative 'methods' need to be research-specific. Jayaratne and Stewart (1991: 223) suggest that quantitative methods may never provide the kind of richly textured 'feeling for the data' that qualitative methods can. Yet, it is also possible to argue that multivariate statistical analyses of large data sets can provide the most truly 'contextual' analyses of people's experience because they allow the incorporation of a large number of variables, permitting the simultaneous testing of elaborate and complex theoretical models.

Indeed, Oakley (1998) goes so far as to suggest that we should avoid the terms 'quantitative' and 'qualitative' when describing the methods we use as they add neither insight nor credibility. She adds that qualitative methods are usually taken to include unstructured or semi-structured interviewing, participant observation, ethnography, focus groups and other approaches that involve researchers in actively 'listening' to what respondents have to say. On the other hand, quantitative methods are equated with questionnaires, surveys, structured observation and experimental studies, including randomized, controlled and other kinds. But she suggests that there are many grey areas. For example, she asks how 'structured' does interviewing have to be to escape the label 'qualitative' and how do we categorize the narratives that are often written (unasked for) on the bottom of questionnaires?

So, as Stanley and Wise (1983: 159) note, 'methods themselves aren't innately anything' and as Oakley (1998: 724) adds 'The critical question remains the appropriateness of the method to the research question'. Rather than assert the primacy of any method, our choice of method(s) should depend on the topic and scale of the study in question. As (Kelly et al. 1994) argue, what makes research 'feminist' is *not* the methods that are used but the particular ways in which they are deployed and the frameworks in which they are located. Kelly et al. support Fonow and Cook (1991) who suggest that a well-designed and executed quantitative study is likely to be more useful to policy makers, and cause less harm to women, than a poorly-crafted qualitative one. Essentially it is important to use the method to suit the project (i.e. the method that is most likely to uncover the real experiences), because as Jayaratne (1983) argues the better quality the research the more likely it will influence others.

Yet despite all of this, qualitative methods remain popular among feminists and there is a tension because, as Maynard (1994: 21) notes, '. . . despite feminist disclaimers the epistemological discussions still point to the overall legitimacy of qualitative studies, while researchers themselves are attempting to rehabilitate approaches that involve measurement and counting'. I am conscious that I may be guilty of this myself in this book (and elsewhere). Early in my research career I too was 'seduced' by the view that the 'best way to find out about women's lives' is through the use of qualitative methods. I still find it much more difficult to find examples of, and write about, quantitative examples. This is a tension then that I (and I would suggest others) need to address for, as Oakley (1998) argues, there is much to be done in adapting 'malestream' methods and models to suit feminist values.

Doing feminist research

So far in this chapter I have suggested that despite the view held by some that qualitative methods (and within this the in-depth interview) are the *only* way that feminists should do research, feminists themselves are very aware of the critiques of the in-depth interview and the danger of supporting a paradigm divide regarding methods and the values of the quantitative. I now develop the view of feminist research as eclectic and non-essentialist in terms of choice of method through a consideration of some feminist work. I am not attempting a complete picture of all types of feminist research, but this review of various research methods and experiences does suggest that feminists use *all* the methods that there are. I give examples of work using various qualitative and quantitative methods, and work which combines methods and is innovative in approach.

Talking, talking, talking

Life history, oral narrative, in-depth interview and biographical interview are all used to describe the qualitative methods that involve an interviewer recording, either on tape or on paper, the words of another. An interview can take place with one person (single interview), a couple or a small group (sometimes called a focus-group interview). Furthermore, as Scott (1998: 7.1) suggests, terms such as 'stories', 'narratives' and 'accounts' are all used variously to describe the data collected. All of these different words have implications for the status of the data and the research:

> The term 'stories' inevitably incorporates the idea of fiction and leans towards locating the main event at the level of discourse. 'Narratives', as well as having the disadvantage of being merely a posh word for 'stories', pushes forward form and structure above content. Even 'accounts' are always-already 'competing accounts' . . .

'Life histories' take themselves more seriously as resources for knowledge . . .
Oral narratives can include a focus on one respondent's life or an aspect of their
life or conversely can involve multiple biographies focusing on aspects of many
people's lives.

Whatever terms are used, the narrative technique of collecting people's
'life histories' (in full or part) is not only seen as a way of developing participatory research but is a method that enables the discovering of the social
experiences of 'silenced women' (or other silenced groups) (Geiger 1986:
335). Life histories, 'tell it like it is' from the lived experience of the narrator
and many writers suggest that as a feminist method they are invaluable
because they do not fracture life experiences but provide a means of evaluating the present, re-evaluating the past and anticipating the future, and offer
a challenge to other 'partial' accounts (see e.g. Geiger 1986; Scott 1998). For
example, Scott (1998: 5.5), writing about her own experience of using life
histories in a study concerned with experiences of researching ritual abuse,
argues that the media and professional responses to ritual abuse are often
removed from the everyday familial existence in which it is embedded and
she hoped that her research, focusing as it did on 'whole lives', would challenge this.

Within the general rubric of in-depth interviewing there are many different approaches. Researchers sometimes have a completely unstructured
agenda, an *aide-mémoire* of themes to cover (that either they themselves have
devised or they have negotiated with respondents), or vignettes (a set of
statements which respondents can respond to in general terms or more
specifically in relation to their own experience). Single interviews may be
used to inform focus-group interviews or vice versa; interviews and focus
groups may take place simultaneously following analysis of a questionnaire
or may inform the development of a questionnaire and so on. 'Life histories'
(or whatever we call them) have been used to collect data about women's
health, family life, work experience, political involvement, in fact just about
all aspects of women's lives (see e.g. Reinharz 1992; Roberts 1992; Afshar and
Maynard 1994; Maynard and Purvis 1994; Ribbens and Edwards 1998).

With reference to the reliability and validity of this approach, Rose (1982:
368) suggests that 'the purely personal account of one individual woman's
oppression while casting brilliant insights may tell us more about the essentially idiosyncratic character of her unique experience than the generality of
experience of all or even most women . . .' Attar (1987: 33), reflecting on the
disadvantages and advantages of experiential material, argues that:

A further problem of purely personal accounts is that they can be used in a token
way, meaning that a one-off story implies a one-off experience and an exceptional
woman. Sometimes, the point we want to make may indeed be that our experiences differ, and that no one woman can represent another. But this should
not be taken to mean that we have wholly different concerns – as if racism,
violence, sexuality, could be issues for some women but not others. When a
woman writes about experiences she has had which have not been shared by most
of her readers – describing specific religious upbringing, perhaps, or writing as an

incest survivor – there will still be connections between the readers' experience and the writer's.

Thus, it is possible to argue that research of this type may have value in explanatory terms, if not in terms of its typicality, and it might therefore be relevant to others who find themselves in similar situations (Clyde Mitchell 1983).

Geiger (1986) suggests that, regardless of difference, women seem to share a 'familial embeddedness' that is central to the way they perceive their social world, and while this may not be true of all women people do seem to make sense of their lives by referring to individual and family transitions. Furthermore, Marchbank (2000) suggests that women's experiences as women are diverse and distinct yet women's experience of, and treatment by, public politics and political bodies are sufficiently equivalent to reveal certain common problems and responses. Life histories facilitate these connections. In a very real sense they are an account of 'group lives' where the narrator weaves her story with those of her 'significant others': her children, parents, partner, lovers, friends and colleagues. So, individual life histories often give us insights into the lives of many. However, it is important to acknowledge that respondents are active in the process of reflection and construction and furthermore that the interview gives us an insight into a point in time: a 'snapshot'. Scott (1998: 5.7) suggests that there are deeply embedded notions and expectations about the 'normal' course of a life, as well as commonly-held views about what constitutes a good story and that these can shape a personal narrative as much as the 'brute facts'.

Another method that involves the researcher reflecting on the spoken word of others is that of conversational analysis, where the conversation may or may not take place for the purpose of the research. Examples include Fishman's (1978) analysis of taped conversations between couples in their homes, which was concerned with how verbal interaction both reflects and perpetuates hierarchical relationships between men and women, and Davis' (1988) analysis of consultations between male doctors and their female patients which challenged the model of dominant male doctor/passive female patient.

Writing, reading and looking
Investigations into women's lives have been carried out by studying autobiographies, journals, diaries and letters of individual women and documentary records of women's organizations. However, writers point out that the literary tradition is essentially an élitist one and that the act of writing, particularly by women, is both class- and culture-bound (Graham 1984; Geiger 1986). As Graham (1984) and Purvis (1994) note, resources allowing individuals to keep written records of their lives are ones which have traditionally not been available to working-class women.

But as Reinharz (1992: 146) notes, cultural artefacts (documents that are produced by people) can come from every aspect of human life including the writings of individuals, 'high' culture, popular culture and organizational life. She adds that the only limit to what can be considered as a cultural artefact is the researcher's imagination. With this in mind she notes that feminist studies of 'texts' include children's books, fairy tales, billboards, feminist non-fiction and fiction, children's art work, fashion, postcards, Girl Scout/Guide handbooks, works of fine art, newspaper rhetoric, clinical records, introductory textbooks, medical texts and cookery books to mention only a few. She suggests that: 'One way to categorize these in terms of gender is to consider artefacts produced *by* women, *about* women and *for* women, artefacts produced *by* men, *about* men and *for* men, or any combination of these . . .'. (p. 147)

Such cultural artefacts are of course not written or produced for the purpose of research, a point which Purvis (1994) makes specifically in relation to the analysis of historical documents. Purvis suggests that what the researcher tries to do is immerse herself in the sources, get a 'feel' for the time and place, and then engage in descriptive analysis, comparing the descriptions of life offered in one account with others and other printed analyses. She adds that it is important to find out as much as possible about how the personal documents were produced, who wrote and created them and why, and what sources of information were drawn upon. Reflecting on her own research, which involved the analysis of the prison letters of suffragettes, Purvis argues that the letters were produced under certain social conditions and this framed the women's writing. Prisoners were permitted to write and receive letters for the purpose of keeping a connection with their respectable friends but not so that they could be kept informed of public events. Furthermore, all letters were read by the prison authorities. Alternatively, letters composed surreptitiously, in contravention of prison rules, and smuggled out, might contain normally censored material. It is also, of course, important to be aware of the fact that these letters, like other forms of autobiographical writing, are written from the perspective of one person (see e.g. Iles 1992; Purvis 1994).

It is not just the written words of others that can be analysed. A feminist sociological analysis of a photograph of Marilyn Monroe by Farran (1990a) shows how gendered meanings and understandings are socially constructed (in this case Marilyn Monroe as a 'sexual' woman). Farran suggests that while on the one hand the dominant image of Marilyn Monroe is that of a sexual woman and an 'object' for other people to view, on the other hand 'we can also recognise that by subordinating herself to a public gaze she thereby gains power over that public: she becomes subject and "it" an object which reacts in ways determined by her' (p. 265). Farran (p. 272) adds that biographies of Marilyn Monroe suggest that she was very often instrumental in initiating poses in photographic sessions and so she helped to produce the form in which 'Marilyn' was publicly consumed as a product, thus operating as both producer and product of her own public sexual self. So although the power she had was on male terms, given/achieved because she played their game, this analysis suggests that, power is always resisted, negotiated and mediated.

Other examples of feminist analyses of cultural artefacts can be found in an edited text by Skeggs (1995). The areas covered include 1950s female film representation, video-recorder usage, responses to TV drama, mothers and TV drama and representations of women at Greenham Common. One example is the work of Hallam and Marshment (1995: 169) which set out to analyse the television version of Jeanette Winterson's *Oranges are Not the Only Fruit* and 'concluded that the familiar pleasures of "quality" realist drama, together with the casting of religious fundamentalism as the villain, were central, not only in persuading viewers to identify with the lesbian character, but also in "naturalising" her sexuality'. Their findings also led them to question the 'identity of the ordinary viewer'.

Having considered the analysis of cultural artefacts not produced for the purpose of the research it is also interesting to consider how feminists have reflected on documents and images produced specifically at the researcher's request. Bell (1998), writing about the use of respondent diaries, distinguishes between 'activity diaries' (which she describes as quasi-observational) and 'personalized diaries' (accounts which reveal emotions and attitudes as well as activities). She argues that issues of interpretation are much more complex in the latter and suggests that analysis can involve connections between diaries written by respondents and researchers' 'own' field diaries.

Similarly, within correspondence research – where respondents and re-searchers exchange letters – interpretation is a complex issue (Letherby and Zdrodowski 1995). Some questions may be ambiguous and may need further qualification. Others may be insensitive and inappropriate (which of course can also be true with questionnaires). Within an interview it is possible to pick up on points, to change direction if answers indicate that some questions are inappropriate and to stop if respondents express a desire to do so. It is impossible to do this with the same spontaneity when receiving and replying to letters or analysing questionnaires. However, respondents may feel less exposed as people if they write rather than speak to researchers, even though written guarantees of confidentiality carry as little weight as verbal ones. Although the research relationship is stretched across time and space, Dawn Zdrodowski and I (1995) argue that rapport is possible using this method. The development from 'Dear Dr Letherby' to 'Dear Gayle' and from 'Yours sincerely' to 'Best wishes' charts the pro-gression of a relationship that affects the disclosures of both the researcher and the researched. Furthermore, when given the opportunity to write about their experiences (in diaries and letters) respondents may feel they have more control in that they can take their time and reflect on what they do and do not want to disclose. As Chester and Nielsen (1987: 17) argue: 'The act of writing itself can be political for women. Learning to organise thoughts on paper, to express feelings, to respond to others is an enormous extension of women's power'. Attar (1987) agrees and argues that many women have found that expressive forms of writing fit well with feminist concerns. Our experience (Letherby and Zdrodowski 1995) supports this, as several of the women who wrote to each of us gave very detailed accounts but added that they would feel unable to talk about their experiences.

Counting and ordering

Statistical techniques exist for generalizing from a small population to a large one; survey research is used to provide information about problems that seemingly occur to only a few people and is useful in demonstrating how a problem is distributed in a particular way throughout a population and whether or not the problem is increasing. It is possible for an understanding of the distribution to lead to an understanding of the factors that contribute to the problem and these factors, in turn, may provide hints as to how the problem can be prevented or remedied through particular forms of action (Reinharz 1992). Reinharz adds that survey research can also help identify differences among groups and changes over time – for example, analysis of statistics that compare men's and women's experience have been used to document inequality and highlight areas where change is needed. Furthermore, statistics have not only been used to document differences between the sexes but also to demonstrate similarities and differences between women.

Mcfarlane (1990: 332) draws attention to the historical background of the collection of official statistics and the main sources of official statistics and data specifically collected about women. She gives examples of ways in which statistics may be misinterpreted, and makes it clear that the ways in which statistics are collected can restrict what we learn from the data. Pugh (1990), on the other hand, demonstrates how statistics can be used *for* those they represent. She suggests that in the case of homeless people, statistics are usually cited to say that there are X numbers of homeless people. On its own, this statistic tells us very little about homelessness. MacFarlane insists that if people working in agencies dealing with the young homeless were able to produce statistics which were servicing a more realistic (in experiential terms) portrayal of young homelessness, these studies might command more serious attention than is currently experienced.

Jayaratne and Stewart (1991: 100) provide some examples of the use of statistics to uncover gendered discrimination and to put things right. For example, Seifert and Martin's (1988) research on maternal deaths in Chicago demonstrated that there was a much higher rate of such deaths among black than among white women, as well as a rate for black women higher than in many Third World countries. In response to this research a new programme was developed by the Illinois Health Commissioners and Chicago Health Department to ensure that pregnant women got antenatal care. Also, Jayaratne and Stewart report that, prior to the court decision of *Griggs* v. *Duke Power Company* 1971, which was argued under the Civil Rights Act of 1964, sex discrimination could be substantiated in court only if one could prove intent on the part of the defendant. However, the decision resulting from this case was that discrimination could be demonstrated by presenting statistics which showed a different and unfair impact on a racial group, sex group or other groups. This case set a new course for discrimination suits.

Like cultural artefacts, statistics may exist prior to the research or may be generated by the researcher(s) through the analysis of a questionnaire. Like research by correspondence the questionnaire is a method which allows individuals to describe things on paper. But unlike processual correspondence, questionnaires are usually anonymous and, as Kelly et al. (1994: 35) argue, 'whatever our topic of investigation individuals will be at different stages in their willingness to discuss it. It means something different to disclose information anonymously on paper or on computer than to speak/communicate it interactively with another person'. For this and other reasons, Jennifer Marchbank and I (Letherby and Marchbank 2001) used an anonymous questionnaire that allowed for quantitative and qualitative analysis (with some agree/disagree type questions and some open-ended questions) for our research on the experience of, and attitudes towards, women's studies. Part of our respondent group was known to us as we gave our questionnaire to students (women's studies and others) whom we taught. Questionnaires were anonymous and we asked students to return them to us via the internal mail, all of which hopefully made it easier for them to be critical than would be the case in face-to-face interviews (I explore this further in Chapter 5). Using this method also enabled us to access the experience of a wide group of respondents fairly easily, both within our own university and in others across the country.

Looking and living

Okley and Callaway (1992: xi) note that participant observation involves either close or superficial rapport with a variety of individuals and ethnography can provide detailed and valuable insight into a multitude of social settings and experiments. Yet, Okley and Callaway add that the specificity of individuals is often lost or generalized in the standard anthropological texts which tend to present the society from the perspective of the author.

With this in mind, D. Bell (1993: 41) argues that: 'What distinguishes this moment from earlier ones is the sophistication of the discourse regarding the exotic other, the critique of anthropology as complicit in the colonial encounter, and the voices, often angry, of indigenous scholars'. Macintyre (1993: 60) adds to this, arguing for the importance of reflexivity:

> The implications of reflexive modes of writing are important for feminist anthropology. But in setting out to expose to critical scrutiny, the process and results of field research as an individual activity, we are perhaps more likely to be exclusive and ethnocentric than might otherwise have been the case. In truth, I think that my experiences and the self-awareness I gained during the time I lived on Tubetude [Island, Papua New Guinea] are far less interesting than Tubetude people's history and their perceptions of their social universe as they disclosed them to me.

Some of these tensions are evident in Roseneil's (1993) research on the Greenham Common peace camp. Roseneil acknowledges that she is heavily influenced by feminist values and, more specifically, the values of the Greenham peace camp. She thus 'takes sides *with* Greenham women *against* the values of militarism and patriarchal state violence' (Devine and Heath 1999: 185). Devine and Heath suggest that, in her research, Roseneil is concerned with using the experience of Greenham as the basis for celebrating and theorizing women's agency and activism and uses Greenham as a means of developing a feminist perspective on social movement theory. Also, she is determined to 'tell it how it is' and challenge inaccurate representations of Greenham, including those advanced by feminists who have been critical of some aspects of the Greenham camp and those who assume that the protest was mobilized around the duty of women as mothers to protect life. Roseneil suggested that this owed rather more to media representation than it did to the reality of many women's motivation for involvement:

> Greenham was far from being a harmonious, tranquil idyll, in which some innate womanly peacefulness reigned supreme. A community of strong-minded women, who grew stronger over time, there were many differences of opinion, often vociferously expressed. Conflict sometimes rocked the camp, and arguments about money, hierarchy, class and, to some extent race, created real divisions.
>
> (Roseneil 1993: 172)

Devine and Heath (1999: 194) suggest that Roseneil provides a powerful portrayal in that she focuses on the changes in consciousness and identity which Greenham wrought in women's lives, paying particular attention to the liberating experience of living in a women-only environment and, more specifically, of living within an environment in which, in a complete reversal of the world outside Greenham Common, heterosexuality was rendered strange.

Researchers such as Cavendish (1982), Westwood (1984), Purcell (1987), R. Bell (1993) and Ramsay (1996) have undertaken ethnographic studies in the worlds of work, employment and education. As well as the data on gendered practices and experiences of respondents that emerge from these studies they are also interesting because of the way in which researchers place themselves and are 'placed' by respondents in the field. This itself gives valuable insight into gender relations. Warren (1988: 19), reflecting on her own experience of working in various medical, psychiatric and legal organizations, writes that when in the mental health court young women were typically treated as either law students or assistants, or as visiting nursing students, and adds that she was treated as one or another of these social types even by people she had told, more than once, that she was a researcher. On the other hand, male visitors were more often taken for attorneys, psychiatrists, or (again) law students, but never nursing students or nurses. There are also many examples of women in the field being characterized as lesbians, whores, potential girlfriends or wives, emotional props and also as honorary males when researching male-dominated settings such as the police force, the criminal underworld and higher education institutions (Foster 1994; Ramsay 1996; Horn 1997). Furthermore, who the researcher is researching influences the perception of the importance or not of the research. For example, when researching secretaries the study may be seen as trivial, but as valid when researching executives (Pringle 1989).

Triangulation and innovation

It should now be clear from this brief account that there is no such thing as *the* feminist method. Furthermore, feminists have used all available methods and have, as Reinharz (1992) notes, 'invented' new ones. In order to find out more about women's (and men's) lives, feminists have used group diaries, drama, videotaping, photo-novellas and unplanned personal experience: what Cook and Fonow (1986) call 'use of situation at hand'. For example, Stanley and Wise (1979) analysed the content of obscene phone calls that they received over a number of years after their names and phone numbers were used in advertisements for local gay and lesbian groups. Stacey (1994) was a member of the General Medical Council for nine years and spent two years engaged in research based on her membership. Mies' (1983) research grew from informal discussions at a shelter for battered women and involved collecting and analysing life histories of shelter residents. Paget (1990) studied the process of confronting terminal illness while terminally ill herself and Fine (1983/4) used her own experience as a volunteer rape counsellor to re-evaluate assumptions by social psychologists.

Many feminists not only draw on their own autobiographies when deciding what to study, when collecting the data and when analysing and writing up, but many are also keen to acknowledge that the 'self' is a resource for helping to make sense of the lives of others (e.g. Okley and Callaway 1992; Cotterill and Letherby 1993; Stanley 1993). As Ribbens (1993: 88) argues:

> A critical and reflexive form of autobiography has the sociological potential for considering the extent to which our subjectivity is not something that gets in the way of our social analysis but is itself social . . . I would suggest that the key point is that 'society' can be seen to be, not 'out there' but precisely *located 'inside our heads'*, that is, in our socially located and structured understandings of 'my-self', 'my-life', 'me-as-a-person' and so forth.

Reinharz (1992: 197) suggests that the use of multiple methods enables feminist researchers to link the past and present and relate individual action and experience to social frameworks. She adds that feminist researchers use multiple methods because of changes that occur to them and to others, so sometimes multiple methods reflect the desire to be responsive to respondents. If our aim is to understand the critical issues in women's lives this type of flexibility is important. As Reinharz suggests, we can enhance our understanding both by adding layers of information and by using one type of data to validate or refine another. Innovation is therefore evident in the approaches to the use of methods as well as in the choice of methods. Furthermore, this often extends to the writing and presentation of the data as well as to the relationships within research teams (see Chapters 5, 6 and 7 for further detail).

End points

Like Harding (1987) I would suggest that disputes and tensions among feminists about exactly how to put feminist theory into practice are valuable, as they encourage change and self-criticism, which is important if feminism is not to become static and complacent. Although some feminists insist on one way of working, the (largely) general agreement is that feminism should be eclectic in its approach and its use of techniques. This ensures adaptation to research programmes rather than research programmes being chosen to 'fit' favourite techniques (e.g. Bowles and Klein 1983; Harding 1987; Stanley and Wise 1993).

Harding (1987: 187) further argues that, because feminism insists on the validity of the subjective, eliminates sexism and is self-reflexive, it provides a more complete and less distorting view – i.e. a 'truer or less false image'. However, as Stanley and Wise (1993) insist, it is important that feminists do not go further and argue that their methodology eliminates the bias of sexism and, therefore, is value-neutral. Feminist research does not help to uncover the 'pure and uncontaminated truth' but should be respected for what it *does* do: provide another way of seeing the world (Stanley and Wise 1993: 158). Thus, as Holland and Ramazanoglu (1994: 116) argue: 'Our conclusions should always be open to criticism'.

This returns us to the concerns of Chapters 1 to 3 and links us to Chapters 5, 6 and 7. In the debate on what method to use and the implications of their uses there is much discussion among feminists concerned with what Scott (1998: 1.2) calls 'feminist friendly epistemology'. Thus, feminists are concerned with who has the right to know, the nature and value of knowledge and feminist knowledge within this, the relationship between the method you use and how you use it and the 'knowledge' you get. Thus, the main concern is with the relationship between the process and the product of feminist research and how epistemology becomes translated into practice. Kelly et al. (1994: 32) criticize what they call the 'romance with epistemology' which they argue: '. . . seems more concerned with attempting to convince the predominantly male academy that a privileged status should be accorded to "women's ways of knowing" than with enabling us to better discover and understand what is happening in women's lives, and how we might change it'.

For me (at least), though 'knowing' and 'doing' are intertwined, and from my reading of the plethora of writing concerned with both doing feminist research and theorizing about feminist understandings, I would suggest that this 'knowing/doing relationship', and not the 'gendered paradigm divide', is the central debate among feminists. The important point here is that 'the power of feminist theory' implies a constant critical engagement with the issue and the responses. Like many others referred to in this book, my central concern as a feminist researcher is not what I do but how I do it and the implications of this for what I get. I am aware of, and I think sensitive to, the critique of both quantitative and qualitative approaches and agree with

Kelly et al. (1994: 35–6) that: 'Rather than assert the primacy of any method, we are not working with a flexible position: our choice of method(s) depends on the topic and scale of the study in question. Whenever possible we would combine and compare methods, in order to discover the limitations and possibilities of each'.

Yet, it is important to acknowledge that people may work within departments which (not contractually but in practice) discriminate in favour of some kinds of research and against others, and some research contracts do not always permit the complete freedom of choice and approach that we might wish. With these provisos in mind I now consider further the 'doing of research' and the implications of this for 'knowledge production'.

Suggested further reading

Reinharz, S. (1992) *Feminist Methods in Social Research* (Oxford: Oxford University Press) is a comprehensive text with lots of detail about the doing of feminist research. There are also several edited texts which provide examples of qualitative and quantitative research accounts. For example: Roberts, H. (ed.) (1990) *Doing Feminist Research*, 2nd edn (London: Routledge); Wilkinson, S. (ed.) (1986) *Feminist Social Psychology: Developing Theory and Practice* (Buckingham: Open University Press); Stanley, L. (1990) *Feminist Praxis: Research, Theory and Epistemology in Feminist Sociology* (London: Routledge); Afshar, H. and Maynard, M. (1994) *The Dynamics of 'Race' and Gender: Some Feminist Interventions* (London: Taylor & Francis); and Women and Geography Study Group (1997) *Feminist Geographies: Explorations in Diversity and Difference* (Edinburgh: Longman). See also Roberts, H. (ed.) (1990) *Women's Health Counts* (London: Routledge) and (1992) *Women's Health Matters* (London: Routledge) for examples of quantitative and qualitative studies respectively.

Chapter five

Whose life is it anyway? Issues of power, empowerment, ethics and responsibility

Introduction

Having considered issues surrounding the status and construction of knowledge (Chapters 1 and 2) and the relationship between knowledge, theory and action (Chapters 3 and 4), in Chapters 5 and 6 I explore further some of the detail of doing research. Throughout I highlight the relationship between 'process' and 'product'. Thus, I am concerned in this chapter and the next with how what researchers *do* affects what they *get*. These two chapters also stand as a challenge to the view that research can be 'hygienic', in that I aim to highlight the 'messiness' of it all. In this chapter I consider issues of power, empowerment, emotion, ethics and responsibility in relation to the research process in general and research relationships in particular. However, the chapter is not subdivided around these topics but instead focuses on the stages of the research process and the importance of these issues at each stage. I also demonstrate that, throughout the research process – through choice of study through to analysis and presentation of data – the choices that researchers make, the practicalities that need to be considered when doing research and the process of actually doing the research are all likely to affect not only the dynamics of particular research relationships and the research process, but also the research 'product(s)': the 'findings', the 'results', the 'knowledge'. In this chapter (and the next) I use my own individual and collaborative research experience as a resource in exploring some of the difficulties and the positive aspects of attempting feminist research.

The chapter is divided into three main sections. In 'Getting started' I consider the things that affect initial choices in relation to topic, approach and research population. This is followed by 'Feminist research in action' in which I focus on early and developing research relationships, presentation of self and emotional labour, and reflect on issues of power and empowerment. In 'Leavings and endings' I consider how researchers manage the end-of-data collection and the end of a project in terms of data analysis and presenta-tion. Overall, I highlight some tensions between the philosophy and practice of feminist research, with a particular emphasis on researcher/respondent relationships and the dynamics between the process and the product. I do not argue that the power balance is always in favour of the researcher but explore the implications of shifting power for everyone involved in the research process at all stages.

Getting started

Project parameters and research populations

'Research design' is very often presented as orderly and static and the public conception of research is that it is 'ordered, academic and rational' (Miller 1998: 61). However, much research is actually very different to this and our initial plans may turn out to be very different in reality. When writing a research proposal, or planning the project, researchers think about who they need to reach (as a respondent group), and what method they should use in order to have the best chance of uncovering people's experience. But the best-laid plans do not always work out. For example, if studying fathers as well as mothers of children who attend the local playgroup, the fathers may all be out at work, many of the women may be bringing up their children alone or the men may just not be willing to speak to us (McKee and O'Brien

1983; Cotterill 1992; Letherby 1993). When planning a project on patient experience we may intend to give our questionnaire to a large group of individuals to discover different illness experiences, as well as differences of age, ethnicity and class, but many of these people may not want to be involved for a variety of reasons: because they are too ill, because they do not want to complain about the nurses and doctors who are caring for them or because cultural norms and language differences make it difficult for them to be involved. Researchers who are committed to incorporating respondents from different 'races' and classes in their work must be prepared to allow more time and money for respondent recruitment and data collection (Cannon et al. 1991). For their research on the relationship between race, class and gender inequality and well-being and mental health among full-time employed professional, managerial and administrative women in the USA, Cannon et al. (1991) spoke at meetings, wrote for newspapers and used 'snowballing' techniques (word of mouth among respondents). Glucksmann (1994) and Standing (1998) both argue that working-class women are less likely to respond to requests for research in written form, especially on 'official' stationery. Standing suggests that the reasons for this are complex and include a mistrust of authority and the style and language that requests are written in. Similarly, when undertaking research with children we need to be aware that significant adults in their lives may not only act as gate-keepers to respondents but may also wish to vet the research output (Mayall 1999).

Furthermore, what should we do if those who come forward do not match our original intended 'respondent characteristics' and ask to be involved in a project because they feel that they meet the criteria or have something important to say? What if those involved decide that the method that you have devised is not appropriate and although they want to be involved they want to dictate the terms of their involvement (see e.g. Kelly et al. 1994; Letherby and Zdrodowski 1995; Letherby 1997)? Respondents may willingly agree to be involved in the research at the first data collection stage but may decide that they do not want to be involved for the second interview, the keeping of the research diary, the questionnaire stage. This may be because they are busy or because they are worried that their experience does not resonate with the dominant one, and they will be characterized as 'unusual' or 'abnormal' (Millen 1997).

Obviously, all of these issues affect the process and the product of the research, as does the position and status of the researcher. A postgraduate funding her or himself doing a small-scale qualitative project has very different resources from a team of researchers working on government-funded, large-scale multi-method longitudinal research projects. Not having much money or much opportunity for large-scale work is not always a disadvantage, as the researcher may be able to be more flexible and responsive to changes which the respondents, or the project, require. So a single researcher may find it easier to adapt their method and introduce new techniques and new questions, and even a new respondent group. For example, a researcher may aim to study the culture of a school by talking to the pupils and then realize on reflection that she really needs to talk to the teachers or, having intended to use only a questionnaire, then decide that some focus-group interviews would add to the richness of the data (see Reinharz 1992 for some examples). However, as Leonard and Coate (2002) note, some funding councils may withdraw their funding if researchers change the focus of their research.

Furthermore, and as highlighted in earlier chapters, the researcher who identifies as feminist (pro-feminist) needs to choose a method which enables women's experiences and voices to be distinct and discernible, and this does not only mean choosing an appropriate method (see Chapter 4) but also adopting a flexible research approach which adapts to the emerging data. Miller (1998: 60), whose research was concerned with women's ante- and postnatal experiences, adopted a longitudinal approach in order to capture episodes in the stories of women's experiences as they unfolded.

At this stage, when forming a study group, unless they are researching a specific target population (see below), the researcher is likely to feel vulnerable: what if no one comes forward, or if those who do all wish to drop out halfway through a project? Because of this, when respondents do come forward, the researcher may feel initially excited and satisfied, which in turn may lead to feelings of guilt and anxiety if the research topic is a sensitive or emotive one. Researchers may worry about making things worse for their respondents and feel distressed by the experience of potential respondents. A personal experience illustrates this. The following was sent to me early in my doctoral research and made me question both my motives and approach:

> Dear Gayle
> I read in today's *Guardian* that you are studying infertility and childlessness. I have experienced both of these, and I would be very interested in helping you. I tried for 15 years to get pregnant, lost a total of 10 potential children, had 2 ectopic pregnancies, 2 attempts at IVF and have now given up.
> We were turned down for adoption in 1985 as I WAS 35 – too old!
> If you would like to contact me, I will happily fill in a questionnaire or answer questions etc.
> Yours, LF

Although I continued with the data collection I opened further letters with some trepidation and reflected on my earlier 'enthusiasm' for respondent recruitment. It is important to remember that 'respondents' are people first, people who may have had difficult and distressing experiences.

Access

Projects that involve gatekeepers and/or translators (i.e. the researcher needs help from others in order to get access to respondents) often appear to discourage respondents who feel that these 'others' may then have access to what they have divulged through the course of the research which may, in turn and when relevant affect their treatment and their care from these individuals (Cannon 1989; Afshar 1994). Most obviously, this is relevant when researching individuals' experience in the public sphere (the world of work, education, health etc.). For example, reflecting on Yvonne Jewkes' research inside a prison, she and I (Jewkes and Letherby 2001) detailed the strategies she used to distance herself from the prison officers. These included wearing clothes which could in no way be seen as reminiscent of a uniform, using prison jargon and making it clear to each (inmate) respondent that she was a researcher independent of the Home Office and the prison service. Similarly, Miller (1998), when studying women's ante- and postnatal experience, was concerned that women recruited through antenatal clinics by midwives and health visitors might perceive the research as in some way linked to the delivery of health care services and feel inhibited and/or feel obliged to present their experiences in a way that mirrored public accounts given by health professionals.

Gatekeeping issues are also relevant when trying to reach respondents in the private sphere, and when researching personal and family issues. Song (1998) discovered this when considering competing siblings' perceptions as part of her research on labour participation in the Chinese take-away business in Britain. She asked one respondent if his older sister would like to speak to her and was told that she was too busy. Likewise, Cotterill (1992), when researching mothers and daughters-in-law had a similar experience in that she found it was not possible to interview women who were related. She suggests that if she had done so, not only would her respondents have felt very uncomfortable, but her data would have been completely different as women would not have wanted to say anything critical about the other woman she was going to interview. Further complications may arise when the researcher and some, or all, of the respondent group do not speak the same language, when respondents are children or have a disability which is likely to involve them telling their story through another (see Afshar and Maynard 1994; Hood et al. 1999 for some examples).

Study group formation

In terms of researcher/respondent experience and data collection there are differences between studies where respondents are self-selecting or specifically targeted. In order to consider the implications of these two methods of study group construction in further detail I am going to outline two pieces of research that I have been involved in recently: namely my doctoral research ('Infertility' and 'involuntary childlessness': definition and self-identity, which I completed in 1997) and a project which I undertook with a colleague (Jennifer Marchbank) during 1997–9 ('Why do Women's Studies?') (Letherby and Marchbank 2001).

My doctoral research was a qualitative study and the respondent group was self-selecting and comprised women and men (mostly women) who defined themselves at that time, or at some time in the past, as 'infertile' and/or 'involuntarily childless'. Unlike many other studies in this area I did not focus on a group of people or a set population (i.e. a group of people undergoing treatment, or going through the adoption process, or reflecting on their experience of donor insemination). The resulting study group was diverse and included:

- individuals who were childless through non-medical reasons;
- cases where the source of infertility was with the man, the woman, both or unknown;
- cases where infertility was the primary problem and cases where infertility was secondary as a result of endometriosis or some other physical problem;
- people who had become parents: through unaided biological means; as the result of assisted conception; through adoption; and step-parents and non-parents.

Overall, I was concerned to include individuals who defined themselves as 'infertile' and/or 'involuntarily childless' at the time of the fieldwork, or at some time in the past, and not just people who were defined in this way by others. I also wanted to explore the emotional and social aspects of their experience, as well as the medical aspects.

To get access to this group of diverse people I used a variety of techniques (e.g. letters in national and local newspapers, letters in women's magazines, letters in support group magazines; snowballing – in that some respondents suggested others to me – and occasionally through people who had heard about the research from one of my colleagues or another respondent approaching me). These approaches, and the nature of the topic at issue, affected the data I obtained. Originally I thought that my data would all be collected via in-depth interviews but more of my respondents (51 out of 87) ended up writing, rather than talking, to me because some lived a long way away and others preferred to write rather than talk about their experiences. Also, as there were no clear theoretical criteria determining the size or nature of the study group and the aim was to consider the range and diversity of experience and to focus on self-identity and self-selection my respondent groups were fluid rather than rigid in composition – i.e. some of the respondents would not necessarily be considered 'infertile' and/or 'involuntarily childless' by either the medical profession, some of the other respondents, or me.

I wrote to 38 different local and national newspapers, women's magazines and support group magazines about my project. Eleven printed my letter or an article about me asking for women to contact me. I was concerned that individuals who felt that their experience was relevant were included and that their inclusion in the research was not dependent solely on my criteria. This was not totally selfless as the problematization of definition and identity was a central issue within the research. Sometimes relying on the media in this way caused me distress in that my letter was edited, which changed the meaning slightly and, in one extreme case when I was interviewed by the editor of the women's pages of a local newspaper, my request (and quite a few personal details about me) was written up under the headline 'Learning from the pain and suffering of childlessness'. At the time I felt this was emotive, patronizing and sensational. However, the women who came forward as a result of this article were not offended by it. I realized that if I had stressed more forcibly the complexity of experience rather than stereotypical desperateness, the headline could have been worse. For example, imagine the response to 'Childlessness can be fun says researcher'! Four women did come forward after reading the article and I asked each of them what they thought about the headline. They all said that it had not bothered them, but I cannot know how many people were put off the research by the article and its headline. However, I got no fewer responses as a result of this article than from other less emotive publications.

When replying to initial letters from respondents by letter or telephone I tried to make it clear what my project was and was not about, to ensure that respondents had a clear idea of what was expected from them and of my motivations and emphasis. However, a couple of people did write initially for advice about their treatment and I made it clear that I was not a medical expert and sent them some details about support groups (I explore the political motivation of respondents, including the implications of this for the research process and product further in Chapter 6).

On reflection, I realize that I could have accessed a group of very different people using this method if my request for respondents had asked for a more specific, or conversely more general, group of people. With respect to being more specific, if I had 'advertised' just for respondents who were currently engaged in 'infertility' treatment or the adoption process, or for those with experience of either, my group would have been somewhat different. I now wish that my advert had been more 'general', as my resultant study group was largely middle class and heterosexual. Yet the inclusion of others may have caused me further problems. For example, in order to include all nationalities I may have needed an interpreter, which I could not afford and in any case, as previously noted, for some cultural groups talking about intimate issues such as sex and family life to a stranger is deemed inappropriate. I did talk to one woman, who identified herself as lesbian, who had experienced donor insemination. Including more women with this kind of experience is likely to have influenced the definition of the 'problem' of 'infertility' and 'involuntary childlessness' and influenced my 'findings': the 'product' of my research.

Although I advertised for women, some men did come forward and I included them in the research but did not change subsequent adverts. The inclusion of these men meant that the parameters of the project changed from what I had originally intended. Arguably, I could have included more men in order to get a fuller picture of their experience. Indeed, some of my female respondents said I should have. I chose not to mention my personal involvement in the issue (I fit the medical definition of 'infertility' and at the time of the fieldwork I was 'involuntarily childless') until first letters and interviews and some respondents said/wrote that they would have got in touch sooner had they known about my experience earlier. A couple of respondents who got in touch following adverts and then discovered that we had met before through a mutual friend were wary of being involved (see Chapter 6 for more on how prior knowledge of the researcher may encourage or inhibit respondent involvement).

Clearly, self-selection as a recruitment method has an influence on the data in that it affects what respondents say and how they say it. In my research, those who did not come forward but would have been willing to be involved if targeted were likely to have had different things to say, for their 'infertility'/'involuntary childlessness' may or may not have been an issue for them. Alternatively, some individuals may not have come forward because the issue was 'too painful' to share, or indeed because it was less significant in their lives (see Letherby 1997).

The aim of the 'Why do women's studies?' research (Letherby and Marchbank 2001) was to explore students' experience and views of women's studies. This was a multi-method project and we used a mixture of quantitative and qualitative data collection. We began the research with two focus groups using women's studies students in a university not represented elsewhere in the study. From this we generated a questionnaire on which there were a mixture of quantitative and qualitative questions. We administered our questionnaire to several groups. Within our own institution we gave the questionnaire to students that we taught: women's studies students, students taking women's studies modules, social science students who were not taking women's studies modules and students that we had not had any previous contact with (i.e. students who had no contact with women's studies or social science). We also sent copies of our questionnaire to colleagues at three other universities, and these were distributed to women's studies students and students taking women's studies modules, and then sent back to us.

Clearly, there were complex issues here in terms of access and power. For example, in our own institution women's studies students may have felt obliged to be involved and may have felt that their involvement (or non-involvement) and their answers to our questions would affect their relationships with us, their teachers (people already in a position of power). So, even though we stressed that involvement was voluntary and asked students to 'post' their responses back to us, and even though we promised confidentiality and anonymity, it was often obvious to us who a respondent was, and, we think, obvious to them that we would know who they were. Clearly, all of this was likely to affect what these respondents wrote and some may have tried to please us. However, it did appear that some respondents also found it possible to express dissatisfaction about their courses, their modules and us, their teachers: it appeared to us that it was easier to criticize us on paper and for 'the purposes of research' than either face-to-face or on module evaluation forms. Similar but different issues are relevant when considering the involvement of the students from other universities whose responses may have been affected by their relationships with their own tutors who may have looked at the responses before returning the questionnaire to us. Readers will notice that I appear to be contradicting myself here because in Chapter 4, when I mentioned this research project, I suggested that it was the fact that the questionnaire was anonymous that made it possible for respondents to criticize us. In fact we think both these explanations are valid: an example of the complex dynamics between respondents and researchers and evidence of the need for researchers to recognize that respondents are thoughtful, reflective and possibly, at times, manipulative.

With reference to the students we did not know within our own institution, as researchers we were much more vulnerable. In these instances, we decided to approach potential respondents in student bars and cafés and some of these people assumed we were students ourselves and made it clear that they had very little respect for us or our work. Obviously, this too affected the data we obtained, because, although some of the respondents who had no contact with us took the issue seriously, others ridiculed the research to our faces and on the questionnaire (e.g. writing derogatory and abusive comments about women's studies staff and students in answer to several questions). It is possible to argue that many see women's studies and those associated with it as an easy target and, indeed, we would suggest that the defacing of questionnaires was data in itself, as it told us quite clearly the attitudes of some towards women's studies (for a fuller discussion see Letherby and Marchbank 1998, 2001).

It is necessary to consider a different set of issues when looking at the study of secondary data (data not collected for the purpose of the study), such as statistics or cultural artefacts. A researcher may or may not need permission to get access to the data they require and when this is achieved (if relevant) it is important to remember that the material was not created for the purpose of the research (see Chapter 4) and therefore may be partial or incomplete. It is also important to remember that many of the anxieties that characterize the collection of primary data are relevant here too.

Feminist research in action

Beginnings
First contact with respondents can include the distribution of a questionnaire, a first letter, a first interview, participation in a slimming club for the first time, an initial visit to a police station or a village and so on. At this time, shyness and embarrassment is likely for both respondents and researchers. Yet it is important at this stage for the researcher to fully explain the research aim and their interest and to talk about issues of confidentiality and anonymity, making it clear what they are doing and what they are not. Yet, this can be complex.

Some feminist research takes place with those close to us. For example, Stanley (1993) interviewed her mother and Scott (1998) her stepdaughter and it is possible to find other references to research with friends, family, colleagues and acquaintances. I explore the significance of these connections further in Chapter 6 but for now it is worth noting that the beginnings of research relationships may be characterized by shyness and embarrassment, and a tension between engagement and distance, whether or not the respondent is known to us.

At this stage of the research, respondents may be concerned about what will happen to the material that they are providing for the researcher(s). In addition, within the same project, respondents' concerns may be different: in my doctoral research, for example, Hazel stressed the importance of confidentiality with respect to what she was telling me as 'No one in the family knows about this'; Della wrote at the end of her letter, 'Please contact me to say you have received this and I trust that total confidentiality will be enforced – even in your home and office', and some women wrote anonymously (e.g. 'This is my only declaration of this history and therefore I'd rather not sign'). However, others showed much less concern about confidentiality. As Jean said, 'Well you can change my name but I don't expect anyone in my family will read it'; and Jane wrote, 'Everybody knows about me anyway'. Clearly, it is not only respondents and their significant others that may be identified but workplaces, government agencies, communities, streets and so on and it may be necessary to omit data that makes a person or a location obvious. The ethical guidelines of most professional associations suggest that the only time when confidentiality should be broken is if respondents disclose details of abuse (of themselves or others, by themselves or others). Of course even when this is the case some methods do not allow for the tracking of respondents and sometimes this poses other problems for the researcher (e.g. in the case of sexual or violent behaviour and drug use).[1]

If the research focus is exploratory the researcher may not have a rigid agenda and clearly this fluidity is relevant to the data and to the research relationships. Giving respondents a list of themes for discussion prior to an interview, deciding with them what you will focus on, going with a list of specific questions that you do not deviate from or asking them what they think is important to discuss all result in very different encounters and very different 'results'. Likewise, initially deciding to collect data through a questionnaire and then realizing that focus groups, photo-diaries etc. would enlarge the data, is likely to make the project very different (e.g. Reinharz 1992).

Space and place are also important in research terms. When doing research on emotive or sensitive issues, respondents may or may not feel more comfortable when the research takes place in their own home, workplace, social club etc., and it may be important to offer an alternative venue. Doing research in a respondent's own space will usually make them feel more in control and when this involves visiting respondents in their own homes the research relationship is also likely to be affected. During my doctoral research I was only once not offered a drink. On many occasions respondents greeted me with, 'I've got us something nice for lunch'. I helped children with homework, washed dishes, read bedtime stories and even named a kitten (Bunty). Clearly, research of this nature often prompts a temporary closeness initiated by shared experience.

As Ribbens (1989) notes, research relationships are complicated social encounters. Research may involve listening to a story that has never been told to anyone before, working closely alongside others in a workplace or community during difficult times, going into an institution such as a residential home or a prison where respondents may feel (or are literally) trapped. In all of these situations respondents are likely to tell you private and personal things because, as Cotterill (1992) suggests, research relationships are often seen as 'safe' (for further detail see Chapter 6). Furthermore, as Parr (1998: 95) suggests, it is important to listen to what is *not* being said as well as what is, which means that researchers need to pay attention to verbal cues such as intonations, nuances, pauses and inflections and to pay attention to body language. Silences are as important as noise in research and the interpretation of silence is as important as the interpretation of what is being said.

Identity, impression management and emotion work

'The intensity of the fieldwork process is typically accompanied by a psychological anxiety resulting in a continuous presentation and management of self when in the presence of those studied' (Shaffir et al. 1980: 4). While male social scientists have rarely been interested in the sphere of women, women social scientists have, historically, sought access to male worlds (Fleuhr-Lobban and Lobban 1986). Women who have carried out research in male-dominated organizations have been able to obtain rich data because of their perceived 'invisibility'. As Warren (1988) points out, women in organizations have traditionally been employed as filing clerks, secretaries and in other service jobs. This had some advantages for her as a researcher in a court of law, as her presence drew 'hardly a glance from the males engaged on "more important" business' (p. 18). Alternatively, women doing research in female-dominated areas appear to be 'noticed' by respondents. Oboler (1986: 45), writing about her experiences of fieldwork in Kenya, while pregnant, notes the positive effect that her pregnancy had on her field relationships. She writes that her identity as a 'childbearing woman' improved her rapport with the women she was researching. Conversely, Chrisler (1996: 95) found that 'a veil seemed to descend' between her and the women in a weight-loss group meeting when, in reply to their questions, she told them that she herself had never had a 'weight problem'.

Clearly, there are some aspects of our identity that it is difficult to disguise (even assuming that we would want to) and it is important to acknowledge that our sex, age, skin colour, accent and so on are all likely to have an effect on how we are seen by respondents, and this will subsequently affect that data we collect. However, there are other aspects of ourselves (e.g. adornment and dress) that can be easily adapted to the research situation. As mentioned earlier, when doing research with prison inmates it is likely that a researcher wearing a suit would be viewed with suspicion (see Jewkes and Letherby 2001). Similarly, Cannon (1989) writes of how, when doing research with breast cancer patients in hospital, she rejected the advice that she should wear white as this would identify her as a medic. Yet, 'When everyone else was wearing either a nursing uniform or a white coat it felt conspicuous to be wearing "civvies". I used to avoid over-bright colours, sticking to dark blue or grey to try to blend in with the nurses' (p. 69).

On the other hand Ramsay (1993: 8), when undertaking research in male-dominated university departments, felt the need to accentuate her 'outsider' status:

> I also managed the impression I gave of myself as researcher. I wore smart clothes, arranged my hair and wore make-up. Lipstick was particularly important. Lipstick represents femininity to me, and it is unusual for me to wear it; by putting it on each morning I reminded myself that I was doing something unusual, I was assuming a role. In this I experienced myself, and was perceived by others, as an outsider.

Dressing up or dressing down in this way is not just about 'getting the best data' but about enabling respondents and researcher to feel comfortable. Clearly, when going into a prison or a hostel for the homeless, to appear in expensive clothes and accessories is less than sensitive, whereas wearing jeans and a T-shirt when engaged in observation in a bank means one is less likely to be treated seriously as a researcher.

Issues of emotional involvement, management and work are also an aspect of research relationships. With Hochschild's (1983) *The Managed Heart* in mind, Frith and Kitzinger (1998) note that 'emotion work' includes regulating and managing the feelings of others and oneself in order to conform to dominant expectations in a given situation. In other words, as Dunscombe and Marsden (1998) note, individuals perform emotion work on and for others and on and for themselves. Several writers have argued that emotion work is an inevitable part of fieldwork (e.g. Ramsay 1993; Young and Lee 1996). Like Ramsay (1993: 19), I think that:

> Attending to *emotional responses* to experiences in the field is a method of finding out where the researcher stands in relation to those being studied . . . and exploration of the level of *emotional management* required in the relationship between researcher and respondent places the researcher clearly within the research process . . . viewing qualitative research . . . as *emotional labour* locates the process clearly within a discussion of the academic mode of production.

The display of emotions is gendered, in that it is less acceptable for women to display stereotypical masculine emotions such as anger and less acceptable for men to display stereotypical feminine emotions such as distress (Hochschild 1990). James (1989) argues that the result of the gender division of labour is that men are held responsible for bringing in the income and women for the routine running of the home and the care of children, and within this allotted role women are primarily responsible for 'working with emotions'. Thus, women are responsible for others' emotional needs and men are not. This is relevant to women fieldworkers who, as Warren (1988:

45) notes, have traditionally been portrayed as 'more accessible and less threatening than men' which coupled with their 'superior' communicative abilities makes the interactions of fieldwork generally easier (see Chapter 4). This is not only sexist but denies the hard work involved in 'doing research' (for both researchers and respondents).

Clearly, displays of emotion can be difficult and even dangerous for both the researcher and the researched and, as McRobbie (1982: 5) argues, at times the researcher may feel that she is 'holidaying on people's misery' and then leaving the respondent to deal with the consequences alone while she goes off with what she came for. However, others have argued that it is morally indefensible to distract someone from talking about something that they feel the need to talk about, and being able to reflect on and re-evaluate experiences as part of the research can be therapeutic and/or help the respondent to re-evaluate their position (see e.g. Cotterill 1992; Opie 1992; Letherby 2002). Indeed, it may be easier to talk to a researcher than a significant other, as demonstrated by the following account from a terminally ill woman:

> I can quite happily sit there and chat and laugh and tell her [an acquaintance at the hospital] all about myself, and listen to her tell me all about herself, and it doesn't bother me. But when it comes to somebody who I'm really close to, who I really love, or who I know loves me I can't do it. I can talk to you, 'cos I don't love you, you're outside the family, but I just can't talk to the family.
>
> (Exley and Letherby 2001: 122)

Yet, giving people a chance to talk and write about an experience which is often 'taboo' can bring forward vulnerable people who may 'give away' more (both substantively and emotionally) than they later feel comfortable with (Finch 1984).

Researchers, too, may feel strong emotions in the field. In my doctoral research I found that listening to the accounts of my respondents was often very distressing, and this was compounded by the fact that what they were describing often resonated with my own feelings and experiences. However, as well as feeling empathy with my respondents I sometimes felt irritation or anger. For example, during an interview with Jean which lasted three hours, she became very distressed and pulled me towards her in an embrace. Although I am myself a tactile, demonstrative person, I felt extremely uncomfortable with this. I felt 'used' by Jean and thought her behaviour was inappropriate. Also, I sometimes found respondents' views of my experience difficult to cope with. In many letters and interviews respondents asked questions about me and asked me what treatments I had undergone. Many expressed surprise that since my miscarriage I had not had 'fertility' treatment of any sort. Several who lived locally suggested that I go to visit this or that doctor and/or clinic. May went as far as to say, 'I can see you with a baby in your arms yet'. I felt ambivalent about this. I thought it ironic that May should say just the kind of thing that she felt it was insensitive of others to say to her, yet at the same time I realized that she was only showing concern for me. I felt only anger when both Bob and Neil (partners of women I interviewed) suggested that it was my own fault that I had no children if I was not prepared to have treatment. In all of these situations I 'managed' my emotions. I recognize that my respondents may have had a different view of our relationship to me, especially as there are no laid-down prescriptions of behaviour for the researched. After all, why shouldn't they say what they think of me, given the personal aspects of the topics I was asking them to talk about? Marshall's (1994) and Scott's (1998) experience is also relevant here:

> Staying in an unfamiliar house after one interview I walked in my sleep for the first time in my life, and during the weeks of transcription I endured stomach cramps and nausea on a regular basis. Annecka Marshall has pointed out doing research can seriously damage your health (Marshall, 1994). I would add that it can make a nasty dent in our ontological security. My research diary during this period records my own struggles with disbelief . . . to anxiety about the truth status of ritual abuse accounts . . .
>
> (Scott 1998: 5.14)

Similar accounts of emotional management are provided by Ramsay (1996) and R. Bell (1993) who both write about managing anger in work-based research situations when respondents displayed sexist and racist views. Their research accounts highlight the fact that issues of emotion are not just relevant when researching so-called emotive issues but in all research situations. These accounts also demonstrate how the management of emotion is complex. If a respondent displays very obvious prejudice it would seem that, given our feminist politics, we should challenge this. However, if we allow the respondent(s) to continue we may discover an insight to the extent and roots of these prejudiced views which, in turn, may help us to challenge them in the future (Phoenix 1994; Ramsay 1996). Furthermore, if we make a challenge, this may affect the research from then on, as Westwood (1984) found. For her fieldwork she worked as a packer in a factory and, after challenging sexism at a works social event, found that this had some influence on the women she was working with. It is difficult to be clear on the right course of action here and most researchers probably end up going with their (politically and intellectually informed) 'instinct'. But, this is often likely to leave you feeling that you have done it wrong:

> In one instance a man was telling me about how there were two types of women students in engineering. One type were conscious of their gender and used it to get their own way; they wore make-up and skirts. The other type looked like any other student on the course (male) and concentrated on getting on with people (men) and getting the job done. The first type were a problem while the second type were the best students. This was a lovely piece of data and I had no wish as a researcher to stop him. I listened, giving feedback in terms of head nods and indistinguishable 'umms'. However, as a feminist who did not share his assumptions about sexuality and power, I wanted to challenge him. When I left the office I was exhausted and unhappy about the interview. I had some good data but I had colluded with a powerful man in recreating understandings about women, sexuality and power.
>
> (Ramsay 1996: 138)

What is important in terms of the production of knowledge is being aware of the implications of what we do or do not do.

Emotion work is relevant to questionnaires as well as face-to-face research methods (see e.g. Katz-Rothman 1986). During the questionnaire stage of her research on amniocentesis Katz-Rothman received questionnaires detailing respondents' experience of 'a bad result' and writes how she also grieved for the babies her respondents had 'lost'. Kelly et al. (1994: 155) also write about their feelings during the coding of the data they gathered from their research on sexual abuse: 'We learnt very quickly to pick up on each other's distress – tears, rage and despair were seldom far away'. Furthermore, as Kelly et al. note, it is important not to forget that data inputters, transcribers and typists are likely to feel emotionally connected to data too.

Difficulties for researchers (and others) when managing emotions in the field are compounded by the fact that there are no formal support systems. Brannen (1988: 562) points out that 'Even professional confidants – counsellors and psychotherapists – have their own confessors. On most research projects these issues are rarely considered and researchers are left to find their own individual solutions outside their formally prescribed roles'. Lee-Treweek (2000), drawing on the work of Kleinman and Copp (1993: 33), notes that one suggested way of dealing with discomforting emotion in the research process is to ignore or 'repress it'. An example of this is given by Meerabeau (1989), who when interviewing 'sub-fertile' couples about potentially embarrassing subjects, followed the advice of Owens (1986) and avoided eye-contact with her respondents. Lee-Treweek (2000) adds that it is also possible to intellectualize away emotion by focusing upon other aspects of data. However, as she and others argue, by using and analysing our emotional experiences we can add to our understandings of respondents' lives (see Lee-Treweek and Linkogle 2000).

With all of this in mind some researchers go so far as to argue that emotion is central to the whole issue. For example, Katz-Rothman (1986: 5) writes: 'I could not have understood it intellectually I don't think, if I had not experienced it emotionally', and Wilkins (1993) similarly argues that she would not have attempted her research on motherhood if she did not have personal experience to draw on. Yet there is a danger here, as the suggestion is that emotional involvement is a prerequisite for good research. Although it is possible to argue that all research can be potentially sensitive and has emotional aspects to it, and feminist research practice is important in highlighting this fact, this should not be used to downgrade work that draws less on emotive and personal issues – i.e. there is no prescriptive view of 'what feminist research is'. It is also important to be aware that emotional involvement, of researchers and respondents, can take the form of manipulation. For example, although a researcher may feel sympathy or empathy with respondents, her involvement with them affects her working life, her career. Similarly, respondents may consciously be using the research and the researcher as a receptacle for their emotions. So is emotion work caring or using, empathy or manipulation? These are possible contradictions that the researcher needs to acknowledge.

Power, empowerment and 'emancipatory' research

It should already be evident that issues of power are complex within research. There is an assumption that the researcher is always in control of the research situation and is the one who holds the balance of power but it is often more complicated in reality. As Giddens (1985) notes, power is in one way or another an aspect of all relationships. He makes the distinction between two types of resources involved in power – control of material resources (money, time, research 'tools') and control of authoritative resources (as in holding the status of 'researcher'). Within research it is us, the researchers, who have the time, resources and skills to conduct methodological work, to make sense of experience and locate individuals in historical and social contexts (see e.g. Kelly et al. 1994; Millen 1997; Letherby 2002). Furthermore, it is an illusion to think that, in anything short of a fully participatory research project, respondents can have anything approaching 'equal' knowledge (about what is going on) to the researcher. Yet, it may also be simplistic to assume that an approach which includes the respondents at all levels is ultimately empowering for respondents. As Wolf (1996: 26) notes, so-called 'participatory' research 'can entail very disparate levels of input from research subjects' [sic] and respondents may not wish this type of involvement. Thus, there may be a tension between the desire to give women a voice and the making of knowledge (see e.g. Maynard and Purvis 1994; Millen 1997), not least because individuals may not necessarily possess the knowledge (or have the desire) to explain everything about their lives.

It is important to acknowledge that researchers often have the objective balance of power throughout the research process. Yet, as Giddens (1985) adds, power is not a simple have/have not aspect of a relationship and in terms of research the subjective experience of power is often ambivalent for both the researcher and the respondent. The researcher usually has control over the order in which the questions are asked and has control over the tape-recorder, a pen, and the associated authority that this brings. Furthermore, it is the researcher who is more often than not responsible for the final analysis and presentation of the data (see below). Stanley and Wise (1993) argue that as researchers we should make ourselves vulnerable and try and 'equalize' our relationship with respondents, and Cook and Fonow (1986) argue for 'transformation' and 'empowerment' through research.

As highlighted earlier, Oakley (1981) suggests that by appealing to sisterhood, researchers can do this. But as Miller's (1998) experience suggests it is easy to get things wrong. Reflecting on the fact that what she chose to disclose of her own experiences of childbirth mirrored the public wall of silence surrounding discussions about pain, she notes that one respondent said to her: 'To be honest . . . even you didn't tell what it would be like!'. Furthermore, Morley (1996: 133) argues that research defined by researchers as 'feminist research' may not always be experienced as feminist by respondents. Drawing on her own experience as a respondent she describes how she has been interviewed by several 'feminist researchers' who have shown 'an ignorance of the micropolitics of power in interpersonal transactions' by, for example, pushing her to talk about things that she did not want to talk about and pushing for more time than she wanted to give; setting up a tape-recorder without her permission with no reassurances about how the tapes might be used; and revealing confidential information in social settings.

With all of this in mind Josselson and Lieblich (1996: 3.4) suggest that we should continue to work 'in anguish', aiming to invest ourselves in research encounters and set agendas with respondents. Yet the desire to invest one-self within the fieldwork stage of research is at least in part structured by the wishes of respondents (Ribbens 1989). In my doctoral research every respondent asked me why I was interested in researching 'infertility' and 'involuntary childlessness'. I was concerned that each interview should con-tain as much of my experience as my respondents wished. But my own experience was referred to by me and the other person/people variably. Once told, a few appeared to accept this as justification for my interest and it was rarely mentioned again; on the other hand many of the interviews involved a lot of two-way discussion. Several women wrote or said that they were worried that what they were saying might upset me (even when our experi-ences had little in common). When embarking on the study I did believe that my personal experience would make it easier, rather than harder, to do research in this area. This proved to be the case in terms of the 'collection of data' as, once respondents had 'placed me' as one of them (Finch 1984) they felt happier to talk (see Chapter 6 for further discussion).

In terms of the power balance there are serious problems with the trust that this implies. Making people feel more powerful does not necessarily change the objective material circumstances. As Millen (1997: 2.2) notes:

> what we as researchers and as feminists might see as empowering women by giving them the tools to analyse their situation in terms of gender and power may actually *disempower* them in the short term by undermining immediate coping strategies which do not involve any long-term structural change for women . . .

On the other hand, Cotterill (1992), Millen (1997), Collins (1998) and Luff (1999) all argue that the research relationship *is* fluid and changing and is always jointly constructed. Thus, researchers do not always hold the balance of power or even have control over their own involvement, let alone the respondent's involvement. This may be relevant when researching indi-viduals who are older, more experienced, more knowledgeable, and so on, than us. It may also be relevant when the women we interview are secure in their own 'power'. With reference to her research with women scientists, Millen (1997) notes that even the more junior PhD students and technicians has access to a certain amount of social privilege compared to many other women. Millen's study of women scientists highlighted the need for a more subtle and detailed characterization of power within feminist research. She adds that power is multi-layered and also dynamic and therefore we need to accept that empowerment is also situational and fractured in that some women do have access to some social power and privilege, all of which impinges upon any notion of their empowerment. The point here is to recognize that our respondents may not necessarily feel that they need to be empowered by us. So it is important not to over-passify respondents within the research situation. They can refuse to answer, take part, tell the truth even, and while it is important that we as researchers remain critically reflexive of our position it is patronizing of us to always place the respondent in the role of potential victim.

There may also of course be people that we feel we do not want to empower in any way. Here I return to my earlier example of the sexist, racist, homophobic etc. respondent. Indeed, at times we may feel that we have to struggle to maintain a sense of self. Many examples of this have been given by women researching men, for example, Foster (1994) and Horn (1997) researching the police, Scott and Porter (1983) and Ramsay (1996) who undertook research in higher education, and Westwood (1984) and R. Bell (1993) who did fieldwork in factories and male-dominated companies. R. Bell (1993), for example, recounts her experience of doing fieldwork in an engineering company when she herself had a first degree in engineering. After spending four weeks in the company and being told on numerous occasions that 'women don't make good engineers' she 'came out' as an engineer. The benefits of this admission were that more people seemed willing to speak to her (which of course had an impact on the data collected), but the disadvantages were that she had to listen to descriptions of 'test procedures in minute detail' (R. Bell 1993: 37).

Before ending this section on empowerment in research it is important to give some attention to issues of power and empowerment within the research community itself, which as Millen (1997) suggests is an issue that has been largely overlooked. In agreement with this, Kelly et al. (1994) suggest that it is ironic that so much discussion is given in research accounts to the empowerment of respondents, while the possibility that members of the research community may be experiencing oppression is ignored. Low pay, insufficient information about the project to engage fully with the issues, short contracts which concentrate on the collection of data and not the analysis and writing stages of the project, characterize the contract researcher's job. It is important that we consider the impact of our work on colleagues as well as on respondents because, 'An agenda which intends to be "for women" cannot uncritically be founded on the exploitation of the low-status and poorly paid skills of female typists, transcribers and data analysts' (Kelly et al. 1994: 41).

Leavings and endings

Leaving the field
Just as beginnings of research relationships often take a considerable amount of negotiation, so do endings. There is a need to reflect on the 'ends' of relationships in research: when to leave the field; when to end each interview

or set of interviews, etc. It may feel inappropriate or artificial to carry on, or it may feel 'wrong' to stop. Sometimes the problem may be taken out of the researcher's hands as respondents may finish it themselves: 'Well that's it, I've told you everything now' or 'Let's have a cup of coffee shall we?'

Leaving the field may or may not signify the beginning of a new type of relationship. This is likely to be structured by the research topic and also by the perceived 'role' of the researcher within the research relationship. Cannon (1989), writing about her research with women living with and dying from breast cancer, recalls that long before she left the field she felt that she could not, and indeed did not want to, say 'thank you and goodbye'. She writes that some of the women in her study would have experienced this as abandonment as they linked it in their minds to the point when the medical staff could no longer help them. Cotterill (1992) outlines an opposite scenario. At the end of her fieldwork on mother-in-law–daughter-in-law relationships she felt that she would like to maintain contact with one of the daughters-in-law that she had interviewed, but was unwilling to impose a 'friendship' on a woman who did not want this. She was thus pleased when the woman herself suggested that they meet and ultimately disappointed when, in reality, this never happened. These two examples indicate the 'flow' of power between the researcher and the researched. Unwilling to exploit the relationship, the researcher has to play a less active role than she may otherwise wish or, indeed, may feel obliged to maintain a relationship against her wishes.

Whether or not the relationship becomes one based on friendliness or friendship, I would suggest that the relationship itself does not end with the completion of fieldwork. Research involves commitment from respondents as well as researchers and the epistemological position of feminist researchers necessitates a recognition of this and the responsibilities it brings. So although in many research projects leaving the field ends the interaction between researchers and respondents, often we know what our respondents want us to write.

Analysing the data

After leaving the field and while writing the research 'findings', the researcher has ultimate control over the material and authoritative resources. At this stage of the research the researcher holds the balance in that they take away the 'words' and have the power of editorship (Stacey 1991; Cotterill 1992; Iles 1992). As Stacey (1991: 114) notes:

> With very rare exceptions, it is the researcher who narrates, who 'authors' the ethnography. In the last instance, [a research account] is a written document structured primarily by a researcher's purposes, offering a researcher's interpretations, registered in a researcher's voice.

So the active role of the respondents is over and because of this Stacey argues that 'elements of inequality, exploitation, and even betrayal are endemic to [research]' (p. 114). Researchers are themselves people, with their own 'responses, values, beliefs, and prejudices' (Morley 1996: 139) and research involves selection, explanation, interpretation and judgement. So as Fine (1994: 22) argues, research involves 'carving out pieces of narrative evidence that we select, edit and deploy to border our arguments'. Because of this it is important that the processes involved in research procedures are clearly outlined in order to uncover the differences that we as researchers make (Jones 1997). This makes our work more accountable to our respondents and to the wider feminist and academic community (Stanley 1991). However, this is not an easy task and we may find that we have to make compromises along the way. To illustrate this I will again refer to my doctoral research experience.

I carried out 99 interviews (lasting between one and three hours) and received more than 100 letters. Although 'quantity' is not central to qualitative research and analysis, having data which included a broad range of experience (in relation to 'infertility' and 'involuntary childlessness') was beneficial to my research both theoretically and politically, as the focus was on issues of definition and identity. Yet this large amount of data also resulted in less available 'space' in which I could discuss any one individual's life and experience. In my data analysis I was concerned with themes and issues and I selected extracts from narratives and accounts that for *me* exemplified groups of respondents' views on the issues that *I* felt were most salient. I also emphasized commonality and difference among my respondents. While I tried to present as many viewpoints as possible, it is also fair to say that in *my* view some respondents had 'more to say' than others. In my thesis as a whole some respondents appeared more than others or in some chapters more than others. For some respondents it is easier to follow the life history of the experience of 'infertility'/'involuntary childlessness' and/or of non-motherhood to motherhood than for others. Thus, it is possible to argue that my approach led to the fragmented representation of many of my respondents' lives. This was accentuated by the fact that *I* decided not to write the thesis following a life course format – for example, from the decision to try to become pregnant, through the discovery that this might be difficult, through investigation and treatment, through to resignation to childlessness. *My* intention was to challenge simplistic representations of resolution in relation to the issues of 'infertility' and 'involuntary childlessness' which was, I think, valuable substantively but I am aware that this approach led to further fragmentation of individual stories.

I do not believe that I generated the true story of 'infertility' and 'involuntary childlessness' but I do think that my work stands as a challenge to what has gone before. I agree with Stanley (1991: 208) that 'people theorize their own experience . . .' and 'observe, categorize, analyse, reach conclusions', so I accept that 'researchers of the social are faced with an already "first order" theorized material social reality'. But I also think it important that I should acknowledge my intellectual privilege (privilege, not superiority) given that I had access to the intellectual and material resources of the academy as well as to the stories of so many people. As I have argued elsewhere:

Wilkinson and Kitzinger (1996) point out that 'our work should not be so much about the other as about the interplay between the researcher and the other (p18). But as they themselves add, 'many feminists want both to enable the voices of Others to be heard, and to create social and political change for or on behalf of those Others' (p20). This creates a dilemma and involves us in a struggle between acknowledgement of the impossibility of full representation and the assertion that our work makes a difference. This leaves me then supporting an approach which may possibly involve a less than complete representation of the other, but I suggest that this is better than no representation at all.

(Letherby 2002: 4.2)

As well as problems of 'full' representation there is also the issue of 'cleaning up the text'. Standing (1998: 190) considers this when relating her experiences of researching lone mothers' involvement in their children's schooling. She writes about how she became aware when listening to the tapes of her interviews that there was very little difference between the spoken language of herself and her respondents but that attempting to 'put the women's voices in the written text in this way looked "wrong"'. Agreeing with Skeggs (1994) that writing in this way had the effect of making the respondents' accounts look 'authentic and simple' and in response to the requests of the respondents themselves she decided to 'tidy up' the accounts. This left her with the worry that she was '"playing" into the hands of the establishment by suggesting that black and white working-class women's speech are wrong, are inadequate, are not as valid as the academic discourse' (Standing 1998: 191).

Even if respondents do have total access to what the researcher has written about their experiences, if they feel that the researcher has 'got it wrong' and this makes them angry or distressed they have an unequal role in terms of response. It is us who turn what Patai (1991) calls the 'raw material' into a feminist account of *their* experience. The worst that can happen is the production of an account that respondents cannot identify with at all. With this in mind we need to be careful not to generalize people's subjective accounts out of all recognition, or to claim to have found an objective account by multiplying together lots of subjective accounts (Stanley and Wise 1993). As Patai (1991: 147) notes, the only projects that avoid these problems 'are those that are at all stages genuinely in control of a community, with the community assuming the role of both researched and researcher'. Yet, as noted earlier, respondents may not want this type of involvement once the fieldwork is over and given our intellectual privileges it is likely that in many cases it is us and not the respondents who will have the resources to undertake this analysis. So as Patai (1991: 147) suggests some measure of 'objectification', or separation and distance, is not only inevitable but, indeed, desirable in most research situations.

Nevertheless, if we recognize respondents as people, and not just research subjects/objects, we must acknowledge that they are not completely passive. However wrong the researcher gets it in terms of meaning it is unlikely that respondents' sense of self-identity and self-assurance will be damaged (unless

of course a researcher's inaccurate 'findings' are translated into policy statements) (see Chapter 3). Researchers take away words not experiences (Skeggs
1994; Millen 1997). Finally, it is important to remember that through the
publication of the research it is the researcher and not the respondent who
gains privileges and advantages: a PhD, a promotion, an enhanced reputation and so on.

End points

In this chapter I have begun a detailed consideration of the relationship
between the process and the product of feminist research. Within this I
have considered the beginning, middle and ending of research relationships
and demonstrated that although feminist research assumes a relationship
between researcher and respondent this is much more complicated in reality
than deciding to adopt a 'participatory approach' and then doing it. Issues of
involvement, emotion and power are evident at all stages of the research
process and the ways in which we as researchers respond to the many dilemmas that we are likely to face affects the process from then on, which in turn
affects the 'results' of our (respondents' and researchers') labours. My aim in
this chapter has been to demonstrate that although some traditional research
accounts make research appear ordered and static, in fact the research process (from choice of project to publication of the 'findings') involves constant
adaptation, re-evaluation and negotiation. Through a further consideration
of the relationship between researchers and respondents I continue this theme
in Chapter 6.

In this chapter and the next (indeed, in the whole of this book) I am
conscious that I may appear guilty of what Glucksmann (1994: 151) calls the
'search for feminism within the research situation'. Glucksmann argues that
this is a response to the lack of external political work by feminists in the
academy and she writes that while 'no one actually argues explicitly that
feminist research *is* feminist politics I do detect an undercurrent, an unwit-
ting implication . . . in many of the best known writings on the subject'.
I agree with Glucksmann that we should have a realistic view of the limits
of research and not claim it as feminist politics, but I also believe that we
need to adopt a consciously political approach to our research practice. This
book represents my understanding of what this entails.

Note

1 Ethical guidelines for many disciplines/professional organizations can be found
  on the Web. Examples include: www.essex.ac.uk/aualidata/forms/bibliog.html
  (British Psychological Society); www.britsoc.org.uk/about/ethic.html (British Sociological Association); www.nmgw.ac.uk/~ohs/ethics.html (Oral History Society);
  http://les1.man.ac.uk/asa/ethics/html (Social Anthropologists of the UK and the

Commonwealth) and www.hsph.harvard.edu/bioethics/guidelines/ethical6.html (Ethical Guidelines for Social Science Research in Health).

Suggested further reading

The thing to do here is to read some research accounts and see for yourself how feminists (and others) reflect on the relationship between the process and the product. As well as the feminist edited collections already mentioned try Bell, C. and Roberts, H. (eds) (1984) *Social Researching: Politics, Problems and Practice* (London: Routledge & Kegan Paul); Hammersley, M. (1993) *Social Research: Philosophy, Politics and Practice* (London: Sage); Hood, S., Mayall, B. and Oliver, S. (eds) (1999) *Critical Issues in Social Research: Power and Prejudice* (Buckingham: Open University Press); and Lee-Treweek, G. and Linkogle, S. (2000) *Danger in the Field: Risk and Ethics in Social Research* (London: Routledge). You will also find articles on the research experience in feminist journals such as *Feminist Review, Journal of Gender Studies, Women's Studies International Forum* and *Feminism and Psychology,* as well as in mainstream journals. Examples from my own discipline include *Sociology, Sociological Research Online* (socresonline.org.uk) and *Sociological Review.* Go looking for more.

Chapter SIX

Texts of many lives: the implications for feminist research

Introduction

Having begun to consider the complex aspects of 'doing feminist research' in Chapter 5 I continue with this theme here and consider further researcher/

respondent relationships and the relevance of these to the research process and product. How we identify ourselves and how we are identified by respondents affects not only relationships during the research process but also the data collected. By 'identity' here I mean 'fixed' aspects of the self including sex, age, ethnicity and so on, and identifying aspects that are possible to change – such as dress and possibly accent. The roles and behaviours that we 'expect' of ourselves and/or respondents 'expect' of us are also significant.

So, in this chapter, I focus particularly on the relationships between the 'self' and 'other' in respect of researcher/respondent relationships. The chapter is divided into three main sections. In 'Roles and relationships' I explore different aspects of researchers' and respondents' selves and their relevance to relationships during the research process and to the research product. In 'Us and them' I consider issues of sameness, difference and representation, and in 'Auto/biography in research' I concentrate on motivation and involvement from the perspective of the researcher and the researched. In this chapter, as in the last, I draw heavily on my own research experiences as well as on the research experiences of others.

Roles and relationships

> Part of the research process, as we see it, is the need to negotiate meanings with subjects [sic] and allow frameworks for understanding to evolve through time . . . The use of self – the influence/impact of self – plays an important part in the unfolding of multiple realities.
>
> (Atkinson and Shakespeare 1993: 6)

Issues of self are paramount. With this in mind Finch (1984) suggests that during her study of clergymen's wives the fact that she too was a clergyman's wife (at that time) meant that she was perceived as 'one of them' by respondents, which she argues both equalized the relationship and justified her interest in the issue. Writing about the development of researcher/respondent relationships in his research with people experiencing chronic job insecurity, Collins (1998) suggests that during the research process a number of overlapping selves are constructed. For example, he notes that he implicitly defined himself, and was defined by, respondents as 'an expert' – or at least as someone who could give an 'expert opinion', and as a 'sympathetic ear' to respondents' views that were not shared by other people. As such Collins suggests that his relationships with respondents did not develop into friendships but he did become something other than a stranger to them, and even though he made it clear to his respondents that he was not a counsellor many still said things like, 'I have to get this off my chest, I have a real problem at the moment'.

Pamela Cotterill and I (Cotterill and Letherby 1994) have similarly written about roles that the feminist researcher may place herself in, feel placed in by respondents or jointly construct with respondents during research encounters. The roles we considered were: 'expert' or 'kindred spirit', 'friends and family', 'counsellor' and 'counselled', and 'friendly strangers'. I further explore the relevance of these and other roles and identities within research here.

Expert or kindred spirit?

Although, as highlighted in Chapter 5, power in research relationships is dynamic, it is easy to see how respondents may think that the researcher, accompanied by the material and authoritative resources (e.g. the time and opportunity to study the issue, the academic backing and status) that they hold, is an expert in the area they are studying. This of course is often not the case and respondents often hold more knowledge about an experience that for the researcher at this stage is 'just' an interest: an area that they hope to explore and understand further, a methodological stance that problematizes the notion of 'expertise'. During my undergraduate research on miscarriage and my doctoral research, in which I was concerned to explore the experience of 'infertility' and 'involuntary childlessness', I was only occasionally defined as an expert, and this always happened at the beginning of the research relationship. Even though I stressed that I was a social scientist and not a medical expert, some women wrote and asked for advice on whether or not to undergo a particular treatment and/or how to 'deal with' their doctor. I always wrote back and clarified my position and some of the women withdrew from the research at this stage. For those that continued, the relationship shifted and I was not considered to be the medical expert they had once thought I was. For other researchers, the respondents' view of them as expert has been relevant throughout the research process. Jewkes (Jewkes and Letherby 2001), whose research was concerned with male prisoners' use of media, found that an episode in a prison dialogue group highlighted for her the fact that some respondents saw her as expert. Following a minor disagreement between herself and another prison dialogue representative (Chris) one inmate participant started to shout at Chris and said, 'Why should we believe you? She's the expert, she's the researcher, she hasn't got an axe to grind or a profit to make from it'. This was particularly ironic as the disagreement was about genetically modified crops, not one of Jewkes' areas of expertise but one of Chris' (Jewkes and Letherby 2001: 48).

Even in the same project it is possible to be ascribed the role of 'expert' and that of 'kindred sprit' by respondents. The 'kindred spirit' role implies two-way exchange and mutual support. Prior to my research on miscarriage I had never spoken in detail to another woman who had miscarried and I found that in many interviews (at the respondent's request) I was able to voice and/or compare some feelings for the first time. As noted in the Introduction, my primary aim was not initially to 'find people to share an experience with' but to draw attention to an experience that I felt was underreported. Yet, the opportunity to 'talk' was helpful to me personally and I could only agree when one respondent said, 'Has this project helped you? I bet it has'. Similarly, in my doctoral research, although first meetings were sometimes stilted and characterized by embarrassment, such reticence was soon overcome and all research relationships became open and to a certain degree intimate, with many respondents referring to our 'shared experience'. This sometimes led respondents not only to reveal very private and personal aspects of their lives to me but to place a great deal of trust in me. An example is when I was asked by one respondent if I would like to take away a picture of her miscarried baby, 'if it would help with your research'. In a similar vein, Birch (1998: 177), reflecting on her experience of researching alternative therapy groups, writes how she was herself in a therapeutic relationship at that time:

> I did not need such words as 'professional stranger' (Agar 1980), 'subjects', 'collaborators' or 'informants' (Okley and Callaway 1992) to describe research relationships, but I was able to refer to friends and group members of which I was one. The term I adopted to satisfy the demands of both being in the research world and present in the academic setting is 'participant'. With this term I am also included; we are all participants.
>
> (Birch 1998: 177)

Like Birch, my first experience of research led me to write about 'participants' and about 'conversations' rather than interviews (see Cotterill and Letherby 1994). However, I now see potential problems with this, for the use of these words implies an equal relationship that is generally not possible in research, as it is the researcher who has the ultimate control over the data collection and presentation (see Introduction and Chapter 5). 'Going native' or 'being native' within research has historically been defined as the ultimate sin, as it is the very antithesis to remaining detached, objective and value free. This analogy is borrowed from colonialist language with 'going native' being defined as 'a commitment to seeing and living the world from the viewpoint of "them", the natives who are "there" and emotionally involved, rather than "us", the rulers who are "here" and rationally detached' (Stanley 1995: 183). (Interestingly, it also implies a contempt for the 'natives'.) Like Stanley, I would suggest that being committed to seeing things from the perspective of respondents is a necessary aspect of feminist research and not something to avoid, but I would suggest that it is also important that researchers remain aware of their 'privileged position' within the research relationship. That is, at the same time that researchers are submitting to the respondent's setting and acquiring a variety of peripheral and membership roles, they also retain formal ties to the academic world (see Hunt 1989 and also Chapter 5).

Nevertheless, it is important to note that sympathy and empathy can exist in research relationships and not just when researching issues that may be viewed as especially sensitive. Connections can be made unexpectedly, and between people who have little in common, as Jewkes (Jewkes and Letherby 2001: 46) discovered when a chance remark during her interview with an armed robber led him to say, 'I can't believe I've met someone else who is scared of magpies as I am – I thought I was the only wuss [sic]'.

Friends and family

In research projects that do not have ready-made sampling frames and where there are no obvious places to recruit respondents, researchers sometimes explore individual friendship and family networks. Most research relationships are at least initially seen as formal but obviously this is not the case when interviewing a friend or family member. The researcher may be seen as a friend or family member who is doing research, a researcher who happens to be a friend or member of the family, or maybe it is not possible to differentiate between the two roles. When researching people close to us it may be difficult to know when to 'begin' and establishing what can and cannot be used as data may be difficult. Thus, it is likely that there will be a tension in a research relationship based on friendship or family affection as the researcher's goal is to gather information. As Stacey (1991: 113) suggests: 'The lives, loves and tragedies that fieldwork informants [*sic*] share with the researcher are ultimately data, grist for the ethnographic mill, a mill that has a truly grinding power'. In this case respondents may feel under pressure to help you and/or may feel that they have to reveal things that they would rather not (Cotterill and Letherby 1994; Scott 1998; Wilson 1998). As Scott (1998: 4.5) who interviewed her stepdaughter during her study of ritual abuse writes: 'Given how much I know about her life, it would be hard for her to edit her story as she might for a stranger, and so decide what would enter the public sphere and what remain private'.

Furthermore, when researching friends and family there is the need to acknowledge the existence of prior knowledge on both sides. This can present difficulties for the researcher because it is easier to make implicit assumptions and to avoid 'probing' so as not to be thought 'naïve'. Burgess (1984) suggests that in research it is essential to make the familiar seem strange by adopting an artificial naïvety, but this can feel inappropriate with all respondents, and especially with friends and family. Constantly questioning the obvious can make the researcher 'appear odd, insensitive or even stupid' (Cotterill and Letherby 1994: 123). This display of ignorance may even irritate or hurt respondents, which is likely to affect both the research and the friendship or family relationship afterwards. For all of these reasons, including friends and family members in research may be something that researcher and respondent may later regret.

Deciding not to ask those close to you to be involved in a project that is relevant to their lives may also feel like the wrong thing for a researcher to do. Scott's experience is again relevant here:

> However, during the course of my fieldwork it became apparent to me that there was not a clean line between Sinead being involved in the research and being excluded from it. Her life story was so much part of *my* knowledge of ritual abuse that it was always with me as a point of comparison and contrast with each new account I collected. I was struggling with how I could acknowledge this knowledge without bringing in Sinead's story 'by the back door', when she approached me and asked to be interviewed as part of the research . . . 'If you don't interview

me, I'll be in there anyway as a voice without a name. I'd rather be included as myself'.

(1998: 4.5)

Involvement in research, for both respondents and researchers, is likely to impinge on other relationships in our life and this becomes even more complex when researching people that are previously known to us.

'Counselling' and research

Whether or not they were previously known to the researcher, when people reveal painful aspects of their lives, perhaps getting distressed or angry in the process, what should a researcher do? As noted in Chapter 5, respondents may find it beneficial to talk or write about their experience but it is necessary to be aware that, even if the researcher possesses counselling skills, research relationships are *not* counselling relationships. Indeed, respondents may feel patronized if they sense that the researcher is taking on the role of counsellor (McRobbie 1982; Brannen 1988). Furthermore, although as researchers we may feel that we want to 'help' our respondents, it is important to acknowledge that such feelings may reflect our own needs – the need to feel better about the research and our involvement in it, or the need to feel useful – rather than those of respondents (Brannen 1988).

Yet not being able to 'help', especially when we think that we that caused a respondent to become distressed by bringing up a particular topic, may be difficult to cope with. These feelings may be accentuated when doing research with friends and family members as researchers struggle with their personal and research roles. This is clearly illustrated by Wilson (1998: 23), who in writing about her experience of researching abortion, notes:

how should the researcher react? Ellie is my friend and it was my instigation of talk about her abortion that had caused her to become tearful and upset. My position as researcher and friend seemed an impossible one. As a friend I would have given her a hug, we would have talked then the conversation would have naturally progressed onto something else. That is how Ellie and I would have coped with the situation as friends. As a researcher and interviewee, in the middle of an interview, our relationship had changed, even though if only temporarily, and the formality of the situation had deemed actions, that would otherwise have been natural to us, seem somewhat inappropriate. After a momentary silence, we just carried on . . .

Taking a break or providing respondents with information on relevant support groups are other ways to manage difficult disclosures but it is still likely that when a respondent gets upset the researcher may be left wondering if they handled things in the right way. Although it is likely to be an unusual occurrence, being placed in the position of the counselled can be equally difficult for a researcher to manage (see p. 14 for an example).

Just good friends?

Relatively little attention has been given to researching 'unloved groups' and Lee (1993) suggests that researchers find it easier to study those that they like or have some sympathy with. He adds that researchers need to like respondents in order to make sense of what they are saying: to understand their worldview. Drawing on Lee's work, Horn (1997: 305) writes that she was unable to 'understand the worldview' of the policemen that she was researching. This type of problem may be a big aspect of the research process when researching a group of people whose views we deplore or have little in common with. For example, the person who voices explicit sexist or racist views or those who we know discriminate against or abuse other people. However, in any research project we may come across people of whom we disapprove or just do not like. In my doctoral research I felt ambivalent about my relationships with Tracey and Mike who I interviewed five times. On all of those occasions I felt like a facilitator to a row and I also felt that Mike placed me in the same 'irrational woman' category in which he had placed Tracey. I found some of their views on parenthood frightening, and consequently developed some very judgemental views on their ability to parent. I also found it particularly difficult when asked by one of them to side with them against the other. Not only did I have to work hard not to take sides, on several occasions I had to manage my dislike of them and their attitudes. At times like this 'detachment' and the adoption of the role of unopinionated seeker of information can be an advantage (Marchbank 2000).

Sometimes the discomfort that researchers feel is linked to the sexual overtones present in the research relationship. Warren (1988) writes that it is male researchers who are more likely to write about 'sexual liaisons' during fieldwork. She draws on the work of Whitehead and Price (1986) who suggest that this imbalance in the literature does not mean that sexual encounters within research are less of an issue for women but reflects the double standard of sexuality whereby it is much less appropriate for women to admit to 'having sex', particularly within casual relationships. Furthermore, whereas sex in the field is a threat to 'scientific objectivity' for any researcher, men, who are credited with being 'non-emotional' and 'rational', are thought to be able to put aside their involvement when analysing the data – this being made easier by the fact that men are (it is stereotypically assumed) less emotional about sex. If women do write about sexual encounters within research they are more likely to refer to 'offers of marriage' and 'boyfriends' rather than the temporary sexual encounters (both heterosexual and homosexual) that male researchers have historically included in their research reports (Warren 1988; Newton 1993). An exception to this is Newton (1993) who suggests that the 'exotic' dimension is absent from anthropological work and argues for its inclusion. She writes of the 'emotional and erotic equation' in her own fieldwork experience, focusing in particular on her loving relationship with her 'key informant' [sic], Kay (1993: 9). In answer to the challenge of 'bias' she notes that 'until we are more honest about how we feel about informants [sic] we can't try to compensate for, incorporate, or acknowledge desire and repulsion in our analysis of subjects or in our discourse about text construction' (1993: 16). The counter-argument to this would be that sex has no place in the research relationship as, like 'friendship', it could be used to manipulate respondents or (although less likely) could be used by respondents to manipulate us. If we recognize the imbalance of power and privilege within research relationships this would also suggest that researchers who have sex with their respondents are abusing their positions.

Friendly strangers

Whereas some have suggested that the transition from the researcher/ respondent relationship to friendship is likely (Oakley 1981; see also Cannon 1989) Measor (1985) argues that the research relationship is not friendship and nor ought it to be. Others suggest that real friendship is not possible during the research process although it may develop once the research is complete (Wise 1987) (which could be extended to the situation when respondent and researcher find themselves sexually attracted to each other). It is unlikely that respondents will agree to take part in research in order to make new friends but they may value the opportunity to talk something through with another person:

> the structural position of women and in particular their consignment to the privatised domestic sphere (Stacey 1981) makes it particularly likely that they will welcome the opportunity to talk to a sympathetic listener.
>
> (Finch 1984: 74)

> People often derive considerable satisfaction from talking about what they are doing to a disinterested but sympathetic ear.
>
> (Robson 1993: 297)

However, as Pamela Cotterill and I (Cotterill and Letherby 1994) have argued, many women do not need a sympathetic listener – a friendly stranger – because they have friends and family in whom they can confide. On the other hand, the friendly stranger, unlike a friend, does not exercise social control over respondents because the relationship exists for the purpose of the research and is terminated when the research is complete. Indeed, respondents may feel more comfortable with a friendly stranger because it allows them to exercise some control over the relationship and because the elements of judgement often present in relationships with friends and family members are less significant. It may be easier to reveal feelings such as guilt, envy and jealousy or express prejudicial opinions in interviews or questionnaires if you are never likely to meet the researcher again and if anonymity is guaranteed. Clearly, this questions Oakley's view that a woman interviewing women should always be socially close to her respondents (Cotterill and Letherby 1994).

Further personal reflections

To a large extent I felt that my first experience of research – my undergraduate dissertation on women's experiences of miscarriage – was characterized by the 'kindred spirit' role. My second experience of research, with its much larger and more heterogeneous study group, was more complex in terms of research relationships. As noted in Chapter 5, in first letters and first interviews I always talked or wrote a little about my own experience. Once told, a few respondents appeared to accept this as justification for my interest and my experience was rarely referred to again. Occasionally I felt silenced. This accords with Ribbens' (1989) view that research provides an opportunity for respondents to talk about themselves at length and that if the researcher volunteers information about her/himself unasked, this may be seen as an unwelcome intrusion and not part of the research contract. Yet many respondents wrote or told me that they felt comfortable relating their story to me *because* I 'understood what they were going through'. For example, Mo wrote: '. . . unless you really know what it is like to be childless and all the heartaches and hopes that go with it, you could never fully understand how people really think and feel'.

This rapport was often accentuated over time. For example, the fifth time we met, Gloria told me about an encounter with a woman she met on a course. She explained how the woman had heard from a mutual friend about Gloria's childlessness and had wanted to talk to Gloria about this. This upset Gloria. After telling me what happened and how she felt, she said: 'I haven't told him [husband], I haven't said that I needed a cuddle and need to talk. He'll just say "Oh dear". He won't feel my pain and then I'll feel guilty because he'll say to himself "She's not over it". I thought, I can tell Gayle tomorrow and get it off my chest'. Thus, it would appear that our shared experience and identification affected the data that I obtained. However, for some respondents it was my status as 'stranger' that made them feel comfortable in writing or talking to me. Several of those who wrote (including three who wrote anonymously) stressed the fact that they would not have been able to talk about these issues face to face. Kate, who I had known slightly before the fieldwork, said that she only decided to be involved when she realized that I had moved away from the geographical area and it was unlikely that she would see me socially. Similarly, Beth said: 'I'm inclined to think that I shouldn't have said that. If I talk a lot I make myself vulnerable. I'm doing it now. But talking to you is easy and you're a relative stranger'. Similarly, when I asked Clare if it was different talking to me than to friends and family, she said: 'Yes it's different. Preferable really. It's something to do with emotions. It doesn't matter very much if I express emotions in this context. Somehow it's preferable than talking with friends. Yes'.

It is useful to draw on Simmel's work on the stranger here. Simmel (Wolff 1950: 404) describes the stranger as a potential wanderer, the 'person who comes today and stays tomorrow', a person who is perceived as being unlikely to censure confidences and unlikely to gossip to other members of the group. Thus: 'The stranger also often meets with the most surprising openness: confidences characteristic of a confessional which would be carefully withheld from a more closely related person. This is chiefly, but not exclusively, true of the stranger who moves on'.

Whatever our involvement with the issue and the respondents, at some level we remain 'outsiders': strangers. Writing specifically about research with women Stanley (1995: 185) argues that by 'becoming academics' as women and as feminists we position ourselves both as insiders and outsiders. We are, she suggests, 'perpetual strangers' but 'strangers within'. Like Stanley I believe that an involvement with an issue on whatever level does not disempower us intellectually, as it is still possible to be critical and analytical about the issue (just as respondents often are). But involvement does make a difference and it is important to acknowledge and to theorize on this and also to recognize that 'closeness' in research is not inevitable nor indeed always desirable and, sometimes, the researcher's status as 'stranger' makes it easier for both respondents and researchers.

'Involvement' with respondents at whatever level is complex and is affected by the power dynamics of the research relationship. Although I may appear to be warning against (some) involvement – in terms of friendship, sexual relationships and so on – to deny the possibility(ies) of identification, friendship, even sex is to deny the reality of research relationships *as* relationships. Genuinely mutual relationships *are* possible within research, as anywhere else. The point is that within the research relationship the research itself is relevant to any understanding of that relationship.

Us and them

Knotty entanglements

Clearly the relationship between the self and other within research is complex. As Fine (1994: 72) argues:

> Self and Other are knottily entangled . . . researchers are always implicated at the hyphen . . . By *working the hyphen* [between Self and Other], I mean to suggest that researchers probe how we are in relation with the contexts we study and with our informants, [sic] understanding that we are multiple in all those relations.

Further to this, Katz-Rothman (1996: 50) suggests that there has been a fundamental shift in methodological thinking where an 'ethic of involvement has replaced an ethic of objectivity'. From this perspective, writing from personal experience rather than from a position of 'detached objectivity' is likely to give the writer 'credentials'. Katz-Rothman adds:

> In the circles I travel in now, if you see an article by a colleague on breast cancer, you write to see how she is, wonder when she was diagnosed. If you see an article on Alzheimer's you assume someone's got a parent or in-law to help. I can track my colleagues' progression through the life cycle, through crises and passages, by article and book titles.

Obviously, the ability to draw and reflect on one's own physical experiences and psychic resources can allow connections to be made and rapport to be developed during fieldwork yet, as highlighted in the previous section, roles and relationships within research are complex and identification is not always possible or even desirable. Furthermore, although many feminist researchers write about identification with respondents this should not be seen as a prerequisite to 'good feminist research'. So, as Katz-Rothman (1996) notes, it is inappropriate to assume that all research is grounded in the autobiography of researchers. Also, as Dawn Zdrodowski and I (Letherby and Zdrodowski 1995) discovered, researchers do not always identify with respondents, even when they seem to be sharing an experience and/or identity. Reflecting on my doctoral research and on her doctoral study (which was concerned to explore women's experience of body image with a primary focus on the experience of being overweight in a society that values thinness) we argued that our own experiences were both similar to and different from those of our respondents. At times we felt empathy with our respondents and at other times we could not identify with their experience or feelings. We both identified with the general theme of our projects, but each study indicated that experience is much more complex than the definitions of 'infertility', 'childlessness', 'overweight' and 'eating disorder' imply. We found that we felt a strong sense of identification with some of our respondents, whereas at other times we found it difficult, if not impossible, to relate to their personal definitions.

In my case I interviewed and wrote to women who had pursued 'infertility' treatment or adoption for years in order to achieve motherhood, women whose children had died and women who were distressed when previous partners went on to have children in another relationship. None of this had happened to me. Likewise, even though Zdrodowski defined herself as overweight, this did not cause her much distress and she had not pursued any weight loss programme. Thus, empathy is not automatically linked to shared gender or experience.

In a piece that I have written with another colleague (again comparing our doctoral experiences) (Jewkes and Letherby 2001) I/we again reflect on complexities of identification and difference. Yvonne Jewkes' study was concerned to explore the use of media by long-term male prisoners, and as a woman on the 'outside' researching men on the 'inside' she could clearly be defined as 'other' by her respondents. On the other hand, given my 'closeness' to the issue of my study I could equally be thought to be more like a 'kindred spirit' than a 'stranger' to my respondents. However, we suggested that this separation of insider and outsider is simplistic. Researcher/ respondent involvement is complex and connections are sometimes present in unexpected situations (as in Yvonne's project) whereas sometimes the relationship causes unexpected tensions (as in my project).

In my doctoral study respondents seem to feel that my interest was more 'genuine' and less voyeuristic because of my personal experience and respondents in Yvonne's study were encouraged by the fact that she stated at the outset that she was not interested in their day-to-day experiences of imprisonment, nor in their prison histories. Yet in each project there were also times when we found it more difficult to make connections with respondents. Despite Yvonne asking all respondents to call her by her first name, a small number continued to call her 'Miss', a title usually reserved for female prison officers, psychologists, teachers and other staff. The respondents who insisted on continuing to call Yvonne 'Miss' were more restrained in their interviews and more likely to resist Yvonne's attempts to try to build up a relationship with them. So it is important to recognize that, as well as the researcher establishing a 'distance', the researched are likely to do this as well.

Clearly, despite the connection between myself and my respondents, there were times when I did not feel the rapport with them that they seemed to feel with me. As highlighted in my earlier piece with Dawn Zdrodowksi (1995), I sometimes did not feel that I could identify with their experience, feelings or views and I experienced discomfort when respondents assumed that I would agree with them. One example concerned differing definitions of feminism and reproductive rights for women, and is expressed through the following extract from Connie's letter:

> it is a nonsense that IVF costs £2,000 per attempt when it is easier and cheaper than ever to get an abortion. The argument that it is wrong to have an unwanted child is totally spurious. Someone would want it – there are thousands of women like me who will never have a chance of adopting, because our society – through *feminist* influence (which in other respects I am) – considers it 'better' and preferable to kill your child rather than let someone else have it. Where's the sisterhood in that?

Although, as highlighted earlier, there were times in each of our projects when we felt uncomfortably positioned as 'expert', we were also both positioned by respondents as academics in a far more inclusive way. In my research some of the respondents were themselves academics, teachers or researchers and others wrote pieces for support group magazines and newspapers etc. On the whole, these women (and men) were an extremely knowledgeable and politically active group who were keen to make an intellectual connection with me. Some of Yvonne's respondents also seemed to be trying to make connections with her as a fellow scholar and introduced themselves as such with reference to the courses they were taking. In each project respondents gave us copies of their work (written for study or publication) or shared with us articles and information that they thought might be of interest and/or use to us.

Thus, the research process is a complex endeavour, and the researcher's status as 'insider' and 'outsider' is subject to constant negotiation between all parties. In all cases it is important to be aware of the danger of positioning the researcher's experience as the norm against which others are judged. As Temple (1997: 5.2) argues, 'It is by listening and learning from other people's experiences that the researcher can learn that "the truth" is not the same for everyone'.

Just as respondents' identities are likely to shift and change so are researchers', and researchers may see themselves as moving from an 'insider' to a 'outsider' position over time. Reflecting on her experience of researching 'infertility' over a number of years Woollett (1996) suggests that she was able to represent some women more than others. She notes that, although she remained constant in her commitment to resisting common designations of 'infertile' women as 'mad', 'sad' or 'desperate', her perspective on the issue inevitably began to differ after she stopped having 'infertility' treatment and as she began to imagine ways of living a fulfilled life without children.

Speaking for 'others'

As highlighted in Chapter 2, it is simplistic and inaccurate to suggest that shared gender can override all other differences between women. So, representations of 'women' which imply a homogeneous category of 'otherness' render invisible the different experiences of women of varied ethnic, sexual and class (and so on) locations. Yet, as many writers suggest, western white feminist academics have themselves contributed to the 'othering' of women unlike themselves and so have added to the academic tradition of speaking about and for 'others' (see e.g. Hill Collins 1990; Wilkinson and Kitzinger 1996). This tendency has included, as Wilkinson and Kitzinger (1996: 13 drawing on the work of Olson and Shopes) point out, 'the temptation to exaggerate the exotic, the heroic, or the tragic aspects of the lives of people with little power'. Wilkinson and Kitzinger themselves suggest that accounts of 'others' tell us as much or more about their authors than about the people the authors aim to represent: 'One way of knowing what "white" people are like (how they construct themselves) may be to look at their representations of black people; one way of knowing what "heterosexual" women are like may be to look at their representations of lesbians – and so on' (1996: 10). They add that however well-intentioned our speech on behalf of an 'other', by the very fact that we are aiming to represent an 'other' we reinforce precisely that 'otherness' which, by speaking, we intended to undermine: 'The Other is silenced *because* she is Other, and the speech of the dominant group on her behalf reinscribes her Otherness simply through the fact of its being spoken' (Wilkinson and Kitzinger 1996: 10–11; see also Minh-ha 1989; bell hooks 1990). All of this suggests that instead of 'speaking for others' as researchers and as writers we should attempt only to 'speak for ourselves'. However, there are problems if we 'speak only for ourselves' and leave others to represent themselves. Speaking only for ourselves implies maintaining a respectful silence while working to create the social and political conditions which might enable 'others' to speak (and to be heard) in their own terms, but there is a problem in defining who, exactly, 'we' are, and what constitutes 'our community'. Attempts to define 'us' inevitably become reductionist: for example, can I speak on behalf of all women, or only on behalf of all white women, all white professional women of working-class background, all white professional women of working-class background who are childless, and so on and so on (see also Wilkinson and Kitzinger 1996). The danger here is that it becomes impossible for anyone to speak for anyone else and 'we' result in 'communities' of single women. As highlighted in Chapter 2, although it is necessary to avoid essentialism it is also necessary to acknowledge the commonalities between us and to remember that gender is a difference that makes a difference. As Stanley and Wise (1990: 23) suggest, an important aspect of research is to understand 'intersubjectivity' – 'the fact that in spite of our ontological distinctness none the less we assume we can, and indeed we do, "share experiences" such that we recognise ourselves in others and they in us and can speak of "common experiences"'. Mies (1991) calls this 'partial identification' and argues that it is important as it enables a recognition of what binds us to other women as well as what separates us from them.

Furthermore, sometimes the definitions on which we base an analysis of sameness and difference may themselves be problematic:

> Therefore, as a Chinese woman researching other Chinese women, it would be methodologically misleading for me to assume that I 'belonged' simply because I am myself Chinese, if I neglected to account for other social differences based on ethnicity, sexuality, class, religion and so on. The racialized category 'Chinese' is itself problematic. Anderson (1991) claims that it is largely an imagined identity that can be traced to early European imperialism of the 'east'. Only in choosing to privilege the racialization of myself and my research participants [sic] can I say that we belong to the same group, because the moment we admit the possibility of other concurrent categories of Otherness, group membership becomes repeatedly re-negotiable.
>
> (Ang-Lygate 1996: 54)

Speaking only for ourselves could also lead to much more research on already privileged groups and implies that women who come from minority groups have a 'duty' to represent 'others' like them. Bola (1996), an Asian woman with no experience of pregnancy research who also had vitiligo (white patches of skin), experienced this when researching the pregnancy experience of white middle-class women. She gives several examples of people assuming that her work was about the pregnancy experience of Asian women or about vitiligo. As she notes:

> There is on the one hand, a need for the experiences of ethnic minorities to be explored by black researchers but, on the other hand, it could also become an exercise in marginalization, where black researchers are deemed only to be able to research black participants. This can be a 'no-win' situation: if one examines non-race matters then one is being treacherous, but if one *does*, then this might be seen as typical and the research be considered low status.
>
> (Bola 1996: 127)

Furthermore, if we cannot speak for 'others' then 'others' cannot speak about 'us', which inevitably stifles criticism and critique. For example: 'in relation to the hegemony of heterosexuality, speaking only for oneself, while authorizing lesbians to speak *qua* lesbians *on lesbianism*, serves equally to *dis*authorize lesbian theories of heterosexuality' (Wilkinson and Kitzinger 1996: 12).

Feminists and non-feminists

As feminists researching and representing the lives of other women, the feminist/not feminist identification is one aspect of 'sameness' and 'otherhood' that we need to consider (Griffin 1989; Morley 1996; Millen 1997). Like Griffin, in her research on young women, I found in my doctoral research that although women often did not define themselves as feminist, they often spoke about gender identity and gender roles in a way that could be defined as feminist: what Griffin calls the 'I'm not a feminist but . . .' syndrome. With reference to political identification, Sarah (a respondent in my study) said:

> I'm not sure [pause] I don't know what feminism is [pause] not sure [pause] I don't know if I [pause] I'm just keen on equal opportunity for all and access to all sorts of opportunities. Whether that's feminism I don't know. I'm not sure what feminism is. But yes for equal opportunities and stuff.

And Kate, in answer to my question, 'Do you think that men and women have equal roles in society?', said with (what I interpreted as) exasperation, 'Oh come on Gayle'.

Feminism is not a unitary category which encapsulates a consistent set of ideas within an identifiable framework. It is not a neat and coherent phenomenon which can be measured in quantitative terms (Griffin 1989). So, as Griffin notes, the concept of feminism is under continual negotiation and there is not one feminism but many. So, for most women, the identification of oneself as a feminist is not straightforward and involves social, political and personal decisions and choices.

With all of this in mind, it is necessary to be aware of what Stanley (1984: 201) calls 'the conundrum of how not to undercut, discredit or write-off women's consciousness different from our own'. As Kelly et al. (1994) add, our understandings and interpretations of women's lives may not only be shared by them but may represent a challenge or threat to their perceptions; their own 'safety of being'. This may be even more of an issue when as feminists we research women who actively define themselves as non-feminist for there is the added question of whether or not we should attempt to raise their consciousness (Millen 1997). Millen writes of how difficult she found it to listen to 'repeated characterisations of feminists as "bra-burners", "lesbians", "hippies" and "trouble-makers"' yet suggests that 'attempting to empower these individuals would also constitute an imposition of my interpretation, which simultaneously denies any notion of an attempt at equality within the research relationship' (1997: 5.9).

As feminist researchers and writers we not only represent the women whom we research but also the work of other feminists. Richardson (1996: 105), writing about the representation of radical feminism in the feminist literature, suggests that the (mis)representation and oversimplification of radical feminism as biologically reductionist leads to the frequent dismissal of radical feminism as 'extreme, outdated, misguided, theoretically naïve and "prescriptive"'. As Richardson notes, our political identity and chosen theoretical perspective can interact with how we as researchers and writers are positioned as 'other'. Through our political identification, we are positioned, and position ourselves, as 'other' to the mainstream. It is also important to remember that, as highlighted in Chapters 1 and 2, feminists often have sympathies with more than one approach and it is important to avoid simplistic characterizations of perspectives and approaches that we do not agree with.

Men

I am conscious that in various places already in this book I have written '(and men)'. Taking 'gender seriously' means 'bringing men back in', for in order to fully understand what is going on in women's lives we need to know what is going on in men's lives also (e.g. Morgan 1981; Laws 1990; Annandale and Clark 1996). Just as there are differences between women there are also differences between men, and it is just as simplistic to characterize all men as powerful as it is to view all women as inevitable victims (Jacobson et al. 2000). So it is necessary to consider when the gender order works against men and when men's and women's lives intersect. With reference to one of my own areas of interest, Annandale and Clark (1996) suggest that by focusing only on women when studying experiences of reproduction we compound the view that reproduction is 'women's business' and that when things 'go wrong' it is women's 'fault'. Thus, for example, we need to be aware that men 'suffer' from 'infertility' too (see e.g. Meerabeau 1989; Mason 1993; Monach 1993). However, there is a danger in focusing on men as victims and, as Ramazanoglu (1992: 346) notes, 'the exploration of men's pain is then an area which needs very careful critical attention if men are not to emerge both as the dominant gender and as the "real" victims of masculinity'.

A feminist analysis of men's experience is also necessary, because as the dominant gender male activities and attitudes have historically been hidden from critical scrutiny (Morgan 1981; Hearn and Morgan 1990; Laws 1990). Laws, explaining why she decided to research men's attitudes towards menstruation rather than women's experience of menstruation, writes:

> much of what is written about menstruation places the problem squarely in the minds of women. If many people in Western culture share one 'sociological' idea about periods, it is that women's bad attitudes are responsible for period pain. By interviewing women, especially if that was the only empirical work I did, I could do little to question such notions ... I must emphasise that I believe that research which reflects women's experiences back to women can be extremely useful: it is possible in this way to reveal aspects of women's condition which are not immediately apparent to the individual. A great deal of very useful work has resulted from this approach. But feminist research must go beyond the study of women to work out ways of studying for women ...
>
> (1990: 12)

Yet, some writers suggest that interviewing men brings different problems. For example, McKee and O'Brien (1983), with reference to their own research on fatherhood, noted that it is difficult to get men to talk about family matters and that they generally have less to say and take less time to say it. On the other hand, as McKee and O'Brien also suggest, being a female interviewer may have advantages with male respondents if the topic is one socially defined as 'female'/'feminine' (see Chapters 4 and 5). They suggest that for men, cross-gender talk about intimate matters may be easier, more appropriate and less threatening than talking to other men. In my own undergraduate research I found it very difficult to recruit men to the study (see Introduction) and this was one of the reasons that I decided not to include men in my doctoral project. However, all of the women I interviewed or wrote to told me about their partners and I felt that through this I did have some insight into male experience. However, I appreciate that we should not assume that women can always be the reliable biographers of men (Goldscheider and Kaufman 1996). The men that I did speak to about 'infertility' and 'involuntary childlessness' did find it more difficult to go into detail about emotional issues and the one man who spoke to me in depth about how his 'infertility' had led to feelings of sexual insecurity appeared embarrassed afterwards and was 'not available' for a second interview. However, as Padfield and Proctor (1996: 356) (drawing on Rapoport and Rapoport) argue, there is a lack of comparative work concerned with male and female researchers in the 'same' situation and much of what we do know is gathered from reflections on 'different' situations. So, more thoughtful and reflective methodological work which will help us to understand the role and significance of the gender mix of respondent and researcher in relation to the research process and product is needed.

One of the most difficult aspects of being a woman researcher researching men is having to cope with overt and covert sexism (see e.g. Laws 1990; Foster 1994; Horn 1997; Chapter 5). Foster (1994), for example, while researching attitudes to law and order in South London, was driven home from the pub by male respondents because 'it isn't safe for a young girl out on the streets' (p. 90) and was also described as 'a left-wing tart' (p. 92) by a police officer who she refused a date. So, although the continued belief by some in women's 'harmlessness' may result in them getting access to areas from which male researchers are barred, this very 'harmlessness' may make female researchers vulnerable to sexual advances from male respondents (Foster 1994; Horn 1997). Thus, safety and danger are important issues for consideration when researching in the public or the private sphere and accusations of 'contributory negligence' (attack as one's own fault) may be more significant when a female researcher goes willingly into a male respondent's home. Reynolds (1993) felt very anxious after two interviews with a male respondent who referred constantly to his own acts of physical and verbal violence towards his neighbours and who implicitly suggested that his epilepsy was caused by too much masturbation. Because of this she decided not to return for a third interview. However, committed as she was to the goals of participatory and emancipatory research, she was left feeling uncomfortable with this decision during her research which was concerned to explore the concepts of philanthropy and physical/sensory impairment. Clearly, shared gender is not the only power dynamic within the research process and feminist researchers may feel guilty that they are breaking their own ethical research code in order to feel safe. But, on the other hand, shouldn't an ethical research code (for women and men) incorporate safety in potentially threatening situations?

If we accept that 'bringing men back in' is as important to the feminist project as 'bringing women in' we need to continue to address the particular issues and problems that this may bring. Perhaps one solution is to encourage more like-minded men to work with us. However, this then leads to the difficult questions of whether men can be feminists and whether men can do feminist research. Although I have indicated above the dangers in 'only speaking for ourselves', it may appear to be a contradiction that I believe that only women can be feminists as only women live with the day-to-day awareness of living as a woman in a male-dominated world, which for me (at least) is a condition for calling oneself a feminist. Feminism is grounded in the experience of women and while men can have an empathic understanding, they do not (obviously) experience womanhood in the same way. I am not saying that men cannot do research 'for women' and indeed there are examples of much work by pro-feminist men which not only problematizes traditional research processes but also (like feminist work) provides a critical analysis of gender and in turn informs feminist work. However, just as a sophisticated analysis of sameness and difference is necessary within feminist work, the men who work with us also need to be aware of the fact that 'gender is a difference that makes a difference' to the process and the product of research as well as to our experience of everyday life. As (David) Morgan (1981: 96) suggests:

> 'taking gender into account' is particularly a problem for male [researchers] . . . The male researcher needs, as it were, a small voice at his shoulder reminding him at each point that he is a man . . . the massive weight of the taken-for-granted (probably the most pervasive domain assumption) conspires with the researcher's own gender to render silent what should be spoken.

The implication being that it is not only feminists who should challenge the accepted domain of assumptions.

Researchers' identities
Before leaving this section on the relationships between 'us' and 'them' it is important to acknowledge that different identities and identifications are often a dimension of research teams as well as being relevant to researcher/ respondent relationships. Within a project, where two or more researchers are working together, roles and relationships and differences and similarities among researchers are also relevant to the research process and product. Therefore, all of the issues and tensions considered in this chapter can be applied to researcher/researcher relationships too. The multiple identities of researchers who are part of research teams are also relevant when considering researcher/respondent relationships. What follows are three examples of this and what must be borne in mind is that researchers are partly in control of and partly 'apart' from the research process.

- In our 'Why do women's studies?' research the fact that Jennifer Marchbank and I went *together* to the student bars and coffee shops to ask students we did not know to fill in our questionnaire helped us to cope with the hostility to our topic and the 'mild' sexual harassment that we encountered (see Letherby and Marchbank 1998, 2001).
- In a recent research project concerned to explore the experience of young mothers the fact that the three researchers who collected the data were all young mothers themselves is likely to have affected both the research process and the data. Things may have been very different if I (an older, childless woman) had been part of the data collection team (see Bailey et al. 2002).
- I was recently in a project concerned to explore institutional racism in The Children's Society. During the construction of our questionnaire, and our planning and undertaking of the focus groups, our identities as two white women, one black man and three academics were at all times significant (Letherby et al. 2002).

More critical consideration of the dimensions and dynamics of research team relationships is needed.

Auto/biography in research

Motivations and coming out
Although I have argued (see Chapter 3) that respondents are not always the best people to represent themselves, I am not suggesting that 'ordinary' people do not express themselves adequately and need academics to translate for them (see Laws 1990 for further discussion). Rather, I have noted that as academic researchers we have an intellectual privilege that is not available to respondents. Furthermore, it is important to note that the interests and priorities of the researcher and the researched are likely to be very different (Scott 1998). Respondents have different motivations for being involved in social research. Sometimes they are willing to do it for the researcher (to help the researcher with their studies); at the same and other times respondents may wish to be involved or be willing to be involved to help themselves (in order to get something 'off their chest'); and some also wish to help to 'set the record straight', to 'educate the world' on an important issue. In my doctoral research in all first interviews and letters I asked respondents why they had decided to be involved in the research. They always gave one of two answers: either they saw their involvement as a way of making themselves feel better or they were concerned to educate others; for example: 'People need to understand the experience better'. Many respondents expressed both of these motivations. In the 'Why do women's studies?' research, the women's studies respondents/students in our own university used the questionnaire to support us, their teachers, and to make it clear that they felt they were getting a raw deal which was not of our making:

WOMEN'S STUDIES STAFF ARE: brilliant. They are helpful and clever, well prepared, caring human beings – and we love them. But, unfortunately there aren't
enough of them!!! – We want more and we want them now!

WOMEN'S STUDIES MODULES ARE: inadequate – the ones we've got are BRIL-
LIANT – But how can you have a degree with only one designated module in the
third year???

(Letherby and Marchbank 2001: 594/595)

In addition, involvement in research is also sometimes a better alternative
to 'going public' oneself: 'The latest change is to "go public" (I still find this
very difficult). I felt I have learned a lot and I want to help others in my
situation – in private lives and/or in research' (Samantha in Letherby 1997).

In her research on ritual abuse, Scott (1998: 4.10) also found that her
respondents were happy for her to 'summarize and contextualize their lives'
partly because (like the respondents in my doctoral research), they were
unhappy about (and aware of) the possible price of 'coming out'. So through
an involvement in research, respondents can 'speak out' anonymously about
something that is important to them while at the same time leaving the
responsibility of how the material is presented to the researcher. As Scott
(1998: 4.10) writes: 'One survivor told me she had felt able to talk with such
candour because it was my responsibility not hers to decide what entered the
public sphere'.

However, 'coming out' is not just relevant to respondents' experience but
also to the researcher who identifies her/himself in the research account (see
below).

Auto/biography in research and research writing

As highlighted in the Introduction to this book the use of 'I' in our research
accounts and other writing has a particular value. Stanley (1993: 49–50)
argues that the 'autobiographical I' is 'inquiring and analytical' and adds
that: 'The use of "I" explicitly recognises that such knowledge is contextual,
situational and specific, and that it will differ systematically according to the
social location (as a gendered, raced, classed, sexualised person) of the particular knowledge-producer'. Thus, writing in the first person helps to make
clear the author's role in constructing rather than discovering the story/
knowledge (Stanley 1993; Mykhalovskiy 1996; Bertram 1998; Letherby 2000b).
Many feminists accept this and, indeed, celebrate this type of 'autobiographical' writing. Some go further and draw on their own autobiography throughout the research and presentation process, including themselves when
analysing the data and writing up. So, this type of autobiographical writing
explicitly draws on the experience of the researcher as data. As I am sure it
will be obvious by now, some of my own work is autobiographical in this
way and some of my differing experiences demonstrate the different ways
in which feminists (and others) include themselves in their work. In my
doctoral research on 'infertility' and 'involuntary childlessness' my own
experience was referred to in interviews and letters and, although I did not

include myself as a respondent in the thesis, I did refer to some similarities and differences between us (respondents and researcher) and I wrote about the ways in which the research led to changes in my own feelings and understandings. In my work on higher education (including the 'Why do women's studies?' research) I draw explicitly on my experience of working and learning in the academy and have written some pieces grounded solely in my experience, with no reference to empirical research. In a study I am undertaking at present, which is concerned with the changing processes of work and leisure with reference to the train (i.e. we are concerned not with why people take the train, but with what work and leisure activities they do on the train) I and my co-researcher Gillian Reynolds are including ourselves as respondents within the research, giving ourselves pseudonyms alongside other respondents (this study is not personally or politically sensitive and we interviewed each other early in the data collection process before we began interviews with others).

Clearly there are different ways to include the autobiographical and it is important to remember that writing about the self always involves writing about the 'other', and writing about the 'other' always involves some reference (even if not expressed on paper) to the self. Within research, issues of auto/biography are complex with the '/' itself helping to demonstrate this complexity. As Pamela Cotterill and I argue:

> As feminist researchers studying women's lives, we take their autobiographies and become their biographers, while recognizing that the autobiographies we are given are influenced by the research relationship. In other words respondents have their own view of what the researcher might like to hear. Moreover, we draw on our own experiences to help us to understand those of our respondents. Thus, their lives are filtered through us and the filtered stories of our lives are present (whether we admit it or not) in our written accounts.
>
> (Cotterill and Letherby 1993: 74)

But respondents do not tell us everything about themselves and we do not include all aspects of ourselves in our research writings. Indeed, I am aware of omissions in everything that I write. Thus, auto/biography is partial not least because researchers who write with reference to their own experience are not protected by anonymity in the way that respondents are. Auto/biographical research writing, then, is 'a representation of self and other and it is likely to have connections for the researched, the researcher and the reader but does not represent the "truth"' (Letherby and Ramsay 1999: 40) yet, given the material and authoritative resources that we have, is a 'privileged' version of the 'truth'.

It is becoming usual for researchers to include aspects of the self in their research and their writing yet there still appears to be a tendency to keep personal details outside of the main report of a study. Despite the increased support for auto/biographical approaches, I think that many people still feel uncomfortable with this way of writing. Reasons include the protection of oneself, one's significant others and one's respondents (who may be more identifiable if the researcher writes auto/biographically), and the fear that the writer may be criticized for self-indulgence and sloppy intellectual work (Katz-Rothman 1986, Scott 1998; Letherby 2000):

> There is the fear . . . that mixing the personal with the academic will discredit the work in some quarters, and that in disavowing the stance of the objective scientist I will let down my informants [*sic*]. Second, there is the additional responsibility for the safety and privacy of someone I love. I am still sometimes unsure whether the better moral choice is to acknowledge or deny the connection between us. Each time I present my research in a public forum I remake the decision about how much of myself and herself I reveal: there is no once and for all distinction between alienated and unalientated knowledge.
>
> (Rose 1983 cited in Scott 1998: 4.6)

Furthermore, even a detailed description of the room in which the writing takes place, and/or the feelings of the writer, written by a relatively unknown person, may not be received with the same degree of interest or tolerance as that offered to one of the 'big names' of the academic world (feminist or otherwise) (Bertram 1998).

So, because of the possible threat to professional, intellectual and emotional danger, sometimes researchers and writers write about 'the personal' outside of the main report of a study. For example, as McMahon (1996: 320) writes in the abstract of her article concerned with her own experience as a non-mother researching and writing about motherhood:

> This article looks at how research accounts can conceal stories about the experiences of those who do not appear to be present in the research project. Some of those who do not appear to be present may be called 'significantly absent' because their invisibility holds particular significance for the sorts of research stories researchers tell.

It is possible to suggest that there is a fine line between 'situating oneself' and 'egotistical self-absorbtion' but, like Okley and Callaway (1992: 2), I would argue that reflexivity and autobiography is neither 'mere navel gazing' or a form of 'self-adoration'. As Okley (1992) adds, 'self-adoration' is quite different from self-awareness and a critical scrutiny of the self. Indeed, those who protect the self from scrutiny could well be labelled self-satisfied and arrogant in presuming their presence and relations with others to be unproblematic. However, as Bertram (1998) notes, the auto/biographical 'voices' within feminism are still predominantly the voices of white, educated, middle-class women from the West and we must be careful to point to the limited perspective from which the individual writes.

End points

Pamela Cotterill and I (Cotterill and Letherby 1994) have argued for the need to acknowledge the 'person' in the researcher. Researchers' multiple identities as people are as relevant to the research process and product as the personhood of respondents. Furthermore, as I have indicated in this chapter and the preceding one, no two research situations are the same and it is necessary to be constantly aware of how what we are doing affects what we are getting/presenting. Last, but definitely not least, it is important to acknowledge that both researchers and respondents are likely to be affected by what goes on in 'the complex social encounters that we call research' (Ribbens 1989: 590). So as Stanley and Wise (1993: 161) suggest: 'One's self cannot be left behind, it can only be omitted from discussions and written accounts of the research process, but this is an omission, a failure to discuss something which has been present within the research itself'.

Suggested further reading

As well as the feminist and other research collections suggested elsewhere in this book, new researchers will also find Bell, J. (1993) *Doing Your Research Project: A Guide for First-time Researchers in Education and Social Science* (Buckingham: Open University Press) useful. For more on sameness and difference, self and other, see Wilkinson, S. and Kitzinger, C. (eds) (1996) *Representing the Other: A Feminism and Psychology Reader* (London: Sage), which is a really interesting read and with so many pieces is good value for money. For those interested in reading more about the auto/ biographical approach, the journal *Auto/Biography* is a good resource.

Chapter **seven**

Close encounters: presentations and audiences

Contents   Introduction

Introduction

Having considered in detail the historical and contemporary debates in feminist epistemology (Chapters 1 and 2), the relationship between theory and practice (Chapters 3 and 4) and the relationship between the process of research and the research product (Chapters 5 and 6), in this final chapter I consider the ways in which feminist work is presented and received within the academic community and by lay audiences. The chapter is presented in two main sections. In 'Presenting our work' I focus on the opportunities and barriers to feminist work, both in the academic community and elsewhere, and in 'Responses and receptions' I consider some of the tensions present in our relationships with 'audiences'.

Presenting our work

Spreading the word

Once the project is finished we need to think about how best to present our work. Speaking at conferences, writing academic books and articles, writing for newspapers, general and specialist magazines, appearing on local and national radio and television programmes and talking to journalists about our work are all ways in which feminist (and other) research is presented to both academic and lay audiences. Just as there are many texts on doing research there are also some on writing and presenting. When I first began to present my work as a postgraduate I found books such as *Writing for Social Scientists* by Becker (1986), *How to get a PhD* by Phillips and Pugh (1987) and *In Other Words: Writing as a Feminist* edited by Chester and Nielsen (1987) particularly helpful. Yet I was surprised that most of the advice related to writing, with very little reference to verbal presentation (such as conference papers or defence of one's work at the PhD viva) or speaking to the media.

One reason for the literary stress on the written work is its political and historical importance. For example, as Chester and Nielsen (1987: 110) argue: 'Writing is essential to women's struggle for liberation from second-class status, poverty and enforced silence. Feminism, literacy and education for women are closely linked world-wide; illiteracy is a central part of women's subordination'. Chester and Nielsen and other writers in their edited collection argue that it is important to write down thoughts, conversations and orations in order not to lose our discoveries and triumphs. Arguably, this is of particular importance to feminists, for as Rysman (1977) notes, the negative use of the word 'gossiping', applied to female talk, has been used as a means of preventing female communication and solidarity. So writing is a powerful contradiction to the silencing of women's ideas (Morley 1995).

Yet historically and to date, women have had particular difficulties that may stop them from writing. Woolf ([1929] 1977) argued that women's opportunity to write was severely restricted by lack of material resources and insisted that, if she is to write, a woman 'must have money and a room of her own' (Woolf [1929] 1977: 7). More recently, others have noted that women's roles and responsibilities also sometimes hinder the academic process. For example, motherhood and other caring responsibilities often get in the way (Munn-Giddings 1998; Letherby and Ramsay 2001) as it is still women academics (like other working women) who are likely to bear the 'double burden' of managing home and work (see e.g. Letherby and Cotterill 2001). For feminist academics living with men the pressures that this brings may be intensified by having to admit to a lack of support from a partner, as this exposes contradictions in personal politics and practice (Leonard and Malina 1994). Furthermore, as highlighted in Chapter 1, women academics often also bear more than their fair share of the 'burden' of teaching, administration and emotion work in the academy. So there may be many reasons why the feminist academic does not have the 'psychological' space to concentrate on research and writing (Chester and Neilsen 1987; Thornborrow 1996).

When feminists do write, they often do so in conflict with the norms and expectations of the academy. The academy promotes a competitive, combative culture and the collaborative working relationships that many feminists favour are made difficult within an environment that focuses on an individualistic mode of production (Silverstein 1974; Ward and Grant 1991; Morley 1995). Despite the rhetoric that honours collaboration and cooperation, academia values single-authored work more than that which is jointly authored (Kaplan and Rose 1993; Cotterill and Letherby 1997). At 'Getting into Print' sessions at conferences I have listened to warnings against collaborative writing. The consensus view here seems to be that such work invokes questions about the quality of input and the division of labour. The difference between collaborative work and co-authored work is crucial here as there is much anecdotal and some published evidence of some 'joint' authors doing little, if any, work and passing off the work of another as their own. (See Ward and Grant 1991 for a further analysis of the relationship between co-authorship and gender, and also Emslie et al. 1999. Surely this is another example of the need to consider the power dynamics of research 'teams' as closely as the power dynamics of the researcher/respondent relationship.) Because of this, jointly-written pieces are often valued less in terms of the research ratings and promotion (see below). This works against feminists working in the academy, because truly collaborative work – with its 'emphasis on mutuality, concern and support' (Gray 1994: 85) can be empowering for women (and men) not least as a survival strategy in an individualistic, male-dominated arena (Ward and Grant 1991; Gray 1994; Cotterill and Letherby 1997).

Within the patriarchal system of the university, many women are excluded (and indeed exclude themselves) from the male-defined culture, and from authorized knowledge production (Morley 1995: 119). All of this leads to self-doubt for women as Trinh T. Minh-ha (1989) highlights nicely: 'Who do you think you are (to be writing a book)? And who cares what you think about anything enough to pay money for it . . .'

Publish or perish

Whatever our fears, though, like all academics women in the academy increasingly find themselves caught in the 'publish or perish' dilemma (Broughton 1994). In order to secure tenure (both in the UK and elsewhere) many academics start their career on short-term research and/or teaching contracts and there are more women than men in these insecure positions (Letherby and Cotterill 2001). To achieve promotion it is necessary to publish our work. Furthermore, one of the ways in which our research can make a difference is for it to influence others, and by publishing it we reach a wider audience. As Spender (1981: 188) notes: 'Research that is not in print does not exist' and to give credibility to our work we need to publish it 'between the covers of a respectable academic journal or book'. Furthermore, what gets published influences those who read it and those who write what comes after, so the written word 'establishes the issues in a discipline – constitutes the parameters and defines the terms of the debate' (Spender 1981: 191).

In recent years the pressure on academics to publish has been accentuated by the Research Assessment Exercise, commonly referred to as the RAE. The RAE is thought to operate as a quality assurance measure of research, rating institutions (and effectively individuals) as research active, or not and as good, or not. The first RAE took place in 1986 (when it was known as the Research Selectivity Exercise) in the context of heavy cuts in university expenditure and a desire by government to impose top-down, bureaucratic and managerialist types of control over academic work (Morley and Walsh 1995, 1996; Cuthbert 1996; Trowler 1998). Basically the 'better' research (demonstrated through published material) a university does the more funding it gets. Thus, 'Proof of performance and productivity requires outputs that can be measured and thus made visible' (Strathern 1997 cited by Mace 2000).

Inevitably this public monitoring of individual research performance is likely to further undermine women academics. Given the burden of their other responsibilities (both within the institution and outside it), the processes of academic gatekeeping and the imposed hierarchies of approaches and outputs (see below) it is likely that women will become increasingly stereotyped as less 'research active' (Morley 1995). With this in mind Malina and Maslin-Prothero (1998) suggest that feminist scholars need more than ever to engage in discussion and debate regarding the barriers to feminist publication.

Academic gatekeeping

The gatekeepers in the academic community are 'the people who set the standards, produce the social knowledge, monitor what is admitted to the systems of distribution, and decree the innovations in thought, or knowledge or values' (Smith 1978 cited by Spender 1981: 287). Furthermore, as Spender adds, many of these people are to be found as editors of journals, as referees or reviewers, or as advisors to publishers and so it is they who are in a position to determine what gets published and what does not. Historically, the academic gatekeepers have predominantly been men so it has been hard for feminists, whose work presents a challenge to the mainstream authorized view, to get their work published – a case of the 'authorized' protecting their authority (Spender 1981). So: 'There is a mistrust of new ideas, unless they come from men whose reputation for scholarship is well assured' (Znaniecki 1968 cited by Morley 1995: 125). And as Morley (1995: 126) adds:

> In the academy, there is a declared value base which privileges publication. But there is a gendered subtext which positions women writers as 'language stealers' (Minh-ha 1989: 19). Margaret Duras outlines the resentment many men feel when women appropriate the right to write: 'Men are the ones who started to speak, to speak alone and to speak for everyone else, on behalf of everyone else' (Duras, 1980: 111). A woman member of the Association of University Teachers reports

how her creativity was described as publishing 'excessively' by her male interviewer in a formal appraisal situation. She was also told that she should wait for
promotion and 'allow her male colleagues to catch up', i.e. 'to stop doing research
and publishing' (AUT, 1991). It would appear that in women's hands, research
and writing are often constructed as forms of arrogance, exhibitionism and
self-aggrandisement.

Thus, academia stifles originality. Furthermore, the word 'feminist' is one
that frightens some people and it would seem that many academics are
frightened of the challenge that feminism offers (Kramarae and Treichler
1985). This is demonstrated, not least, in the fact that the rejection of
women's writing has often been brutal, which Morley (1995) suggests represents a form of violence against women: attack as a form of defence perhaps?
The reviewing of articles and book proposals is usually unpaid (reviewers of
book proposals and readers of books before publication are sometimes paid a
small amount), and appointment onto journal boards has historically been
associated with contacts and friends (Spender 1981). Added to this, the
anonymous referencing system of academic journals and publishing houses
(usually both author(s) and reviewers remain anonymous) places the reviewer
in a powerful position. Articles and books are likely to be sent to someone
who has an interest in the area and if the writer's work represents a challenge
to the reviewer's work it is possible for that reviewer to influence the parameters of the debate by suggesting that the writer's work is not good enough
(Spender 1981; Morley 1995).

With reference to feminist writing and issues of method, methodology
and epistemology, Roberts (1990b), in the second edition of *Doing Feminist
Research*, writes about the production and fortunes of the first edition, published in 1981. She began by sending a book proposal to Allen & Unwin who
had published *Doing Sociological Research* (edited by Bell and Newby and
published in 1977), because although she found the book useful (particularly
because of the personal research reflections) there was no mention of feminism. What follows is the response from the publisher's editor at Allen &
Unwin:

> At the time *Doing Sociological Research* was planned, we were mainly looking for
> major research projects from which important and seminal [*sic*] accounts had
> been published in book form . . . I do not think that the necessity or otherwise
> of a feminist methodological contribution ever really occurred to us. We were
> not intending the book to be comprehensive, or to cover all styles or modes of
> research. So I would not accept what you say about the significance of an absence
> of female research in the Bell and Newby book . . . All that being said, and with
> the omission (if not the admission of it) made, then we are left with a rather
> small and specifically feminist market for the kind of book you have in mind . . .
> (Roberts 1990b: xiv)

Due to these problems, feminist writers sometimes decide to publish their
work in feminist journals and with feminist publishing houses and avoid
mainstream outlets altogether. However, there are problems with this. First,
it could lead to women's work being disregarded, 'discounted' or 'counted as

less' by the academic world, and second, it is important to enter the mainstream in order to extend our influence beyond the already converted: 'if feminists do not submit their material to mainstream journals or publishers and seek publication outside feminist channels, then many men and women have good grounds for pleading ignorance when it comes to feminist analysis and insights' (Spender 1981: 198). This is relevant to both substantive issues and to methodological and epistemological debate. We want the mainstream world to be aware of what we do and how we do it. Ironically, though, there is a further problem associated with the growth of feminist journals and publishing houses in the last 20 years of the twentieth century. At a recent conference I attended, a feminist colleague told the group I was in the story of how she had been told by a male colleague of hers that, given the fact that feminists had their 'own journals' to publish in, they should leave the mainstream alone in order to give men more opportunities to publish!

It is also worth noting that feminists themselves can be guilty of finding unacceptable those articles that do not share their own political beliefs (Spender 1981; Eagleton 1996). I have experience of this myself as, early in my career, I sent an article to a well-established and well-known feminist journal only to have it rejected because the editorial board felt that I 'didn't know what feminism was'.

Reflecting on Spender's (1981) work it is clear that feminists today owe a debt to earlier generations of feminist researchers and writers who have fought and won battles to ensure that feminism can reach a wide audience (Malina and Maslin-Prothero 1998). With respect to their own publishing practices it is important that feminists should continue to challenge: 'competing hierarchies of thought which reinscribe the politics of domination by designating work as either inferior, superior, or more or less worthy of attention' (bell hooks 1994: 64) both within and outside of feminist publishing. As Malina and Maslin-Prothero suggest, it is surprising that, given the established and long-running debates around methodological and epistemological issues, feminists are not more open about the production and presentation of feminist articles and books (single authored, joint authored and edited). In order to produce unalienated knowledge – knowledge that can be evaluated by its readers – we need (as well as making the research process transparent) to make clear the practices and procedures of publication.

Just as, historically, 'male academic experts' have been in part created and sustained by their academic audiences, it is possible to argue that a specialist and élite group of feminist theorists has come into existence, producing a 'professional and indexical category' of feminist theory and research which is perceived by those of us who read and teach it to be at the 'apex of feminist knowledge production' (Stanley and Wise 2000: 262). One way to challenge the heroic theorist style of teaching and learning is to avoid replacing 'Great Men' with 'Great Women' (Stacey 1993; Marchbank and Letherby 2001) and instead introduce students to themes and issues. Nevertheless, it is likely that students, academics (and sometimes other audiences) will always have feminist 'heroes', not least because the media and the publishing industry endorse the ascendancy of particular 'stars'.

Feminism in fashion!

A first look at the shelves of any bookshop or newsagent would certainly suggest that feminism, or at least women's culture, is in fashion. Pegg (1990) notes that 'women's culture' is indeed 'big business' and that many publishing companies have made huge profits from the publication of books by and for women. The interest in and celebration of women's writing and the concern with 'gender issues' is also reflected in popular magazines, such as *Cosmopolitan, New Woman* and *Bella.* Women's magazines today are full of articles on women's position in the public sphere and their experience in the private sphere, as well as including reviews of feminist literature. These are presented alongside the more traditional articles and features on health, fitness, beauty and how to find a man and keep him happy (everything from how to give him better orgasms to how to bake better cakes) (Coppock et al. 1995). So although we know that women have always been authors, and we can assume that women have always wanted to know about the lives of other women, it is only recently that the literary world, dominated as it is by men, has realized that there is a huge market of women and men who want to read what women write. However, we need to be careful here before getting too excited for just because a piece of writing is *about* women does not necessarily mean that it is a feminist piece of writing. Having said this, though, it is no longer the case, as Spender suggested in 1981, that the mainstream media reject materials that smack even faintly of feminism. As Robinson and Richardson (1994) note, some feminism sells, with Faludi's *Backlash* (1992) (which reached number one in the *New York Times* best-seller list) and Wolf's *The Beauty Myth* (1990) being key examples.

Just as there is money to be made through women's writing of both fact and fiction for lay audiences there is also profit in the production of feminist work for the academic community (Robinson and Richardson 1994). For example, the emergence of new feminist presses in the 1990s (such as Scarlet Press in 1992), whose aim was to produce and market feminist non-fiction, suggests that even in a recession (some) feminism sells. Yet it has been primarily mainstream publishers who have coined the profits, and not the specifically feminist publishing houses such as The Women's Press and Pandora (Robinson and Richardson 1994). In the 1990s, though, things began to change a little. Whereas in the 1980s Marxist and feminist work was widely published and influential in the academy, and central to social theory and philosophy, in the 1990s issues of gender and masculinity began to take centre stage. At this time gender began to be increasingly emphasized over 'woman' on and inside the covers of publishing catalogues and women's studies and gender and sexuality catalogues began to contain separate sections entitled 'men's studies'.

Gender, as a category, can be argued to be a neutral term which implies that the 'interests of the sexes have now converged and the differences in life changes (not to mention economic rewards) that exist between women and men are matters of choice' (Evans 1991 cited by Robinson and Richardson 1994: 73). The growth of journals such as *Gender and Education, Gender and Society, Gender and History, Journal of Gender Studies* as well as a growing tendency for bookshops to rename women's studies or feminist sections 'gender studies' is also 'symptomatic of the marketing and packaging of feminism into a diluted and more widely acceptable form' (Robinson and Richardson 1994: 92–3). It is interesting that I was recently told by a (female) colleague researching an aspect of male experience that feminists had 'high-jacked' gender.

In addition, as Robinson and Richardson (1994) note, (and see Chapter 1) it is possible to argue that until recently all academic study has been 'men's studies' because of the omission and misrepresentation of women's experience and the theorizing of men's experience as universal. Given this, the emergence of this 'new' men's studies is worrying. A response to this is offered by Kimmel (1998: 20), editor of *Changing Men: New Directions in Research on Men and Masculinity*, who argues that men's studies 'seeks to buttress, to augment women's studies, to complete the radically redrawn portrait of gender that women's studies has begun'. (The use of terms like 'buttress' and 'augment' sound rather like the patronizing chivalry of men who walk on the outside of pavements to 'protect' women from the traffic.) But, as Robinson and Richardson (1994) note, before we put the focus back on men we need to establish women's studies and feminism more securely (the closure of many women's studies university courses during the 1990s and into the twenty-first century would definitely seem to support this).

Before leaving this section I would like to return to where I started. I am aware that, like the authors cited at the beginning of the chapter, I too have concentrated on written work at the expense of spoken work. Both within the academy and outside of it feminist insight and awareness is also transmitted through verbal presentation. We need to keep talking not least because the written word can 'get lost'. Driven as they are by market forces, journals and books go out of print as 'fashions change'. Furthermore, through conference papers, presentations and teaching we may be able to reach people who would never pick up a piece of feminist writing.

Responses and receptions

Academic and other audiences

As well as reflecting on the importance of barriers to the presentation of feminist work it is also important to consider the responses of academic and lay audiences. Writing specifically about audiences that listen to talks (but making, I think, some generalizable points) Goffman (1981: 137–8) suggests that:

> Audiences hear in a way special to them. Perhaps in connection with the fact that audience members are further removed physically from the speaker [and writer]

than a co-conversationalist might be, they have the right to examine the speaker directly, with an openness that might be offensive in conversation.

Goffman further suggests that the role of the audience is to 'appreciate' remarks made but not to reply or respond to these in any direct way.

I would suggest that academic and other audiences have much more power than this. As noted in the previous section, anonymous reviews of feminist work, including those by other feminists, can, if the reviewers so wish, effectively silence feminist voices. Similarly, written and verbal responses to talks, articles and books can be deliberately politically and personally offensive (proof indeed that the personal is political). However, although it is possible to find many examples of mainstream critiques of feminist work, it is also possible to find examples of support from the mainstream. (With reference to issues of feminist epistemology and methodology see e.g. the debates between Malseed and Oakley in 1987 in *Sociology*; between Hammersley, Ramazanoglu, Gelsthorpe and Williams in *Sociology* in 1992/3 and the debate between Hammersley and Gomm, Humphreys and Temple in *Sociological Research Online* in 1997.) For example, a review of the first edition of Roberts' edited book *Doing Feminist Research* (1981) was written by Colin Bell (joint editor with Howard Newby of *Doing Sociological Research*, mentioned earlier): '. . . it gives me great sexist pleasure to report that it is far less gossipy than other similar collections – that will, I suspect, particularly disappoint male readers' (Bell cited by Roberts 1990b: xv). Yet, Margaret Stacey, another reviewer of the first edition, suggested that the articles in the book demonstrated that there was still a long way to go before 'we achieve . . . a methodology, which can see beyond the confines of the society in which it is embedded' (Stacey 1981 cited by Roberts 1990b: xix). As Roberts (1990b: xix) herself notes, although feminist scholarship is 'causing alarm' and 'winning some influence' it 'is still an outsider saying "yes, but" to the conventional wisdoms, rather than the source of an enhanced perspective which takes gender into account as a matter of course'. This is still relevant today and there is still a long way to go.

Many feminists have written of how and why women's work is devalued and have detailed the ways in which women have been excluded from the making of knowledge (Smith 1988; Stanley and Wise 1993; Chapter 1). Historically, objectivity, rationality and value freedom, rather than involvement, subjectivity and emotion, have been lauded and given academic status (see e.g. Chapter 1). Thus, work which draws on and celebrates the experiential can and has been defined as 'un-academic'. So, work which in any way recognizes the significance of the auto/biographical is less highly valued and open to possible attack. This is relevant to my own work, as shown by the response of Day (1993) who 'reviewed' the 'Weaving stories' article I wrote with Pamela Cotterill (Cotterill and Letherby 1993) and who attacked our approach for being 'sickly self-indulgent' and 'grossly self-advertisement'. I have also been advised by book commissioning editors to leave out my auto/biographical involvement if I wanted to publish books and warned by reviewers of journal articles about putting myself at risk from attack from other colleagues for mentioning my miscarriage and 'fertility' status in my work. The possible implication here is that rather than producing respectable academic outputs, I am producing 'sensational journalism' in order 'to sort myself out' (Katz-Rothman 1986: 53).

This type of experience leads me to agree with Temple (1997: 5.3) who suggests that 'the notion of collegial accountability to a research community is problematic'. Temple cites the work of Mykhalovskiy (1996) whose auto/ biographical writing has been described as 'self-indulgent' by an academic orthodoxy which stands by its view that there is one correct way to write about research and only one audience – a (traditional) academic audience – that knows how to read 'correctly' (Mykhalovskiy 1996; Temple 1997). Again this is attack as a form of defence, as what auto/biographical work does is challenge the traditional and the orthodox.

Returning specifically to feminism, many writers have suggested that, when-ever feminism has appeared to be gaining ground, a whole series of repres-sive, political, social, economic and ideological forces are mobilized in direct response (e.g. Hartsock 1990; Faludi 1992; Coppock et al. 1995). Fuelled by the political arguments of the New Right in Britain and America, the anti-feminist backlash which blames feminists and feminism for the dilemmas facing contemporary women can be supported by hostile audiences both within and outside the academy. Ironically, though, there is a worse fear than an attack from the mainstream. Attar (1987: 35) puts this nicely: 'Poised to write, what do you do about the worst fear of the lot – how will other women react when they find out what you really think?' So, although we may feel anxious about how our work is received and reviewed by the main-stream, we are likely to be even more concerned about whether other femin-ists will approve of our work.

Read all about it: feminism in the media

Whatever the problems that women in the academy may have in relation to writing and presenting their work it is likely that, through academic publish-ing, feminist women will make connections with others who share their political concerns. However, it is unlikely that many of our respondents will ever read our books and articles or attend many of the conferences at which we speak about our 'findings' and our methodological concerns. For this reason some feminists stress the importance of trying to reach a wide audi-ence through the mass media. Not surprisingly though, feminist/media rela-tions are often not straightforward or easy.

Reflecting on her experiences with the media, Roberts (1984) writes about three different encounters and details some of the positive and negative aspects of her experience. The first project she describes, undertaken with Michele Barrett, was concerned with high consultation rates of middle-aged women at their general practitioners' (GPs) surgeries. Following a press release, the research received lots of reportage and several pieces in the 'popular' medical press (the papers funded by drug companies and sent free to GPs) had headlines such as 'Why are Middle Aged Women always in the Surgery?' or 'Why GPs see so many Middle Aged Women' or 'Those Middle Aged Women Never Out of the Surgery'. Added to this misleading impression of the work the description of Roberts and Barrett as 'two sociologists [who] are committed women's libbers' also had the effect of labelling the research in a particular way. Writing about a subsequent piece of research on the aspirations and achievements of 16-year-old girls in Bradford in the UK (Roberts and Sharp 1982) Roberts (1984) describes how she sent an 80-plus page report to the local paper. In this report Roberts and Sharp argued that despite a long history of women working and of working-class radicalism in Bradford, girls were not getting a proper chance to succeed alongside boys and were still going into traditional women's work with low pay and promotion prospects. This was reported in the newspaper as 'Bradford Girls Lack Drive'. The third experience Roberts describes relates to a project undertaken with Alan Graham (a mathematician). The project was called 'Sums for Mums', and as part of the research process the researchers devised numeracy courses for women. The reporting of this project, although slightly inaccurate in places, was much less sensational than the reporting of the other two, with typical headlines including, 'When Mother Counts?'. The most annoying part of the coverage was an over-concentration on human interest issues (including pictures of researchers and respondents drinking tea while 'fiddling' with their calculators, and a description of Graham's wife Hilary, (herself a published feminist sociologist, as 'just' a wife and mother) (Roberts 1984: 207).

Despite these problems Roberts is keen to stress the positive aspects of her encounters with the media. For example, following the newspaper coverage of the 'middle-aged women and GP research' the researchers received unsolicited letters from women about their health and their doctors, and their respondents were encouraged that the research they were involved in must indeed be 'serious and sensible if it was reported nationally' (Roberts 1984: 205). Similarly, the press reportage of the 'Sums for Mums' research led to over 300 extra queries from women asking for information and giving detail about their own early experience with maths. So, in each of these cases, the contact with the media was beneficial for the research, not least in the fact that it led to extra data. As Roberts adds, reporting one's research in the popular media is a way of enabling respondents (and other interested parties) to have access to our work. Furthermore, she suggests that popularity can be good for a discipline as 'One need only look at medicine, which has a wide press, a favourable press and popular press, to see that a discipline need not lose credibility by popularity' (Roberts 1984: 211) – and popularity can in turn lead to effective change. As an example Roberts cites changes in the management of childbirth which have undoubtedly come from pressure from 'below' following media exposure of 'traditional' practices (which although authorized are themselves relatively recent) (see Chapter 1).

In contrast, Richardson's (1991) encounter with the media was somewhat different but equally important to consider in relation to 'spreading the word'.

Following her research on the experiences of single women who have sexual and intimate relationships with married men, she wrote a book for the lay market. One of her findings was that, although a single woman might begin a liaison with a married man believing it would be brief and uninvolving, women often ended up in relationships that were long-term and emotionally costly, due in part 'to the relationship's secrecy in conjunction with over-arching gender inequalities'. Richardson's intention in writing the book was to help women and men make more informed choices about their intimate lives. *The New Other Woman: Contemporary Women in Affairs with Married Men* (1985) (a title she resisted but which was imposed upon her because 'New' is what sells) received a huge amount of media attention and Richardson undertook approximately 200 radio interviews, 40 print interviews and appeared on over a dozen television programmes. On the whole, she felt that the attention given to her work was fair and supportive, although occasionally the focus of the journals was on 'what should a wife do?' (not something that Richardson had considered in her study), which extended to an attack on the 'other woman'. Yet, the message of the book reached mass audiences and was taken up by many feminist journalists who themselves carried the message further into print, radio and television. Furthermore, Richardson received lots of letters from 'other women' and from 'wives' saying how much they had enjoyed the book and how much it had helped them.

So, for those feminist researchers and writers who brave encounters with the media there can be many positive benefits. However, wary of the negative aspects of the encounter many of us do not publicize our work in this way. Despite this, even if you do not go to them, they may come to you: professional associations and universities often get communications from journalists asking if there is someone available to comment on the latest news item. This happened to me recently when I was telephoned by a reporter from the *New Scientist* magazine. She was writing an article about the development of new medical procedures to 'slow down the biological clock' and enable women to get pregnant for a longer period of their lives. She asked me for my opinion and for some details on women's experience of 'infertility' treatment. Having checked that I could ring her back the next day, I spent quite a bit of time preparing what I might say. The next day I spent approximately one and a half hours on the phone and went into considerable detail about the social, emotional and medical experience of 'infertility' and childlessness and about the ambivalence women feel surrounding the experience of motherhood and non-motherhood. This was the result:

> Certainly social expectations have a lot to answer for when it comes to pressurising women to reproduce, and they add to the distress of the involuntary childless. 'Motherhood is still considered to be one of the most important things a woman can ever do', says Gayle Letherby, a sociologist at Coventry University. But a growing number of women have no desire to give birth, and most have mixed feelings about it. 'Motherhood is something women feel really ambivalent about' says Letherby. 'It can be a really tough job'.
>
> (Ainsworth 2001: 41)

Nothing to really get upset about but not likely to enhance my international academic reputation either! In this type of situation we as researchers do not have the power of editorship over the research and those that do are likely to be driven above all by the perceived needs of the marketplace.

My other main contact with the media was during my second year as a postgraduate. After watching a programme called *Female Parts* on Channel 4 (1992) that was concerned with motherhood and non-motherhood I was very disappointed that the programme (I felt) supported, rather than challenged, existing stereotypes. It did not recognize the difference between motherhood as an experience and as an institution, nor did it consider the ambivalence that women as mothers often feel (Rich 1976; Letherby 1994). Furthermore, I felt that it supported the dominant and simplistic image of childless women as 'desperate'. The day after the programme I wrote a letter to the producer outlining all of this. I explained that I was doing research in the area but wrote nothing of my own personal experience. I received a reply that included the following:

> You are as you say 'undertaking research on the experience of involuntary childlessness and infertility' . . . and that is reflected in the tone and content of your letter . . . I am interested in your own age and fertility status . . . I feel your approach is clinical and objective. In a sense it is a justification for making the programme as I did.

I include reference to this experience as an interesting and ironic example of the work of a feminist sociologist who writes in an explicitly auto/biographical way being described as clinical and 'objective'!

Clearly, as Richardson (1991) notes, our research can become the fodder of the media and feminist researchers and writers (as others) are likely at times to find themselves in uncomfortable positions during and following their media encounters. The (difficult) trick, then, is to learn how to use the media rather than be used by it. But these kinds of encounters can be beneficial to us, not just to present our work to a wider audience, but to challenge the negative stereotypical definitions of feminism and feminist research that persist.

End points

For me, and hopefully for you, this chapter has brought us full circle. No longer are men the only ones that produce the outputs that represent 'knowledge'. Indeed, as Gray (1994) drawing on the work of Keller and Moglen (1987) suggests, feminist scholarship is now part of the academic and lay marketplace. Yet the recent proliferation of feminist work both within the academy and outside of it needs itself to be subject to feminist critique. Given the stereotypes of feminism that prevail and the complex systems of 'value' – including public interest value, academic value and monetary value – that exist, we need to reflect on what does not get published as well as on what does, and to read and watch academic and popular work at least a little cynically. Rabinow (1986) refers to 'corridor talk' within research – the material that you talk about with friends and colleagues but do not present; in other words, the material that you do not spread too widely for public (either professional or lay) audiences. As well as a consideration of what we choose not to include we need also to consider what we are not 'allowed' to include.

Feminists in the academy are faced with a dilemma. Should we play the game of academic publishing and write and present our work in ways which are acceptable to others (including external examiners, journal and book referees, funding bodies and so on) or shun these authoritative ways of knowing and run the risk of being ignored, belittled or derided? Furthermore, if the aim of feminist research is to change things for the better for women (and men) living in the world today, isn't it important to publish our work as widely as possible, even if this might mean our work being misunderstood or even ridiculed? In Chapter 1 I suggested that feminist academics need to remain ambivalent about their position in academia, and throughout this book I have pointed to the ways in which as feminist researchers we need to be reflexive and ambivalent about the work that we do. To end this chapter on the same theme I suggest that we also need to be ambivalent about presenting and publicizing our work. We must continue to do it while highlighting the limitations of what we are able to do.

Suggested further reading

Chester, G. and Neilson, S. (eds) (1987) *In Other Words: Writing as a Feminist* (London: Hutchinson) is a collection of short pieces by 40 women writers – some professional, some aspiring. All types of writing and all processes of production are considered. Similarly, Sellers, S. (ed.) (1994) *Taking Reality by Surprise: Writing for Pleasure and Publication* (London: The Women's Press) includes 50 pieces written by women novelists, editors, literary agents and writing tutors, poets, dramatists and journalists and offers a complete guide to writing and getting published. Open University Press have a whole series of study guides on research and writing aimed at undergraduates and postgraduates. These include: Fairbairn, G.J. and Winch, C. (1996) *Reading, Writing and Researching*; Crème, P. and Lea, M.R. (1997) *Writing at University: A Guide for Students*; Blaxter, L., Hughes, C. and Tight, M. (2001) *How to Research* (2nd edn); and Leonard, D. (2001) *A Women's Guide to Doctoral Studies*.

Reflections

This final section of the book is not a traditional conclusion and anyone looking for an overview of the central debates and arguments considered will be disappointed. Rather it is a series of reflections on the why and how of the book in which I revisit some of the reasons for writing it. Before I begin though I'd like to say something briefly about style and presentation. My aim has been to write a book that is accessible, in a style that challenges the (often) mystified language of the academy. Drawing on Lorde's (1984) view that you cannot 'dismantle the master's house using the master's tools' Stanley and Wise, in their first edition of *Breaking Out* aimed to do likewise. However, in their second edition, *Breaking Out Again*, (1993) they defended their decision to write in the specialist language of postmodern and poststructural social science, arguing that as academic feminism has become professionalized and accepted by the mainstream and malestream 'it has become necessary to participate in its language-games in order to be taken seriously as a member of its epistemic community' (Stanley and Wise 1993: 231). Although I agree with the need to influence and inform the mainstream I have tried not to adopt the style that the mainstream, and increasingly the feminist, academic community adopts. Yet this book is a serious contribution to the debate and I still hope to be taken seriously.

Feminist Research in Theory and Practice is essentially a re/presentation of my own relationship with feminism. For me, doing feminist research is a dynamic and exciting endeavour. I know that many others share this view and I hope that this book may persuade a few more. Although I have attempted to provide an overview (from my perspective of course) of the debates and concerns I have also included reference to many research experiences, including some of my own, and considered the perspective of both the researcher and the researched. It is important to provide accounts of the fieldwork involved in empirical research because as many researchers (including feminists) have shown, there is often divergence between how research has actually been done and what is reported in research accounts and in textbooks. The result is that methodological accounts often do not prepare researchers for the problems and satisfactions they are likely to encounter (see e.g. McRobbie 1982; Ribbens 1989; Farran 1990; Cotterill 1992; Foster 1994). So, our experiences of research should be written up for others to consider, reflect on, agree with and reject. Accounts of research experience are therefore 'not simply . . . recipes for action, or . . . warnings or advice, but also . . . a rich folkloric tradition in their own right' (Warren 1988: 64).

Yet, I have not written a 'how to do book' but rather a book which considers some of the practicalities and specifics of feminist research in relation to debates concerning the relationship between knowing and doing. Having said this, I do not posit this book as 'a piece of feminist politics'. I accept that feminist research and writing is not feminist politics (Glucksmann 1994: 164) but at the same time I do believe that a critical consideration of the research process is an essential aspect of the political practice of feminism. I do not agree with Kelly et al. (1994: 32) that feminist researchers have concentrated on issues of epistemology at the expense of the intellectual and the political. They argue that feminist researchers seem:

> more concerned with attempting to convince the predominantly male academy that a privileged status should be accorded to 'women's ways of knowing' than with enabling us to better discover and understand what is happening in women's lives, and how we might change it.

Like many other feminist researchers I hope that my work is grounded in the realities of women's (and men's) lives. I also hope that it challenges traditional research practices and my aim is to provide 'accountable knowledge' in which the reader has access to details of the contextually located reasoning process which gives rise to our 'findings' (Stanley 1991: 209). This is relevant both to the research that I do and to this book. Our work should make a difference and should have an emancipatory element to it (see e.g. Acker et al. 1991; Kelly et al. 1994; Oakley 1998). But, epistemological reflection is central to and not separate from this political aim within feminism. Feminist research is not 'just' good research, it is research undertaken and presented from a specific political perspective. Critical thinking about what we do and the relationship between this and what we get is an essential part of the feminist research process but this is certainly not exclusive to feminism. However, feminists' work combines particular analytical, ethical and political dimensions. Good feminist research does make a difference even though in some cases the difference may be small. At times the only people who listen are the already converted but at other times we can influence the unconverted.

I recognize of course that this particular account of the relationship between method, methodology and epistemology in feminist research is written from my perspective, with reference to my work (reading, researching and writing) over the last decade and a half. Like Mills (1959) I have drawn on ideas and research accounts I have presented elsewhere and I see this book as part of my own critical reflexive attempt to locate the person in the researcher and the research, and in the development and production of knowledge.

With all of this in mind I would like to end this book with an acknowledgement. I owe a debt to all of the other writers and researchers presented here, both those with whom I agree and those with whom I do not. They have all made me think and have influenced *my* academic feminist journey. To make a final analogy I would like to suggest that *Feminist Research in Theory and Practice* is rather like a relay race in which all competitors are on the same team. Participants may pass the baton on or even drop it and then go back and pick it up. Sometimes more than one person run together, sometimes everyone stops and reflects on how the 'race' is going. I hope that some people reading this book will want to run alongside me, but I accept that others may want to change direction. I have not written this book in the hope of ending or winning the race – we need to keep running.

References

Abbott, P. and Wallace, C. (1997) *An Introduction to Sociology: Feminist Perspectives*, 2nd edn. London: Routledge.

Acker, J., Barry, K. and Esseveld (1991) Objectivity and truth: problems in doing feminist research, in M.M. Fonow and J.A. Cook (eds) *Beyond Methodology: Feminist Scholarship as Lived Experience*, Bloomington, IN: Indiana University Press.

Acker, S. (1994) *Gendered Education*. Buckingham: Open University Press.

Adams, M.L. (1994) There's no place like home: on the place of identity in feminist politics, in M. Evans (ed.) *The Woman Question*, 2nd edn. London: Sage.

Adams, S. (1993) A gendered history of the social management of death and dying in Foleshill, Coventry, during the inter war years, in D. Clark (ed.) *The Sociology of Death*. Oxford: Blackwell.

Afshar, H. (1994) Muslim women in West Yorkshire: growing up with real and imaginary values amidst conflicting views of self and society, in H. Afshar and M. Maynard (eds) *The Dynamics of 'Race' and Gender: Some Feminist Interventions*. London: Taylor & Francis.

Afshar, H. and Maynard, M. (eds) (1994) *The Dynamics of 'Race' and Gender: Some Feminist Interventions*. London: Taylor & Francis.

Agar, M. (1980) The Professional Stranger: An Informal Introduction to Ethnography. London: Academic Press.

Ainsworth, C. (2001) Stop the clock, *New Scientist*, 2297: 38–43.

Alcoff, L. (1988) Cultural feminism versus post-structuralism: the identity crisis in feminist theory, *Signs: Journal of Women in Culture and Society*, 13(3): 405–21.

Alcoff, L.M. (1996) Feminist theory and social science: new knowledges, new epistemologies, in N. Duncan (ed.) *Body Space*. London: Routledge.

Anderson, B. (1991) Census, maps, museum, in Imagined Communities. London: Verso.

Ang-Lygate, M. (1996) Waking from a dream of Chinese shadows, in S. Wilkinson and C. Kitzinger (eds) *Representing the Other: a Feminism and Psychology Reader*. London: Sage.

Annandale, E. (1998) *The Sociology of Health and Medicine: A Critical Introduction*. Cambridge: Polity Press.

Annandale, E. and Clark, J. (1996) What is gender? Feminist theory and the sociology of human reproduction, *Sociology of Health and Illness*, 18(1): 17–44.

Atkinson, D. and Shakespeare, P. (1993) Introduction, in P. Shakespeare, D. Atkinson and S. French (eds) *Reflecting on Research Practice: Issues in Health and Social Welfare*. Buckingham: Open University Press.

Attar, D. (1987) The controversial feminist, in G. Chester and S. Nielsen (eds) *In Other Words: Writing as a Feminist*. London: Hutchinson.

AUT (1999) *Pay Gaps and Casual Jobs: An Analysis of the Gender, Pay and Employment of UK Academic Staff*. London: Association of University Teachers.

AUT (2000) *Gender and Average Pay for Academic Staff in the UK*. London: Association of University Teachers.

Badinter, E. (1980) *The Myth of Motherhood: A Historical View of the Maternal Instinct*. London: Souvenir.

Bagilhole, B. (1994) Being different in a very difficult row to hoe: survival strategies of women academics, in S. Davies, C. Lubelska and J. Quinn (eds) *Changing the Subject: Women in Higher Education*. London: Taylor & Francis.

Bailey, N., Brown, G., Letherby, G. and Wilson, C. (2002) The baby brigade: teenage mothers and sexuality, *Journal of the Association for Research on Mothers*, 4(1): 101–10.

Barrett, M. (1992) Words and things: materialism and method in contemporary feminist analysis, in M. Barrett and A. Phillips (eds) *Destabilising Theory: Contemporary Feminist Debates*. Oxford: Polity.

Becker, H. (1971) *Sociological Work*. London: Allen & Unwin.

Becker, H. (1976) Whose side are we on? *Social Problems*, 14: 239–47.

Becker, H. (1986) *Writing for Social Scientists*. Chicago: University of Chicago Press.

Belenky, M.F., Clinchy, B.M., Goldberger, N.R. and Tarule, J.M. (1986) *Women's Ways of Knowing*. New York: Basic Books.

bell hooks (1982) *Ain't I a Woman: Black Women and Feminism*. London: Pluto.

bell hooks (1984) *Feminist Theory: From Margin to Center*. Boston, MA: South End Books.

bell hooks (1986) Sisterhood: political solidarity between women, *Feminist Review*, 23: 125–38.

bell hooks (1990) *Yearning: Race, Gender and Cultural Politics*. Boston, MA: South End Press.

bell hooks (1994) *Teaching to Transgress: Education as the Practice of Freedom*. London: Routledge.

Bell, D. and Klein, R. (1996) *Radically Speaking: Feminism Reclaimed*. London: Zed Books.

Bell, C. and Newby, H. (eds) (1977) *Doing Sociological Research*. London: Allen & Unwin.

Bell, D. (1993) Yes Virginia, there is a feminist ethnography: reflections from three Australian fields, in D. Bell, P. Caplan and W. Jahan Karim (eds) *Gendered Fields: Women, Men and Ethnography*. London: Routledge.

Bell, L. (1998) Public and private meanings in diaries: researching family and childcare, in R. Edwards and J. Ribbens (eds) *Feminist Dilemmas in Qualitative Research: Public Knowledge and Private Lives*. London: Sage.

Bell, R. (1993) Pride and prejudice and participant observation, *Praxis*, 35–8.

Bentilsson, M. (1991) Love's Labour Lost?: A Sociological View, in M. Featherstone, M. Hepworth and B.S. Turner (eds) *The Body: Social Process and Cultural Theory*. London: Sage.

Bertram, V. (1998) Theorising the personal: using autobiography in academic writing, in S. Jackson and G. Jones (eds) *Contemporary Feminist Theories*. Edinburgh: Edinburgh University.

Birch, M. (1998) Re/constructing research narratives: self and sociological identity in alternative settings, in J. Ribbens and R. Edwards (eds) *Feminist Dilemmas in Qualitative Research: Public Knowledge and Private Lives*. London: Sage.

Black, M. and Coward, R. (1998) Linguistic, social and sexual relations: a review of Dale Spender's man made language, in D. Cameron (ed.) *The Feminist Critique of Language: A Reader*, 2nd edn. London: Routledge.

Blake, C.F. (1994) Foot-binding in neo-Confucian China and the appropriation of female labor, *Signs: Journal of Women in Culture and Society*, 19(31): 676–711.

Blaxter, L., Hughes, C. and Tight, M. (1998) Writing on academic careers studies, *Higher Education*, 23(3): 281–95.

Bola, M. (1996) Questions of legitimacy? The fit between researcher and researched, in S. Wilkinson and C. Kitzinger (eds) *Representing the Other: A Feminism and Psychology Reader*. London: Sage.

Bowles, G. and Klein, R.D. (eds) *Theories of Women's Studies*. London: Routledge & Kegan Paul.

Box, S. (1986) *Deviance, Reality and Society*, 2nd edn. London: Cassell.

Brah, A. (1991) Questions of difference and international feminism, in J. Aaron and S. Walby (eds) *Out of the Margins*. London: Falmer Press.

Brah, A. (1992) Difference, diversity and differentiation, in J. Donald and A. Rattansi (eds) *Race, Culture and Difference*. London: Sage.

Brannen, J. (1988) Research note: the study of sensitive subjects, *The Sociological Review*, 36(3): 552–670.

Broughton, T. (1994) Life lines: writing and writer's block in the context of women's studies, in S. Davies, C. Lubelska and J. Quinn (eds) *Changing the Subject: Women in Higher Education*. London: Taylor & Francis.

Brown, G. and Harris, T. (1976) *Social Origins of Depression*. London: Tavistock.

Bryman, A. (1988) *Quality and Quantity in Social Research*. London: Macmillan.

Burgess, R. (1984) *In the Field: An Introduction to Field Research*. London: Allen & Unwin.

Butler, A. and Landells, M. (1995) Taking offence: research as resistance to sexual harassment in academia, in L. Morley and V. Walsh (eds) *Feminist Academics: Creative Agents for Change*. London: Taylor & Francis.

Butler, J. (1990) *Gender Trouble*. London: Routledge.

Cain, M. (1986) Realism, feminism, methodology and law, *Journal of the Sociology of Law*, 14(314): 255–67.

Cain, M. (1990) Realist philosophies and standpoint epistemologies or feminist criminology as a successor science, in L. Gelsthorpe and A. Morris (eds) *Feminist Perspectives in Criminology*. Buckingham: Open University Press.

Cameron, D. (1985) *Feminism and Linguistic Theory*. London: Macmillan.

Cannon, L.W., Higginbotham, E. and Leung, M.L.A. (1991) Race and class bias in qualitative research on women, in M.M. Fonow and J.A. Cook (eds) *Beyond Methodology: Feminist Scholarship as Lived Experience*. Bloomington, IN: Indiana University Press.

Cannon, S. (1989) Social research in stressful settings: difficulties for the sociologist studying the treatment of breast cancer, *Sociology of Health and Illness*, 11(1): 62–77.

Caradine, J. (1996) Heterosexuality and social policy, in D. Richardson (ed.) *Theorising Heterosexuality*. Buckingham: Open University Press.

Carby, H.V. (1982) White women listen! Black feminism and the boundaries of sisterhood, in Centre for Contemporary Cultural Studies (eds) *The Empire Strikes Back: Race and Racism in 70s Britain*. London: Hutchinson.

Cavendish, R. (1982) *Women on the Line*. London: Routledge & Kegan Paul.

Chamberlain, M. (1981) *Old Wives Tales*. London: Virago.

Chapman, J. (1992) *Politics, Feminism and the Reformation of Gender.* London: Routledge.

Chester, G. and Nielsen, S. (eds) (1987) *In Other Words: Writing as a Feminist.* London: Hutchinson.

Chrisler, J.C. (1996) Politics and women's weight, in S. Wilkinson and C. Kitzinger (eds) *Representing the Other: a Feminism and Psychology Reader.* London: Sage.

Clifford, J. (1990) Notes on (field)notes, in R. Sanjek (ed.) *The Makings of Anthropology.* Ithaca, NY: Harvard University Press.

Clyde Mitchell, J. (1983) Case and situation analysis, *The Sociological Review,* 31: 187–211.

Collins, P. (1990) *Black Feminist Thought.* Boston, MA: Unwin Hyman.

Collins, P. (1998) Negotiated selves: reflections on 'unstructured' interviewing, *Sociological Research Online,* 3(3): www.socresonline.org.uk/socresonline/3/3/2.html.

Cook, J.A. and Fonow, M.M. (1986) Knowledge and women's interests: issues of epistemology and methodology in feminist sociological research, *Sociological Inquiry,* 56: 2–29.

Cook, J.A. and Fonow, M.M. (1990) Knowledge and women's interests: issues of epistemology and methodology in feminist sociological research, in J. McCarl Nielsen (ed.) *Feminist Research Methods: Exemplary Readings in the Social Sciences.* Boulder, CO: Westview.

Coppock, V., Haydon, D. and Richter, I. (1995) *The Illusions of 'Post-Feminism': New Women, Old Myths.* London: Taylor & Francis.

Cornwell, J. (1994) *Hard Earned Lives.* London: Tavistock.

Corrin, C. (1994) Fighting back or biting back? Lesbians in higher education, in S. Davies, C. Lubelska and J. Quinn (eds) *Changing the Subject: Women in Higher Education.* London: Taylor & Francis.

Cotterill, P. (1992) Interviewing women: issues of friendship, vulnerability and power, *Women's Studies International Forum,* 15(5/6): 593–606.

Cotterill, P. and Letherby, G. (1993) Weaving stories: personal auto/biographies in feminist research, *Sociology,* 27(1): 67–79.

Cotterill, P. and Letherby, G. (1994) The 'person' in the researcher, in R.G. Burgess (ed.) *Studies in Qualitative Methodology,* vol. 4. London: JAI.

Cotterill, P. and Letherby, G. (1997) Collaborative writing: the pleasures and perils of working together in M. Ang-Lygate, C. Corrin and M.S. Henry (eds) *Desperately Seeking Sisterhood: Still Challenging and Building.* London: Taylor & Francis.

Cotterill, P. and Waterhouse, R. (1998) Women in higher education: the gap between corporate rhetoric and reality of experience, in D. Malina and S. Maslin-Prothero (eds) *Surviving the Academy: Feminist Perspectives.* London: Falmer.

Cuthbert, R. (ed.) *Working in Higher Education.* Buckingham: SRHE & Open University Press.

Daly, M. (1979) *Gyn/Ecology.* Boston, MA: Beacon.

Davis, A. (1981) *Women, Race and Class.* London: The Women's Press.

Davis, K. (1988) *Power Under the Microscope.* Holland: Foris.

Dawson, G. (1994) *Soldier Heroes: British Adventure, Empire and the Imagining of Masculinities.* London: Routledge.

Day, G. (1993) Review . . . special issue of biography and autobiography in sociology, *Times Higher Educational Supplement,* 20 October: 37.

de Beauvoir, S. (1949) *The Second Sex.* London: Four Square Books.

Delphy, C. and Leonard, D. (1992) *Familiar Exploitation: A New Analysis of Marriage in Contemporary Western Societies.* Cambridge: Polity Press.

Devine, F. and Heath, S. (1999) *Sociological Research Methods in Context.* Basingstoke: Macmillan.

Di Stephano, C. (1990) Dilemmas of difference: feminism, modernity and postmodernism, in L. Nicholson (ed.) *Feminism/Postmodernism*. London: Routledge.

Douglas, J. (1998) Meeting the health needs of women from black and minority ethnic communities, in L. Doyal (ed.) *Women and Health Care Services*. Buckingham: Open University Press.

Doyal, L. (1995) *What Makes Women Sick: Gender and the Political Economy of Health*. Basingstoke: Macmillan.

Doyal, L. (ed.) (1998) *Women and Health Care Services*. Buckingham: Open University Press.

DuBois, B. (1983) Passionate Scholarship: notes on values, knowing and method in social science, in G. Bowles and R.D. Klein (eds) *Theories of Women's Studies*. London: Routledge & Kegan Paul.

Duncombe, J. and Marsden, D. (1998) 'Stepson wives' and 'hollow men'?: doing emotion work, doing gender and 'authenticity' in intimate heterosexual relationships, in G. Bendelow and S.J. Williams (eds) *Emotions in Social Life: Critical Themes and Contemporary Issues*. London: Routledge.

Duras, M. (1980) Smothered creativity, in E. Marks and I. DeCountivron (eds) *New French Feminisms*. Amherst, MA: University of Massachusetts Press.

Dworkin, A. (1974) *Woman Hating*. New York: E.P. Dutton.

Eagleton, M. (1996) Who's who and where's where: constructing feminist literary studies, *Feminist Review*, 53: 1–23.

Easlea, B. (1983) *Fathering the Unthinkable: Masculinity, Scientists and the Nuclear Arms Race*. London: Pluto.

Edwards, R. (1993) *Mature Women Students*. London: Taylor & Francis.

Ehrenreich, B. and English, D. (1979) *For Her Own Good: 150 Years of Experts' Advice to Women*. London: Pluto.

Ehrlich, C. (1976) *The Conditions of Feminist Research*. Baltimore, MA: Research Group One.

Eichler, M. (1988) *Non-Sexist Research Methods*. London: Allen & Unwin.

Emslie, C., McKie, L., Letherby, G. et al. (1999) *Writing and Publishing*. Durham: British Sociological Association.

Epstein, D. (1995) In our (new) right minds: the hidden curriculum and the academy, in L. Morley and V. Walsh (eds) *Feminist Academics: Creative Agents for Change*. London: Taylor & Francis.

Evans, J. (1995) *An Introduction to Second Wave Feminism*. London: Sage.

Evans, M. (1983) In praise of theory: the case for women's studies, *Women's Studies International Forum*, 6(3): 325–30.

Evans, M. (1991) The problem of gender for women's studies, in J. Aaron and S. Walby (eds) *Out of the Margins: Women's Studies in the Nineties*. London: Falmer.

Evans, M. (ed.) (1994) *The Woman Question*, 2nd edn. London: Sage.

Evans, M. (1995) Ivory towers: life in the mind, in L. Morley and V. Walsh (eds) *Feminist Academics: Creative Agents for Change*. London: Taylor & Francis.

Evans, M. (1997) *Introducing Contemporary Feminist Thought*. Cambridge: Polity Press.

Exley, C. and Letherby, G. (2001) Managing a disrupted lifecourse: issues of identity and emotion work, *Health*, 5(1): 112–32.

Faludi, S. (1992) *Backlash: The Undeclared War Against Women*. London: Chatto & Windus.

Farran, D. (1990a) Analysing a photograph of Marilyn Monroe, in L. Stanley (ed.) *Feminist Praxis: Research, Theory and Epistemology in Feminist Sociology*. London: Routledge.

Farran, D. (1990b) Seeking Susan: producing statistical information on young people's leisure, in L. Stanley (ed.) *Feminist Praxis: Research, Theory and Epistemology in Feminist Sociology*. London: Routledge.

Finch, J. (1984) 'It's great to have someone to talk to': the ethics and politics of interviewing women, in C. Bell and H. Roberts (eds) *Social Researching: Politics, Problems, Practice.* London: Routledge & Kegan Paul.

Finch, J. and Mason, J. (1993) *Negotiating Family Responsibilities.* London: Routledge.

Fine, M. (1983–4) Coping with rape: critical perspectives on consciousness, *Imagination, Cognition and Personality*, 3: 249–67.

Fine, M. (1994) Dis-stance and other stances: negotiations of power insider feminist research, in A. Gitlin (ed.) *Power and Method: Political Activism and Educational Research.* London: Routledge.

Fishman, P. (1978) Interaction: the work women do, *Social Problems*, 25: 397–406.

Flax, J. (1987) Postmodernism and gender relations in feminist theory, *Signs: Journal of Women in Culture and Society*, 12: 334–51.

Flax, J. (1990) Postmodernism and gender relation in feminist theory, in L.J. Nicholson (ed.) *Feminism/Postmodernism.* London: Routledge.

Fleischman, S. (1998) Gender, the personal, and the voice of scholarship: a viewpoint, *Signs: Journal of Women in Culture and Society*, 23(4): 976–1016.

Fleuhr-Lobban, C. and Lobban, R.A. (1986) Families, gender and methodology in the Sudan, in T.L. Whitehead and M.E. Conway (eds) *Self, Sex and Gender in Cross-Cultural Fieldwork.* Urbana, IL: University of Illinois.

Fonow, M.M. and Cook, J.A. (1991) Back to the future: a look at the second wave of feminist epistemology and methodology, in M.M. Fonow and J.A. Cook (eds) *Beyond Methodology: Feminist Scholarship as Lived Experience.* Bloomington, IN: Indiana University.

Foster, J. (1994) The dynamics of gender in ethnographic research: a personal view in R. Burgess (ed.) *Studies in Qualitative Methodology*, vol. 4. London: JAI.

Fox Keller, E. (1990) Gender and science, in J. McCarl Nielsen (ed.) *Feminist Research Methods: Exemplary Readings in the Social Sciences.* Boulder, CO: Westview.

Francis, B. and Skelton, C. (eds) (2001) *Investigating Gender: Contemporary Perspectives in Education.* Buckingham: Open University Press.

Freedman, R. (1988) *Beauty Bound: Why Women Strive for Physical Perfection.* London: Columbus.

French, S. (1998) Surviving the institution: working as a visually disabled lecturer in higher education, in D. Malina and S. Maslin-Prothero (eds) *Surviving the Academy: Feminist Perspectives.* London: Taylor & Francis.

Frith, H. and Kitzinger, C. (1998) 'Emotion work' as a participant resource: a feminist analysis of young women's talk-in-interaction, *Sociology*, 32(2): 299–320.

Frye, M. (1992) Getting it right, *Signs: Journal of Women in Culture and Society*, 17(4): 781–93.

Gamarnikow, E. (1978) Sexual division of labour: the case of nursing, in A. Kuhn and A.M. Wolpe (eds) *Feminism and Materialism.* London: Routledge & Kegan Paul.

Geiger, S.N.G. (1986) Women's life histories: method and content, *Signs: Journal of Women, Culture and Society*, 11: 334–51.

Gelsthorpe, L. (1990) Feminist methodology in criminology: a new approach or old wine in new bottles? in L. Gelsthorpe and A. Morris (eds) *Feminist Perspectives in Criminology.* Buckingham: Open University Press.

Gelsthorpe, L. (1992) Response to Martyn Hammersley's paper 'On feminist methodology', *Sociology*, 26: 213–18.

Gibbon, M. (1999) *Feminist Perspectives on Language.* London: Longman.

Gibson, R. (1996) Deaf women academics in higher education, in L. Morley and V. Walsh (eds) *Breaking Boundaries: Women in Higher Education.* London: Taylor & Francis.

Giddens, A. (1985) *The Nation State and Violence*. Cambridge: Polity Press.

Gillespie, R. (2000) Virtual violence? Pornography and violence against women on the internet, in J. Radford, M. Friedberg and L. Harne (eds) *Women, Violence and Strategies for Action*. Buckingham: Open University Press.

Gilligan, C. (1982) *In a Different Voice*. Cambridge, MA: Harvard University Press.

Glucksmann, M. (1994) The work of knowledge and the knowledge of women's work, in M. Maynard and J. Purvis (eds) *Researching Women's Lives from a Feminist Perspective*. London: Taylor & Francis.

Goffman, E. (1981) *Forms of Talk*. Oxford: Blackwell.

Goldscheider, F.K. and Kaufman, G. (1996) Fertility and commitment: bringing men back, in J.B. Caterline, R.D. Lee and K.A. Foote (eds) *Fertility in the United States: New Patterns, New Theories* (*Population and Development Review*: A supplement to vol. 22). The Population Council, Inc.

Goode, W.J. and Hatt, P.K. (1952) *Methods in Social Research*. New York: McGraw Hill.

Gouldner, A.W. (1971) *The Coming Crisis in Western Sociology*. London: Heinemann.

Graham, H. (1984) *Women, Health and the Family*. Brighton: Wheatsheaf.

Gray, B. (1994) Women in higher education: what are we doing to ourselves? in S. Davies, C. Lubelska and J. Quinn (eds) *Changing the Subject: Women in Higher Education*. London: Taylor & Francis.

Greer, G. (1999) *The Whole Woman*. London: Doubleday.

Gregory, J. and Lees, S. (1999) *Policing Sexual Assault*. London: Routledge.

Griffin, C. (1989) 'I'm not a women's libber but . . .': feminism, consciousness and identity, in S. Shevington and D. Baker (eds) *The Social Identity of Women*. London: Sage.

Griffin, S. (1983) Introduction, in J. Caldecott and K. Leland (eds) *Reclaim the Earth*. London: The Women's Press.

Grimshaw, J. (1986) *Feminist Philosophers*. London: Wheatsheaf.

Grosz, E. (1990) Contemporary theories of power and subjectivity, in S. Gunew (ed.) *Feminist Knowledge: Critique and Construct*. London: Routledge.

Gunew, S. (ed.) (1990) *Feminist Knowledge: Critique and Construct*. London: Routledge.

Hall, C. (1992) Feminism and feminist history, in C. Hall (ed.) *White, Male and Middle Class: Explorations in Feminism and History*. Cambridge: Polity.

Hallam, J. and Marshment, M. (1995) Questioning the 'ordinary' woman: *Oranges are not the Only Fruit*, text and viewer, in B. Skeggs (ed.) *Feminist Cultural Theory: Process and Production*. Manchester: Manchester University.

Hammersley, M. and Gomm, R. (1997b) Bias in social research, *Sociological Research Online*, 2(1): www.socresonline.org.uk/socresonline/2/4/7.html.

Hannam, J. (1993) Women, history and protest, in D. Richardson and V. Robinson (eds) *Introducing Women's Studies*. London: Macmillan.

Harding, S. (1986) *The Science Question in Feminism*. Ithaca, NY: Cornell University.

Harding, S. (ed.) (1987) *Feminism and Methodology*. Milton Keynes: Open University Press.

Harding, S. (1990) Feminism and theories of scientific knowledge, *Women*, 1(1): 87–98.

Harding, S. (1991) *Whose Science? Whose Knowledge?* Buckingham: Open University Press.

Harding, S. (1993) Rethinking standpoint epistemology: 'what is strong objectivity?', in L. Alcoff and E. Porter (eds) *Feminist Epistemologies*. New York: Routledge.

Harding, S. (1994) Feminism and theories of knowledge, in M. Evans (ed.) *The Woman Question*, 2nd edn. London: Sage.

Harding, S. (1997) Comment on Hekman's 'Truth and Method: feminist standpoint theory revisited': whose standpoint needs the regimes of truth and reality? *Signs: Journal of Women in Culture and Society*, 22(2): 382–91.

Hartsock, N. (1990) Foucault on power: a theory for women? in L.J. Nicholson (ed.) *Feminism/Postmodernism*. London: Routledge.

Hartsock, N.C.M. (1997) Comment on Hekman's 'Truth and method: feminist standpoint theory revisited': truth or justice? *Signs: Journal of Women in Culture and Society*, 22(2): 367–74.

Hearn, J. (1982) Notes on patriarchy, professionalism and the semi-professionals, *Sociology*, 26: 184–202.

Hearn, J. and Morgan, D. (eds) (1990) *Men, Masculinities and Social Theories*. London: Unwin Hyman.

Heckman, S. (1990) *Gender and Knowledge: Elements of a Postmodern Feminism*. Cambridge: Polity.

Hekman, S. (1997) Truth and method: feminist standpoint theory revisited, *Signs: Journal of Women in Culture and Society*, 22(2): 341–65.

Henwood, K. and Pidgeon, N. (1995) Remaking the link: qualitative research and feminist standpoint theory, *Feminism and Psychology*, 5(1): 7–30.

Hester, M. (1992) *Lewd Women and Wicked Witches: A Study of the Dynamics of Male Domination*. London: Routledge.

Hey, V. (1989) A feminist exploration, in V. Hey, C. Itzin, L. Saunders and M.A. Speakman (eds) *Hidden Loss: Miscarriage and Ectopic Pregnancies*. London: The Women's Press.

Hill Collins, P. (1989) Black feminist thought, *Signs: Journal of Women in Culture and Society*, 14(4): 745–73.

Hill Collins, P. (1990) *Black Feminist Thought: Knowledge, Consiousness and the Politics of Empowerment*. Boston, MA: Unwin Hyman.

Hill Collins, P. (1994) The social construction of black feminist thought, in M. Evans (ed.) *The Woman Question*, 2nd edn. London: Sage.

Hill Collins, P. (1997) Comment on Hekman's 'Truth and method: feminist standpoint theory revisited': where's the power? *Signs: Journal of Women in Culture and Society*, 22(2): 375–81.

Hochschild, A.R. (1983) *The Managed Heart: The Commercialisation of Human Feelings*. London: University of California.

Hochschild, A.R. (1990) *The Second Shift*. London: Piatkus.

Hockey, J. (1993) Women and health, in D. Richardson and V. Robinson (eds) *Introducing Women's Studies*. London: Macmillan.

Holland, J. and Ramazanoglu, C. (1994) Coming to conclusions: power and interpretation in researching young women's sexuality, in M. Maynard and J. Purvis (eds) *Researching Women's Lives from a Feminist Perspective*. London: Taylor & Francis.

Holmwood, J. (1995) Feminism and epistemology: what kind of successor science? *Sociology*, 29: 411–18.

Hood, S., Mayall, B. and Oliver, S. (eds) *Critical Issues in Social Research*. Buckingham: Open University Press.

Horn, R. (1997) Not 'One of the Boys': women researching the police, *Journal of Gender Studies*, 6(3): 297–308.

Humm, M. (1996) Equal opportunities and higher education, in L. Morley and V. Walsh (eds) *Breaking Boundaries: Women in Higher Education*. London: Taylor & Francis.

Humm, M. (1997) Seven questions and some answers, *Women's Studies Network UK Newsletter*, 26: 16–17.

Humphries, B. (1998) The baby and the bath water: Hammersley, Cealey Harrison and Hood-Williams and the emancipatory research debate, *Sociological Research Online*, 3(1): www.socresonline/org.uk/socresonline/3/1/9.html.

Hunt, J.C. (1989) *Psychoanalytic Aspects of Fieldwork*. London: Sage.

Iles, T. (ed.) (1992) *All Sides of the Subject: Women and Biography*. New York: Teacher's College.

Jackson, S. (1992) The amazing deconstructing woman, *Trouble and Strife*, 25: 25–31.

Jackson, S. (1993) Women and the family, in D. Richardson and V. Robinson (eds) *Introducing Women's Studies*. Houndmills: Macmillan.

Jacobs, S., Jacobson, R. and Marchbank, J. (eds) (2000) *States of Conflict: Gender, Violence and Resistance*. London: Zed.

James, N. (1989) Emotional labour: skills and work in the social regulation of feelings, *Sociological Review*, 37(1): 5–52.

Jayaratne, T.E. (1983) The value of quantitative methodology for feminist research, in G. Bowles and R.D. Klein (eds) *Theories of Women's Studies*. Boston, MA: Routledge & Kegan Paul.

Jayaratne, T.E. and Stewart, A. (1991) Quantitative and qualitative methods in the social sciences: current feminist issues and practical strategies, in M.M. Fonow and J.A. Cook (eds) *Beyond Methodology: Feminist Scholarship as Lived Experience*. Bloomington, IN: Indiana University.

Jewkes, Y. and Letherby, G. (2001) Insiders and outsiders: complex issues of identification, difference and distance in social research, *Auto/Biography*, IX(1&2): 41–50.

Jones, S.J. (1997) Reflexivity and feminist practice: ethical dilemmas in negotiating meaning, *Feminism and Psychology*, 7(3): 348–51.

Josselson, R. and Lieblich, A. (1996) Ethics and process, in *The Narrative Study of Lives*, vol. 4. London: Sage.

Kahn, R.L. and Cannell, B. (1957) *The Dynamics of Interviewing*. New York: Wiley.

Kaplan, C. and Rose, E.C. (1993) Strange bedfellows: feminist collaborations, *Signs: Journal of Women in Culture and Society*, 18(3): 547–61.

Katz-Rothman, B. (1986) Reflections of hard work, *Qualitative Sociology*, 9: 48–53.

Katz-Rothman, B. (1996) Bearing witness: representing women's experiences of prenatal diagnosis, in S. Wilkinson and C. Kitzinger (eds) *Representing the Other: A Feminism and Psychology Reader*. London: Sage.

Keller, E.F. and Moglen, H. (1987) Competition and feminism: conflicts for academic women, *Signs: Journal of Women in Culture and Society*, 12(3): 493–511.

Kelly, L. (1978) Feminism and research, *Women's International Quarterly*, 225–33.

Kelly, L. (1988) *Surviving Sexual Violence*. Cambridge: Polity.

Kelly, L., Burton, S. and Regan, L. (1994) Researching women's lives or studying women's oppression? Reflections on what constitutes feminist research, in M. Maynard and J. Purvis (eds) *Researching Women's Lives from a Feminist Perspective*. London: Taylor & Francis.

Kemp, S. and Squires, J. (1997) *Feminisms*. Oxford: Oxford University Press.

Kent, J. (2000) *Social Perspectives on Pregnancy and Childbirth for Midwives, Nurses and the Caring Professions*. Buckingham: Open University Press.

Kessler-Harris, A. (1992) The view from women's studies, *Signs: Journal of Women in Culture and Society*, 17(4).

Kimmel, M. (ed.) (1988) *Changing Men: New Directions in Research on Men and Masculinity*. London: Sage.

Kirkham, M.J. (1997) Stories and childbirth, in H.J. Kirkham and E.R. Perkins (eds) *Reflections on Midwifery*. London: Bailliere Tindall.

Klein, R.D. (1983) How do we do what we want to do: thoughts about feminist methodology, in G. Bowles and R.D. Klein (eds) *Theories of Women's Studies*. Boston, MA: Routledge & Kegan Paul.

Kleinman, S. and Copp, M.A. (1993) *Emotions and Fieldwork*. London: Sage.

Kramarae, C. and Treichler, P.A. (1985) *A Feminist Dictionary*. London: Pandora.

Larner, C. (1983) *The Enemies of God*. Oxford: Blackwell.

Laws, S. (1990) *Issues of Blood: The Politics of Menstruation*. Basingstoke: Macmillan.

Lee, R.M. (1993) *Doing Research on Sensitive Topics*. London: Sage.

Lee-Treweek, G. (2000) The insight of emotional danger: research experiences in a home for older people, in G. Lee-Treweek and S. Linkogle (eds) *Danger in the Field: Risk and Ethics in Social Research*. London: Routledge.

Lee-Treweek, G. and Linkogle, S. (eds) (2000) *Danger in the Field: Risk and Ethics in Social Research*. London: Routledge.

Lees, S. (1996) *Carnal Knowledge: Rape on Trial*. London: Hamish Hamilton.

Lees, S. (1997) *Ruling Passions: Sexual Violence, Reputation and the Law*. Buckingham: Open University Press.

Leonard, D. and Coate, K. (2002) Rules that rob our research, *Times Higher Educational Supplement*, 8 March.

Leonard, P. and Malina, D. (1994) Caught between two worlds: mothers as academics, in S. Davies, C. Lubeska and J. Quinn (eds) *Changing the Subject: Women in Higher Education*. London: Taylor & Francis.

Letherby, G. (1993) The meanings of miscarriage, *Women's Studies International Forum* 16(2): 165–80.

Letherby, G. (1994) Mother or not, mother or what? The problem of definition, *Women's Studies International Forum*, 17(5): 525–32.

Letherby, G. (1997) 'Infertility' and 'involuntary childlessness': definition and self-identity. Unpublished PhD thesis, Staffordshire University.

Letherby, G. (1999) Other than mother and mothers as others: the experience of motherhood and non-motherhood in relation to 'infertility' and 'involuntary childlessness', *Women's Studies International Forum*, 22(3): 359–72.

Letherby, G. (2000a) Working and wishing: an auto/biography of managing home and work, *Auto/Biography*, VIII(1&2): 89–98.

Letherby, G. (2000b) Dangerous liaisons: auto/biography in research and research writing, in G. Lee-Treweek and S. Linkogle (eds) *Danger in the Field: Risk and Ethics in Social Research*. London: Routledge.

Letherby, G. (2002) Claims and disclaimers: knowledge, reflexivity and representation in feminist research, *Sociological Research Online*, 6(4): www.socresoline.org.uk/6/4/letherby.html.

Letherby, G. and Cotterill, P. (2001) *Doubly burdened, AUTLOOK*, 129:

Letherby, G. and Marchbank, J. (1998) To boldly go: 'safe' spaces and 'gendered' places in feminist research. Paper presented at the Women's Studies Network UK Conference, Hull.

Letherby, G. and Marchbank, J. (2001) Why do women's studies? A cross-England profile, *Women's Studies International Forum*, 24(5): 587–603.

Letherby, G. and Ramsay, K. (1999) So why are you doing this project? Issues of friendship, research and autobiography, *Auto/Biography*, VII(1&2): 35–42.

Letherby, G. and Shiels, J. (2001) 'Isn't he good, but can we take her seriously?' Gendered expectations in higher education, in P. Anderson and J. Williams (eds) *Identity and Difference in Higher Education: 'Outsiders' Within*. Aldershot: Ashgate.

Letherby, G. and Zdrodowski, D. (1995) 'Dear researcher': the use of correspondence as a method within feminist qualitative research, *Gender and Society*, 9(5): 576–93.

Letherby, G., Coghlan, A. and DuBoulay, D. (2002) *Institutional Racism and the Children's Society*. Coventry: Centre for Social Justice.

Lloyd, A. (1995) *Doubly Deviant, Doubly Damned: Society's Treatment of Violent Women*. London: Penguin.

Lorde, A. (1984) *Sisters, Outsiders: Essays and Speeches*. New York: Crossing Press.

Lovenduski, J. and Randall, V. (1993) *Contemporary Feminist Politics: Women and Power in Britain*. Oxford: Oxford University Press.

Luff, D. (1999) Dialogue across the divides: 'moments of rapport' and power in feminist research with anti-feminist women, *Sociology*, 33(4): 687–704.

Mace, J. (2000) The RAE and university efficiency, *Higher Education Review*, 32(2): 17–36.

MacFarlane, A. (1970) *Witchcraft in Tudor and Stuart England: A Regional and Comparative Study*. London: Routledge & Kegan Paul.

Macintryre, M. (1993) Fictive kinship or mistaken identity? Fieldwork on Tubetude Island, Papua New Guinea, in D. Bell, P. Caplan and W. Jahan Kurim (eds) *Gendered Fields: Women, Men and Ethnography*. London: Routledge.

Maguire, M. (1996) In the prime of their lives? Older women in higher education, in L. Morley and V. Walsh (eds) *Breaking Boundaries: Women in Higher Education*. London: Taylor & Francis.

Malina, D. and Maslin-Prothero, S. (1998) *Surviving the Academy: Feminist Perspectives*. London: Taylor & Francis.

Malson, H. (1996) *The Thin Body*. London: Routledge.

Marchbank, J. (2000) *Women, Power and Policy: Comparative Studies of Childcare*. London: Routledge.

Marchbank, J. and Letherby, G. (2001) Not missing but marginalized? Alternative voices in feminist theory, *Feminist Theory*, 2(1): 104–7.

Marchbank, J. and Letherby, G. (2002) Offensive and defensive: feminist pedagogy, student support and higher education, in G. Howie and A. Tauchert (eds) *Gender, Teaching and Research in Higher Education: Challenges for the 21st Century*. London: Ashgate.

Marshall, A. (1994) Sensuous sapphires: a study of the social construction of black female sexuality, in M. Maynard and J. Purvis (eds) *Researching Women's Lives from a Feminist Perspective*. London: Taylor & Francis.

Mason, J. (1996) *Qualitative Researching*. London: Sage.

Mason, M. (1993) *Male Infertility: Men Talking*. London: Routledge.

Mayall, B. (1999) Children and childhood, in S. Hood, B. Mayall and S. Oliver (eds) *Critical Issues in Social Research*. Buckingham: Open University Press.

Maynard, M. (1994a) Methods, practice and epistemology: the debate about feminism and research, in M. Maynard and J. Purvis (eds) *Researching Women's Lives from a Feminist Perspective*. London: Taylor & Francis.

Maynard, M. (1994b) 'Race', gender and the concept of 'difference' in feminist thought, in H. Afshar and M. Maynard (eds) *The Dynamics of 'Race' and Gender: Some Feminist Interventions*. London: Taylor & Francis.

Maynard, M. and Purvis, J. (1994) *Researching Women's Lives from a Feminist Perspective*. London: Taylor & Francis.

McCarl Neilsen, J. (ed.) (1990) *Feminist Research Methods: Exemplary Readings in the Social Sciences*. Boulder, CO: Westview.

McFarlane, A. (1990) Official statistics and women's health and illness, in H. Roberts (ed.) *Women's Health Counts*. London: Routledge.

McKee, L. and O'Brien, M. (1983) Interviewing men: taking gender seriously, in E. Gamarnikow, D. Morgan, J. Purvis and D. Taylorson (eds) *The Public and the Private*. London: Heinemann.

McLennan, G. (1995) Feminism, epistemology and postmodernism: reflections on current ambivalence, *Sociology*, 29(3): 391–409.

McMahon, M. (1996) Significant absences, *Qualitative Inquiry*, 2(3): 320–36.

McRobbie, A. (1982) The politics of feminist research: between talk, text and action, *Feminist Review*, 12: 26–57.

Measor, L. (1985) Interviewing: a strategy in qualitative research, in R. Burgess (ed.) *Strategies of Educational Research: Qualitative Methods*. Lewes: Falmer.

Meerabeau, L. (1989) Parents in waiting: the experience of subfertile couples. Unpublished PhD thesis, University of London.

Mies, M. (1983) Towards a methodology for feminist research, in G. Bowles and R.D. Klein (eds) *Theories of Women's Studies*. London: Routledge & Kegan Paul.

Mies, M. (1991) Women's research or feminist research? The debate surrounding feminist science and methodology, in M.M. Fonow and J.A. Cook (eds) *Beyond Methodology: Feminist Scholarship as Lived Experience*. Bloomington, IN: Indiana University Press.

Millen, D. (1997) Some methodological and epistemological issues raised by doing feminist research on non-feminist women, *Sociological Research Online*, 2(3): www.socresonline.org,uk/socresonline/2/3/3.html.

Miller, T. (1998) Shifting layers of professional, lay and personal narratives: longitudinal childbirth research, in J. Ribbens and R. Edwards (eds) *Feminist Dilemmas in Qualitative Research: Public Knowledge and Private Lives*. London: Sage.

Mills, C.W. (1959) *The Sociological Imagination*. London: Penguin.

Mills, J. (1991) *Womanwords*. London: Virago.

Minh-ha, T.T. (1989) *Woman, Native, Other: Writing Postcoloniality and Feminism*. Bloomington, IN: Indiana University.

Mizra, H. (1992) *Young, Female and Black*. London: Routledge & Kegan Paul.

Monach, J.H. (1993) *Childless No Choice: The Experience of Involuntary Childlessness*. London: Routledge.

Morgan, D. (1981) Men, masculinity and the process of sociological inquiry, in H. Roberts (ed.) *Doing Feminist Research*. London: Routledge & Kegan Paul.

Morgan, R. (1989) *The Demon Lover: On the Sexuality of Terrorism*. London: Methuen.

Morley, L. (1995) Measuring the muse: feminism, creativity and career development in higher education, in L. Morley and V. Walsh (eds) *Feminist Academics: Creative Agents for Change*. London: Taylor & Francis.

Morley, L. (1996) Interrogating patriarchy: the challenges of feminist research, in L. Morley and C. Walsh (eds) *Breaking Boundaries: Women in Higher Education*. London: Taylor & Francis.

Morley, L. and Walsh, V. (eds) (1995) *Feminist Academics: Creative Agents for Change*. London: Taylor & Francis.

Morley, L. and Walsh, V. (1996) *Breaking Boundaries: Women in Higher Education*. London: Taylor & Francis.

Moser, C.A. (1958) *Survey Methods in Social Investigation*. London: Heinemann.

Munn-Giddings, C. (1998) Mixing motherhood and academia – a lethal cocktail, in D. Malina and S. Maslin-Prothero (eds) *Surviving the Academy: Feminist Perspective*. London: Falmer.

Mykhalovskiy, E. (1996) Reconsidering table talk: critical thoughts on the relationship between sociology, autobiography and self-indulgence, *Qualitative Sociology*, 19(1): 131–51.

Newburn, T. and Stanko, E. (1994) When men are the victims: the failure of criminology, in T. Newburn and E. Stanko (eds) *Just Boys Doing Business? Men, Masculinities and Crime*. London: Routledge.

Newton, E. (1993) By best informant's dress: the erotic equation in fieldwork, *Cultural Anthropology*, 8(1): 3–23.

Nicholson, L.J. (ed.) (1990) *Feminism/Postmodernism*. London: Routledge.

Noddings, N. (1989) *Women and Evil*. Berkeley, CA: University of California.

Oakley, A. (1974) *The Sociology of Housework*. London: Martin Robertson.

Oakley, A. (1979) *From Here to Maternity: Becoming a Mother*. London: Penguin.

Oakley, A. (1981) *Subject Women*. Oxford: Martin Robertson.

Oakley, A. (1990) Interviewing women: a contradiction in terms, in H. Roberts (ed.) *Doing Feminist Research*. London: Routledge.

Oakley, A. (1998) Gender, methodology and people's ways of knowing: some problems with feminism and the paradigm debate in social science, *Sociology*, 32(4): 707–32.

Oakley, A. (1999) People's ways of knowing: gender and methodology, in S. Hood, B. Mayall and S. Oliver (eds) *Critical Issues in Social Research*. Buckingham: Open University Press.

Oakley, A. (2000) *Experiments in Knowing: Gender and Method in the Social Sciences*. Cambridge: Polity.

Oakley, A., McPherson, A. and Roberts, H. (1984) *Miscarriage*. Glasgow: Fontana.

Oboler, R.S. (1986) For better or worse: anthropologists and husbands in the field, in T.L. Whitehead and M.E. Conaway (eds) *Self, Sex and Gender in Cross-Cultural Fieldwork*. Urbana, IL: University of Illinois.

Okley, J. (1992) Anthropology and autobiography: participatory experience and embodied knowledge, in J. Okely and H. Callaway (eds) *Anthropology and Autobiography*. London: Routledge.

Okley, J. and Callaway, H. (eds) (1992) *Anthropology and Autobiography*. London: Routledge.

Olsen, T. (1980) *Silences*. London: Virago.

Opie, A. (1992) Qualitative research, appropriation of the 'other' and empowerment, *Feminist Review*, 40: 52–69.

Owens, D. (1986) The desire for children: a sociological study of involuntary childlessness. Unpublished PhD thesis, University College, Cardiff.

Padfield, M. and Proctor, L. (1996) The effect of interviewer's gender on the interviewing process: a comparative enquiry, *Sociology*, 30(2): 355–66.

Paget, M.A. (1990) Life mirrors work mirrors text mirrors life, *Social Problems*, 37(2): 137–51.

Parr, J. (1998) Theoretical voices and women's own voices: the stories of mature women students, in J. Ribbens and R. Edwards (eds) *Feminist Dilemmas in Qualitative Research: Public Knowledge and Private Lives*. London: Sage.

Parsons, T. and Bales, R. (1955) *Family, Socialisation and International Process*. London: Routledge.

Pascall, G. (1997) *Social Policy: A New Feminist Analysis*. London: Routledge.

Patai, D. (1991) U.S. Academics and Third World women: is ethical research possible? in S. Berger Gluck and D. Patai (eds) *Women's Words, Women's Words, Women's Words: The Feminist Practice of Oral History*. London: Routledge.

Pegg, C. (1990) A 'pretended family', in J. Scanton (ed.) *Surviving the Blues*. London: Virago.

Phillips, E.M. and Pugh, D.S. (1987) *How to Get a PhD: A Handbook for Students and their Supervisors*. Milton Keynes: Open University Press.

Phoenix, A. (1994) Practising feminist research: the intersection of gender and 'race' in the research process, in M. Maynard and J. Purvis (eds) *Researching Women's Lives from a Feminist Perspective*. London: Taylor & Francis.

Potts, T. and Price, J. (1995) 'Out of the blood and spirit of our Lives': the place of the body in academic feminism, in L. Morley and V. Walsh (eds) *Feminist Academics: Creative Agents for Change*. London: Taylor & Francis.

Pringle, R. (1989) *Secretaries Talk: Sexuality, Power and Work*. London: Verso.

Pritchard, C. and Deem, R. (1999) Wo-managing further education: gender and the construction of the manager in the corporate colleges of England, *Gender and Education*, 11(3): 323–42.

Pugh, A. (1990) My statistics and feminism – a true story, in L. Stanley (ed.) *Feminist Praxis: Research, Theory and Epistemology in Feminist Sociology*. London: Routledge.

Purcell, K. (1987) Gender and experience at work, in D. Gallie (ed.) *Employment in Britain*. Blackwell: Oxford.

Purvis, J. (1994) Doing feminist women's history: researching the lives of women in the suffragette movement in Edwardian England, in M. Maynard and J. Purvis (eds) *Researching Women's Lives from a Feminist Perspective*. London: Taylor & Francis.

Rabinow, P. (1986) Representations are social facts, in J. Clifford and G.E. Marcus (eds) *Writing Culture: The Poetics and Politics of Ethnography*. Berkeley, CA: University of California.

Ramazanoglu, C. (ed.) (1993) *Up Against Foucault: Explorations of Some Tensions Between Foucault and Feminism*. London: Routledge.

Ramazanoglu, C. (1992) On feminist methodology: male reason versus female empowerment, *Sociology*, 26: 207–12.

Ramsay, K. (1993) Emotional labour and qualitative research. Paper presented at the British Sociological Association Annual Conference, Essex University.

Ramsay, K. (1996) Emotional labour and organisational research: how I learned not to laugh or cry in the field, in S.E. Lyon and J. Busfield (eds) *Methodological Imaginations*. London: Macmillan.

Randall, V. (1991) Feminism and political analysis, *Political Studies*, XXXIX: 513–32.

Reinharz, A. (1984) *On Becoming a Social Scientist*. New Brunswick, NJ: Transaction Books.

Reinharz, A. (1990) So-called training in the so-called alternative paradigm, in E.G. Guba (ed.) *The Paradigm Dialog*. Newbury Park, CA: Sage.

Reinharz, S. (1983) Experiential research: a contribution to feminist theory, in G. Bowles and R.D. Klein (eds) *Theories of Women's Studies*. London: Routledge.

Reinharz, S. (1992) *Feminist Methods in Social Research*. Oxford: Oxford University Press.

Reinhold, S. (1994) Through the parliamentary looking glass: 'real' and 'pretend' families in contemporary British politics, *Feminist Review*, 48: 61–79.

Reynolds, G. (1993) 'And Gill came tumbling down . . .': gender and a research dilemma, in M. Kennedy, C. Lubelska and V. Walsh (eds) *Making Connections: Women's Studies, Women's Movements, Women's Lives*. London: Taylor & Francis.

Ribbens, J. (1989) Interviewing women: an unnatural situation, *Women's Studies International Forum*, 12(6): 579–92.

Ribbens, J. (1993) Facts or fiction? Aspects of the use of autobiographical writing in undergraduate sociology, *Sociology*, 27(1): 323–42.

Ribbens, J. and Edwards, R. (eds) (1998) *Feminist Dilemmas in Qualitative Research*. London: Sage.

Rich, A. (1976) *Of Woman Born: Motherhood as Experience and Institution*. London: Virago.

Rich, A. (1986) Towards a women-centred university, in A. Rich, *On Lies, Secrets, Silence: Selected Prose 1966–78*. London: Virago.

Richardson, D. (1996) Representing other feminists, in S. Wilkinson and C. Kitzinger (eds) *Representing the Other: A Feminism and Psychology Reader*. London: Sage.

Richardson, L. (1985) *The New Other Woman: Contemporary Women in Affairs with Married Men*. New York: The Free Press.

Richardson, L. (1991) Sharing feminist research with popular audiences: the book tour, in M.M. Fonow and J.A. Cook (eds) *Beyond Methodology: Feminist Scholarship as Lived Experience*. Bloomington, IN: Indiana University Press.

Roberts, H. (ed.) (1981) *Doing Feminist Research*. London: Routledge & Kegan Paul.

Roberts, H. (1984) Putting the show on the road: the dissemination of research findings, in C. Bell and H. Roberts (eds) *Social Researching: Politics, Problems, Practice*. London: Routledge & Kegan Paul.

Roberts, H. (ed.) (1990a) *Women's Health Counts*. London: Routledge.

Roberts, H. (ed.) (1990b) *Doing Feminist Research*, 2nd edn. London: Routledge.

Roberts, H. (ed.) (1992) *Women's Health Matters*. London: Routledge.

Roberts, H. and Sharp, M. (1982) After sixteen: what happens to the girls? Bradford: Bradford Metropolitan Authority.

Robinson, V. (1993) Introducing women's studies, in D. Richardson and V. Robinson (eds) *Introducing Women's Studies*. London: Macmillan.

Robinson, V. and Richardson, D. (1994) Publishing feminism: redefining the women's studies discourse, *Journal of Gender Studies*, 3(1): 87–94.

Robson, C. (1993) *Real World Research*. Oxford: Blackwell.

Rose, H. (1982) Making science feminist, in D. Leonard and E. Whitelegg (eds) *The Changing Experience of Women*. Oxford: Martin Robertson.

Rose, H. (1983) Hand, brain and heart: a feminist epistemology for the natural sciences, *Signs*, 9: 75–90.

Roseneil, S. (1993) Greenham revisited: researching myself and my sisters, in D. Hobbs and T. May (eds) *Interpreting the Field: Accounts of Ethnography*. Oxford: Clarendon.

Rowbotham, S. (1992) *Women in Movement*. London: Routledge.

Ruddick, S. (1990) *Maternal Thinking*. London: The Women's Press.

Rysman, A. (1977) How the 'gossip' became a woman, *Journal of Communication*, 27(1): 176–80.

Scott, S. (1998) Here be dragons, *Sociological Research Online*, 3(3): www.socresonline.org.uk/socresonline/3/3/1html.

Scott, S. and Porter, M. (1983) On the bottom rung, *Women's Studies International Forum*, 6(2): 211–21.

Segal, L. (1987) *Is the Future Female: Troubled Thoughts on Contemporary Feminism*. London: Virago.

Seifert, K. and Martin, L.D. (1998) Preventing black maternal mortality: a challenge for the 90s, *Journal of Primary Prevention*, 9: 57–65.

Sellers, S. (ed.) (1991) *Taking Reality by Surprise: Writing for Pleasure and Publication*. London: The Women's Press.

Sellitz, C., Jahoda, M., Deutsch, M. and Cook, S.W. (1965) *Research Methods in Social Relations*. London: Methuen.

Shaffir, W.B., Stebbins, R.S. and Turowetz, A. (1980) *Fieldwork Experience: Qualitative Approaches to Social Research*. New York: St Martins Press.

Shelley, M. ([1818] 1994) *Frankenstein: The Modern Prometheus*. Ware: Wordsworth Classics.

Showalter, E. (1987) *The Female Malady*. London: Virago.

Silverstein, M. (1974) The history of a short, unsuccessful academic career, in J.H. Peck and J. Sawyer (eds) *Men and Masculinity*. Englewood Cliffs, NJ: Prentice Hall.

Skeggs, B. (1994) Situating the production of feminist ethnography, in M. Maynard and J. Purvis (eds) *Researching Women's Lives from a Feminist Perspective*. London: Taylor & Francis.

Skeggs, B. (ed.) (1995) *Feminist Cultural Theory: Process and Production*. Manchester: Manchester University.

Skelton, C. (1993) Women and education, in D. Richardson, and V. Robinson (eds) *Introducing Women's Studies*. Basingstoke: Macmillan.

Slocum, S. (1982) Woman the gatherer: male bias in anthropology, in M. Evans (ed.) *The Woman Question: Readings on the Subordination of Women*. Oxford: Fontana.

Smart, C. (1990) Feminist approaches to criminology or postmodern woman meets atavistic man, in L. Gelsthorpe and A. Morris (eds) *Feminist Perspectives in Criminology*. Buckingham: Open University Press.

Smeeth, M. (1990) Can you here me at the front? in J. Scanlon (ed.) *Surviving the Blues*. London: Virago.

Smith, D. (1974) Women, the family and corporate capitalism, in M.L. Stephenson (ed.) *Women in Canada*. Toronto: New Press.

Smith, D. (1978) A peculiar eclipsing: women's exclusion from man's culture, *Women's Studies International Quarterly*, 1(4): 281–96.

Smith, D. (1988) *The Everyday World as Problematic: A Feminist Sociology*. Milton Keynes: Open University Press.

Smith, D. (1991) Women's perspective as a radical critique of sociology, in S. Harding (ed.) *Feminism and Methodology: Social Science Issues*. Bloomington, IN: Indiana University Press.

Smith, D. (1997) Comment on Hekman's 'Truth and method: feminist standpoint revisited', *Signs: Journal of Women in Culture and Society*, 22: 392–8.

Smith, J. (1989) *Misogynies*. London: Faber & Faber.

Song, M. (1998) Hearing competing voices: sibling research, in J. Ribbens and R. Edwards (ed.) *Feminist Dilemmas in Qualitative Research: Public Knowledge and Private Lives*. London: Sage.

Sparke, M. (1996) Displacing the field in fieldwork: masculinity, metaphor and space, in N. Duncan (ed.) *BodySpace: Destabilizing Geographies of Gender and Sexuality*. London: Routledge.

Sparkes, A. (1998) Reciprocity in critical research? Some unsettling thoughts, in G. Shaklock and J. Smyth (eds) *Being Reflexive in Critical Educational and Social Research*. London: Falmer.

Spelman, E.V. (1990) *Inessential Woman: Problems of Exclusion in Feminist Thought*. London: The Women's Press.

Spencer, H. (1893) *Principles of Sociology* (3 vols), 3rd edn. Williams and Nongate.

Spender, D. (1980) *Man-Made Language*. London: Routledge & Kegan Paul.

Spender, D. (1981) The gatekeepers: a feminist critique of academic publishing, in H. Roberts (ed.) *Doing Feminist Research*. London: Routledge & Kegan Paul.

Spender, D. (1982) *Women of Ideas and What Men Have Done to Them: From Aphra Behn to Adrienne Rich*. London: Routledge & Kegan Paul.

Spender, L. (1983a) *Intruders on the Rights of Men*. London: Routledge & Kegan Paul.

Stacey, J. (1991) Can there be a feminist ethnography? in S.B. Gluck and D. Patai (eds) *Women's Words, Women's Words, Women's Words: The Feminist Practice of Oral History*. New York: Routledge.

Stacey, J. (1993) Untangling feminist theory, in D. Richardson and V. Robinson (eds) *Introducing Women's Studies*. Basingstoke: Macmillan.

Stacey, M. (1981) The division of labour revisited or overcoming the two Adams, in P. Abrams, R. Deem, J. Finch and P. Rock (eds) *Practice and Progress: British Sociology 1950–1980*. London: Allen & Unwin.

Stacey, M. (1994) From being a native to becoming a researcher: Meg Stacey and the General Medical Council, in R. Burgess (ed.) *Studies in Qualitative Methodology*, vol. 4. London: JAI.

Standing, K. (1998) Writing the voices of the less powerful: research on lone mothers, in J. Ribbens and R. Edwards (eds) *Feminist Dilemmas in Qualitative Research*. London: Sage.

Stanko, E.A. (1985) *Intimate Intrusions: Women's Experience of Male Violence*. London: Virago.

Stanley, L. (1984) How the social science research process discriminates against women, in S. Acker and D. Piper (eds) *Is Higher Education Fair to Women?* London: Routledge.

Stanley, L. (ed.) (1990) *Feminist Praxis: Research, Theory and Epistemology in Feminist Sociology*. London: Routledge.

Stanley, L. (1991) Feminist auto/biography and feminist epistemology, in J. Aaron and S. Walby (eds) *Out of the Margins: Women's Studies in the Nineties*. London: Falmer.

Stanley, L. (1993) On auto/biography in sociology, *Sociology*, 27(1): 41–52.

Stanley, L. (1995) My mother's voice? On becoming a 'native' in academia, in L. Morley and V. Walsh (eds) *Feminist Academics: Creative Agents for Change*. London: Taylor & Francis.

Stanley, L. (1997) Methodology matters, in D. Richardson and V. Robinson (eds) *Introducing Women's Studies*, 2nd edn. London: Macmillan.

Stanley, L. (1999) Children of our time: politics, ethics and feminist research processes. Paper presented at 'Feminism and Educational Research Methodologies' conference, Institute of Education, Manchester Metropolitan University, June.

Stanley, L. and Wise, S. (1979) Feminist research, feminist consciousness and experiences of sexism, *Women's Studies International Quarterly*, 2(3): 359–74.

Stanley, L. and Wise, S. (1990) Method, methodology and epistemology in feminist research processes, in L. Stanley (ed.) *Feminist Praxis: Research, Theory and Epistemology in Feminist Sociology*. London: Routledge.

Stanley, L. and Wise, S. (1993) *Breaking Out Again: Feminist Ontology and Epistemology*. London: Routlege.

Stanley, L. and Wise, S. (2000) But the empress has no clothes! Some awkward questions about the 'missing revolution' in feminist theory, *Feminist Theory*, 1(3): 261–88.

Steier, F. (1991) *Research and Reflexivity*. London: Sage.

Strauss, A. and Corbin, J. (1990) *Basics of Qualitative Research: Grounded Theory Procedures and Techniques*. London: Sage.

Temple, B. (1997) 'Collegiate accountability' and bias: the solution to the problem? *Sociological Research Online*, 2(4): www/socresonline.org.uk/socresonline/2/4/8.html.

Thomas, K. (1990) *Gender and Subject in Higher Education*. Buckingham: Open University Press.

Thornborrow, J. (1996) Women in the arts and media, in B. Madoc-Jones and J. Coates (eds) *An Introduction to Women's Studies*. Oxford: Blackwell.

Toynbee, P. (2000) Comment, *Radio Times*, 15–21 April, 8.

Trowler, P.R. (1998) *Academics Responding to Change: New Higher Education Frameworks and Academic Cultures*. Buckingham: SRHE & Open University Press.

Ussher, J.M. (1991) *Women's Madness: Misogyny or Mental Illness?* Hemel Hempstead: Harvester Wheatsheaf.

Ussher, J.M. (1997) *Fantasies of Femininity: Reframing the Boundaries of Sex.* London: Penguin.

Van der Kwaak, A. (1992) Female circumcision and gender identity: a questionable alliance? *Social Science and Medicine*, 35(6): 777–87.

Verslusyen, M.C. (1981) Midwives, medical men and 'poor women labouring of child': lying-in hospitals in eighteenth-century London, in H. Roberts (ed.) *Women, Health and Reproduction.* London: Routledge & Kegan Paul.

Wajcman, J. (1991) *Feminism Confronts Technology.* Cambridge: Polity.

Ward, K.B. and Grant, L. (1991) Coauthorship, gender and publication among sociologists, in M.M. Fonow and J.A. Cook (eds) *Beyond Methodology: Feminist Scholarship as Lived Experience.* Bloomington, IN: Indiana University Press.

Warren, C. (1988) *Gender Issues in Field Research.* Newbury Park, CA: Sage.

Waugh, P. (1998) Postmodernism and feminism, in S. Jackson and G. Jones (eds) *Contemporary Feminist Theories.* Edinburgh: Edinburgh University.

Webb, C. (1986) *Feminst Practice in Women's Health Care.* Chichester: Wiley.

Weber, M. (1949) *The Methodology of the Social Sciences.* Glencoe, IL: Illinois Free Press.

Weedon, C. (1987) *Feminist Practice and Poststructural Theory.* Oxford: Blackwell.

Weiner, G. (1996) Which of us has a brilliant career? Notes from a higher education survivor, in R. Cuthbert (ed.) *Working in Higher Education.* Buckingham: Open University Press.

Westkott, M. (1990) Feminist criticism of the social sciences, in J. McCarl Nielsen (ed.) *Feminist Research Methods: Exemplary Readings in the Social Sciences.* Boulder, CO: Westview.

Westwood, S. (1984) *All Day Everyday: Factory and Family in the Making of Women's Lives.* London: Pluto.

Whitehead, T.L. and Price, L. (1986) Summary: sex and the fieldwork experience, in T.L. Whitehead and M.E. Conaway (eds) *Self, Sex and Gender in Cross-Cultural Fieldwork.* Urbana, IL: University of Illinois.

Wilkins, R. (1993) Taking it personally: a note on emotions and autobiography, *Sociology*, 27(1): 93–100.

Wilkinson, S. (ed.) (1986) *Feminist Social Psychology: Developing Theory and Practice.* Milton Keynes: Open University Press.

Wilkinson, S. (1991a) Feminism and psychology: from critique to construction, *Feminism and Psychology*, 1(1): 5–18.

Wilkinson, S. (1991b) Why psychology (badly) needs feminism, in J. Aaron and S. Walby (eds) *Out of the Margins: Women's Studies in the Nineties.* London: Falmer.

Wilkinson, S. (ed.) (1996) *Feminist Social Psychology: Developing Theory and Practice.* Buckingham: Open University Press.

Wilkinson, S. and Kitzinger, C. (eds) (1994) *Women and Health: Feminist Perspectives.* London: Taylor & Francis.

Wilkinson, S. and Kitzinger, C. (eds) (1996) *Representing the Other: A Feminism and Psychology Reader.* London: Sage.

Williams, A. (1993) Diversity and agreement in feminist ethnography, *Sociology*, 27: 575–89.

Williams, F. (1996) Postmodernism, feminism and the questions of difference, in N. Parton (ed.) *Social Theory, Social Change and Social Work: An Introduction.* London: Routledge.

Williams, M. and May, T. (1996) *Introduction to the Philosophy of Social Research*. London: UCL Press.

Willis, P. (1977) *Learning to Labour*. London: Saxon House.

Willis, P. (1978) *Profane Culture*. London: Routledge & Kegan Paul.

Wilson, C. (1998) Feminist methodology, friendship and emotive issues. Unpublished dissertation, Coventry University.

Wise, S. (1987) A framework for discussing ethical issues in feminist research: a review of the literature, in *Writing Feminist Biography*, vol. 2. Manchester: University of Manchester.

Witz, A. (1992) *Professions and Patriarchy*. London: Routledge.

Witz, A. (1993) Women at work, in D. Richardson and V. Robinson (eds) *Introducing Women's Studies*. Basingstoke: Macmillan.

Wolf, D.L. (1996) Situating feminist dilemmas in fieldwork, in D.L. Wolf (ed.) *Feminist Dilemmas in Fieldwork*. Boulder, CO: Westview.

Wolf, N. (1990) *The Beauty Myth*. London: Chatto & Windus.

Wolff, K.H. (1950) *The Sociology of Georg Simmel*. New York: The Free Press.

Wollstonecraft, M. ([1792] 1972) *A Vindication of the Rights of Women*. London: Penguin.

Woolf, V. ([1929] 1977) *A Room of One's Own*. London: Virago.

Woolf, V. (1938) *Three Guineas*. London: Penguin.

Woollett, A. (1996) Infertility: from 'inside/out' to 'outside/in', in S. Wilkinson and C. Kitzinger (eds) *Representing the Other: A Feminism and Psychology Reader*. London: Sage.

Young, E.H. and Lee, R. (1996) Fieldworker feelings as data: 'emotion work' and 'feeling rules' in first person accounts of sociological fieldwork, in V. James and J. Gabe (eds) *Health and the Sociology of Emotions*. London: Blackwell.

Zalewski, M. (2000) *Feminism After Postmodernism: Theorising through Practice*. London: Routledge.

Znaniecki (1968) *The Social Role of the Man of Knowledge*. New York: Harper & Row.

Index

Keller, E.F., 37, 157
Kelly, L., 3, 5, 64, 67, 74, 78, 81, 85–7,
  94, 97–8, 101, 113–14, 116, 136,
  160
Kemp, S., 2, 4, 42, 48, 50, 56, 57
Kent, J., 27
Kessler-Harris, A., 34
Kimmel, M., 152
kindred spirit role, 124–5, 129, 132
King, D.K., 56
Kirkham, M.J., 39
Kitzinger, C., 24, 55, 76, 85, 110, 119,
  134, 135
Klein, R.D., 48, 69, 74, 97
Kleinman, S., 113
knotty entanglements (self/other), 131–4
knowers, 20, 63, 75, 77
knowing, 30, 48, 75
  and doing, 2–3, 5, 97, 160
knowledge, 78, 97
  access to, 21, 41
  accountable, 9, 71, 76, 160
  authorized, 20, 22, 24–8, 30–2, 52, 76,
    82, 147
  claims, 15, 20, 45, 49, 51, 69, 75
  experiential, 20, 22, 24–8, 77
  feminist reconstruction, 16, 41–60
  language and, 16, 20, 30–4
  masculinized, *see* masculinized
    knowledge
  power and, 3, 28, 36, 46–7, 52, 54–5,
    75
  production of, 2–5, 9, 19, 21, 28,
    38–9, 66, 70, 77, 81, 98, 150, 161
  subjectivity-based, 71
  unalienated, 62, 71, 73, 143, 150
  see also epistemology
known, 20, 63
Kramarae, C., 149

Landells, M., 37
language
  -games, 159
  knowledge and, 16, 20, 30–4
  male authority and, 20, 30–4
  man-made, 30–3
  power and, 33–4
  reality and, 30, 31–2, 33–4
  sexism in, 31, 33–4, 53
Larner, C., 26

Laws, S., 75, 137, 138, 140
lay audiences, 17, 145, 146, 151–4
leavings (research relationships), 116–20
Lee, R., 110, 127–8
Lee-Treweek, G., 68, 86, 113
Lees, S., 55
leisure activities (on trains), 142
Leonard, D., 55, 102
Leonard, P., 37, 146
lesbianism, 50, 51, 55, 92, 135
Letherby, G., 34, 37–8, 47, 68–9, 76, 92,
  94, 96, 101, 103, 106–7, 110, 111,
  114, 118–19, 123–6, 129, 132,
  140–3, 146–7, 150, 153, 156–7
  academic influences/interests, 9–15
letters, 90, 91, 92
Lieblich, A., 115
life histories, 88–90, 96
linguistic determinism, 33
Linkogle, S., 68, 86, 113
Lloyd, A., 55
Lobban, R.A., 109
lone mothers, 119
Lorde, A., 49, 159
Lovenduski, J., 42, 55
Luff, D., 115
Luther, Martin, 23

McCarl Nielsen, J., 19, 46, 62–3, 66
Mace, J., 148
MacFarlane, A., 25, 65, 93
Macintyre, M., 94
McKee, L., 75, 100, 137
McLennan, G., 52, 71
McMahon, M., 143
McRobbie, A., 69, 74, 111, 127, 160
magazines, 34, 151
Maguire, M., 37
male authority, language and, 30–4
male prisoners, 124, 132
male subjectivity, 67, 70
male youth culture, 66
malestream theory, 88
  critique, 63–72
Malina, D., 37, 146, 148, 150
Malseed, J., 153
Malson, H., 55
man-made language, 30–3
Man-Made Language (Spender), 30–2
Managed Heart, The (Hochschild), 110

FEMINISM

Jane Freedman

- What is the relevance of feminist thought to today's society?
- What do feminists mean by equality and difference?
- Can we find unity in feminist thought, or only conflict?

Feminism provides an introduction to some of the major debates within feminist theory and action. Focusing on the perennial question of equality and difference, the book examines the ways in which this has been played out in different areas of feminist social and political theory. Jane Freedman adopts a refreshing approach by focusing on issues rather than schools of thought. Among the subjects she examines are politics and women's citizenship, paid and unpaid employment and the global economy, sexuality and power, and race and ethnicity. Finally, the book analyses the problem of essentialism for feminism and the challenge of postmodern and poststructuralist theories. Written in a jargon-free style, this book presents a clear and concise introduction to a wide range of feminist thought.

Contents

Introduction: Feminism or feminisms? – Equal or different? The perennial feminist problematic – Feminism and the political: the fight for women's citizenship – Employment and the global economy – Sexuality and power – Ethnicity and identity: the problem of essentialism and the postmodern challenge – Bibliography – Index.

112pp   0 335 20415 5 (Paperback)   0 335 20416 3 (Hardback)

A WOMAN'S GUIDE TO DOCTORAL STUDIES

Diana Leonard

Endorsements from Research Students:

> ... I read it cover-to-cover in one sitting – it was really gripping stuff and I couldn't put it down! I think you've got the mode of address exactly right, and immeasurably more so than what's already on the market. I like the academic feel of it, as it implies you think your readers are intelligent adults, capable of understanding complex issues and wanting to make informed, considered decisions.

> ... Thanks for your input ... about ... PhD assessment/vivas. It made me aware of the sad experience that I went through in the 1980s when I undertook a part-time PhD ... I had little contact with my supervisor ... and had a viva without any preparation or information about what to expect. ... I didn't know of any appeal procedure until you mentioned it.

> ... You manage to cover an enormous amount of ground, while, at the same time, being mindful of the need to provide a certain amount of depth on each issue you address.

This guide is designed to help women – since they are less likely than men to be encouraged to do doctorates, are slower to put themselves forward, and tend to operate on the belief that (in academia at least) they will be judged solely on the quality of their work. This book will help women undertake and enjoy serious scholarly work whilst recognizing the wider 'rules' of the academic game.

The author compares the current situation in the UK with that of North America and Australia, and discusses the pros and cons of PhDs and new professional doctorates. Thought provoking case studies of the diverse experiences of home and international, young and older, heterosexual and lesbian students across the disciplines make illuminating reading.

This book is an essential read for women (and men) starting, midway through or finishing their doctorates.

Contents

304pp   0 335 20252 7 (Paperback)   0 335 20253 5 (Hardback)